Grace Unbound

Grace Unbound

The Sacred Activism of an Orthodox Bishop

Bishop Demetrios C. Kantzavelos
and
Patra McSharry Sevastiades

Foreword by Bill Kurtis

ROWMAN & LITTLEFIELD
Lanham • Boulder • New York • London

Rowman & Littlefield
Bloomsbury Publishing Inc, 1385 Broadway, New York, NY 10018, USA
Bloomsbury Publishing Plc, 50 Bedford Square, London, WC1B 3DP, UK
Bloomsbury Publishing Ireland, 29 Earlsfort Terrace, Dublin 2, D02 AY28, Ireland
www.rowman.com

Copyright © 2025 by Bishop Demetrios C. Kantzavelos and
Patra McSharry Sevastiades

All rights reserved. No part of this publication may be: i) reproduced or transmitted in any form, electronic or mechanical, including photocopying, recording or by means of any information storage or retrieval system without prior permission in writing from the publishers; or ii) used or reproduced in any way for the training, development or operation of artificial intelligence (AI) technologies, including generative AI technologies. The rights holders expressly reserve this publication from the text and data mining exception as per Article 4(3) of the Digital Single Market Directive (EU) 2019/790.

British Library Cataloguing in Publication Information available

Library of Congress Cataloging-in-Publication Data Available

ISBN 9781538194478 (cloth : alk. paper) | ISBN 9781538194485 (ebook)

For product safety related questions contact productsafety@bloomsbury.com.

∞™ The paper used in this publication meets the minimum requirements of American National Standard for Information Sciences—Permanence of Paper for Printed Library Materials, ANSI/NISO Z39.48-1992.

Epilogue	195
Notes	199
Index	215
About the Authors	227

Contents

Acknowledgments ix

Foreword *by Bill Kurtis* xi

1	The Visitor Room	1
2	"Please Don't Do This"	13
3	Meeting Andrew	23
4	It Isn't for Everybody	35
5	Even the Dogs	51
6	Meeting Bob	67
7	Lessons in Advocacy	83
8	Empathy in Action	95
9	Countdown	115
10	"Be Careful the AIDS!"	129
11	Lows and Highs	147
12	Fulfillment amid Heartbreak	165
13	To Sign or Not to Sign	177
14	An End, and a Beginning	185

For my parents:
My father, whose advice should have been heeded,
My mother, whose advice is always heeded.

Acknowledgments

Over twenty years ago my dear friend, Father Philemon Sevastiades of blessed memory, suggested I share my experience in social justice ministry with a broader audience. A man of brilliant mind and letters, it has become clear to me that a great deal of his own success as a writer was due to his beloved spouse, Patra McSharry Sevastiades. A most talented professional editor and author in her own right, Patra has given final form to these chapters after years of encouraging me through our many long conversations and reminiscences. More than anyone, her advice, insights, inquisitiveness, wisdom, empathy, and patience permitted me to articulate the stories that, without her, would remain largely untold. I am indebted to her skill, dedication to this work, and our enduring friendship.

For much of my career in ministry, Reverend David G. Bissias, also a native Chicagoan, collaborated with me in almost all my advocacy and activism, though by his preference, "behind the scenes." I am indebted to him for my own articulation of issues over the years, and his invaluable assistance in the initial preparation of these chapters.

Many others have assisted in this endeavor. This publication appears due to the generosity of so many persons, and I must thank those to whom I ministered and who allowed me to tell their stories here and elsewhere (some names have been changed to respect requests for anonymity). Countless persons made my ministry and the stories related here possible, and I ask forgiveness of those whose names I have forgotten or perhaps never knew.

Among those I can name are the several persons who read drafts and responded to these chapters with useful advice: the award-winning author Eva Apelqvist, my late friend Peter Artemas, Dean Casperson, editor and writer Janie Johns, Catherine McSharry, and Demetrius Sevastiades.

I am indebted to the professional encouragement and advice of Mr. John M. Liston, Esq., and the Honorable Martha Mills (retired) from the legal community, and of Rev. John H. Thomas and Rev. Lydia Veliko, both of the United Church of Christ, for their insights from the ecumenical and interfaith religious community.

I am thankful to have had the pleasure of working with a number of Bloomsbury's wonderfully talented staff. Richard Brown, an editor with a discerning eye and unerring ear, saw something meaningful in my story and then worked to make it so much better. Victoria Shi, assistant editor, reassuringly answered every question I had and capably shepherded the manuscript through the editorial process. Meaghan Menzel, production editor, meticulously attended to every detail of the manuscript, which ensured the accuracy of my story. Thank you all; I could not have asked for a better team. I am also grateful to Andrea Heinecke of the Bindery Agency for believing in this book and for her invaluable efforts in securing a publisher.

Of course, as noted in the text, foremost of all "influences" deserving of gratitude is my spiritual father and mentor, the late Metropolitan Iakovos, first Metropolitan of Chicago, who fostered my ministry, inspiring and supporting all my endeavors prior to his repose in the Lord in 2017. May his memory be eternal!

Yet long before any of these friends, colleagues, and spiritual mentors, I shared in the love of my family. My siblings and I received abundant gifts from the love and commitment of our parents, to whom this work is dedicated. Of course, their love is a gift from God "who loved us first," to whom belongs all glory and thanksgiving to the ages!

+Bishop Demetrios C. Kantzavelos

Foreword

I met Bishop Demetrios of Mokissos in 2004 while promoting a book on the death penalty. To say that book struck a chord would be an understatement. It was one of those lightning strikes at the right place and right time. It struck the bishop in his heart.

Little did I know that the death penalty had played a major role in the bishop's life—as had other major movements over the years.

This book is the remarkable story of a man who chose to serve his God by joining the battle against the social injustice in the world around him. That path was chosen uncommonly early in his life, so early one could easily call it his destiny.

As he climbed through the structure of Greek Orthodox clergy, it seemed specifically designed for Demetrios, leading him headlong into his first major challenge—ministering to persons living with HIV/AIDS. The Greek Orthodox Church was not ready for the deadly virus. Like so many people, priests often treated victims very cautiously, avoiding their duties rather than come in contact with someone living with HIV/AIDS.

By 1992, Demetrios was a priest assuming the administrative duties of the office and coordinating the work of priests in fifty-eight parishes throughout the Midwest. It was not direct contact with parishioners.

It was almost an accident that Demetrios was in the diocese office when he learned of a young man diagnosed with HIV/AIDS. Despite his requests, no one had come to see him. He needed Christian comfort and counseling.

It was Demetrios's first look into the deadly virus sweeping through the community of predominately gay men since the late 1970s, and the young priest realized neither his church nor the rest of the nation was dealing effectively with the menace. With the guidance of his bishop and the help of faith leaders from other religious traditions, he launched the diocese-wide Bishop's Task Force on AIDS, dedicated to educating Greek Orthodox priests and helping those living with the disease. The Task Force educated people about risk-reducing behaviors, like no unprotected sex and no sharing of needles. Demetrios was part of a movement that consolidated powerful religious bodies and pushed forward a general awareness that resulted in a new attitude toward those living with HIV/AIDS, a Christian attitude, a force for good works in social justice.

One can wonder how the desire to end injustice reaches the right souls who are waiting to act upon it, especially Bishop Demetrios. I'll leave the story's details to him but suffice it to say that he began to visit a man on death row at Pontiac Correctional Center in Illinois. Convinced of Andrew's innocence and opposed to capital punishment on theological and moral grounds, Demetrios fought a losing battle against the man's execution. Andrew was convicted of a terrible crime based solely on one piece of evidence: after aggressive interrogation at the Chicago Police Department, he confessed to taking part in the murder. Despite Andrew's having immediately recanted this forced confession, it was used against him.

Appeals were denied, and a date for execution was set.

Bishop Demetrios, along with other religious leaders, sought a meeting with Illinois governor George Ryan, a known supporter of capital punishment. Governor Ryan refused to meet with the group, ignoring their very public arguments against the death penalty. However, looking back, one might conclude that their vociferous arguments lingered in the governor's mind, creating a fertile ground for consideration of a moratorium on the death penalty at a future date.

Andrew was put to death in 1999, leaving the bishop deeply disappointed and feeling he had failed. Over the course of the next four years, thirteen people on death row in Illinois had been proven innocent and been released. This prompted the governor to declare a moratorium on capital punishment in January 2003. The next day, he commuted the death sentences of 164 condemned prisoners to life without the possibility of parole.

Bishop Demetrios had lost a battle, but he played a major role in the final victory of the death penalty being eliminated in Illinois.

He's written a book of courage, determination, hard work, and a laser-like focus on a commitment made as a young man. In an age of terrible uncertainty and calamity, this book should serve as a model for all those who are searching for purpose in their lives.

—Bill Kurtis
Television Journalist, Producer, Narrator, Author

Is not this the fast that I choose:
to loose the bonds of injustice,
to undo the thongs of the yoke,
to let the oppressed go free,
and to break every yoke?
Is it not to share your bread with the hungry,
and bring the homeless poor into your house;
when you see the naked, to cover them,
and not to hide yourself from your own kin?

—Isaiah 58:6–7 (NRSV)

1

✝

The Visitor Room

February 27, 1999

I awoke before my alarm went off and stared into the darkness. Grisly images of crime scenes and murder victims' faces had haunted my sleep, and a sinking feeling of foreboding stirred in my gut. *What am I doing?* I thought. Seminary had not prepared me for this.

A shower didn't dispel my uneasiness, but at least I was up and moving. I dressed quickly. I wanted to get going.

That explained why I was taking the elevator down to the lobby of my building now, fully fifteen minutes before Fred was scheduled to pick me up. The elevator doors opened, and I stepped out into the lobby. Through the building's glass entrance, I saw the empty driveway. I checked my watch, willing time to move faster, then paced, occasionally glancing out the front door. The morning sky was bright blue. *A perfect day for a road trip*, I thought, then caught myself. *Road trip!* I checked my watch again. Eight o'clock.

Right on time, Fred pulled up to the curb. I pushed through the revolving door and stepped outside. A bracing wind off Lake Michigan made me duck my head. It felt like an insult on an already uneasy morning.

"Good morning, Father!" Fred said brightly as I got into his car. His face radiated good cheer, and I had to smile. Fred had generously rearranged his Saturday schedule so he could drive me today so I wouldn't have to be alone; he had even brought two cups of coffee. I gratefully took a sip, and while it wasn't enough to dispel the tension in my stomach, it helped. Fred slid smoothly into traffic, and soon we left Chicago behind, heading

1

southwest. Fred chatted amiably. Out my window, I saw a frosting of snow on an industrial building. I took a couple of slow breaths.

Fred was an attorney and a friend. I was a priest. I worked at the Greek Orthodox Diocese of Chicago, where Fred served pro bono as legal counsel.[1] It was February 27, 1999.

A few days before, I had received a call at the diocese from a woman named Theodora, whom I had known since the earliest days of my ministry. It had been a pressure-filled morning—an afternoon deadline was looming—but when I recognized her voice, I leaned back in my chair, glad for a respite.

"Father Demetri," she said, "I'm wondering if you would be willing to meet with a man on death row?"

The question was so unexpected that I momentarily forgot the paperwork on my desk.

"Of course," I said, pulling out a notepad. "Tell me about him."

Theodora had felt called to prison ministry two years before, she said, and a priest had suggested she visit a man in the Pontiac Correctional Center, not too far from where she lived. "He's on death row," the priest had cautioned. "Are you okay with that?"

Death row? she had thought, but aloud she said, "Okay." The priest had given her the man's name, Andrew Kokoraleis.

Theodora had arranged to visit Andrew. She was used to rolling up her sleeves and getting things done, but she had never visited a prison, much less death row. She'd been a little uneasy, she told me. Andrew didn't know her—what would he think? Yet there she was a few days later, sitting across the table from a man in shackles. Theodora introduced herself, speaking English with a warm Greek accent. She told Andrew that God had not given up on him. She asked him about himself. Andrew answered, but the hardness on his face did not yield.

"It didn't go very well," she admitted to me. The awkward visit had lasted only fifteen minutes.

She was discouraged as she stood up to go, but she asked Andrew, "Would you like me to come again?"

A pause. "Yes," he answered.

"I'll be here next week," she promised.

She kept her word. Little by little, Andrew came to trust this kind weekly visitor. She urged him to pray. She spoke of faith and reassured Andrew that God loved him. His life had purpose, she told him, even on death row.

He gradually let down his defenses, and over the next two years they established a genuine relationship, she said. His bitterness seemed to lessen and then disappear. He started to pray. She gave him a gold cross necklace, and he wore it all the time. He asked Theodora if he could call

1

✟

The Visitor Room

February 27, 1999

I awoke before my alarm went off and stared into the darkness. Grisly images of crime scenes and murder victims' faces had haunted my sleep, and a sinking feeling of foreboding stirred in my gut. *What am I doing?* I thought. Seminary had not prepared me for this.

A shower didn't dispel my uneasiness, but at least I was up and moving. I dressed quickly. I wanted to get going.

That explained why I was taking the elevator down to the lobby of my building now, fully fifteen minutes before Fred was scheduled to pick me up. The elevator doors opened, and I stepped out into the lobby. Through the building's glass entrance, I saw the empty driveway. I checked my watch, willing time to move faster, then paced, occasionally glancing out the front door. The morning sky was bright blue. *A perfect day for a road trip*, I thought, then caught myself. *Road trip!* I checked my watch again. Eight o'clock.

Right on time, Fred pulled up to the curb. I pushed through the revolving door and stepped outside. A bracing wind off Lake Michigan made me duck my head. It felt like an insult on an already uneasy morning.

"Good morning, Father!" Fred said brightly as I got into his car. His face radiated good cheer, and I had to smile. Fred had generously rearranged his Saturday schedule so he could drive me today so I wouldn't have to be alone; he had even brought two cups of coffee. I gratefully took a sip, and while it wasn't enough to dispel the tension in my stomach, it helped. Fred slid smoothly into traffic, and soon we left Chicago behind, heading southwest. Fred chatted amiably. Out my window, I saw a frosting of snow on an industrial building. I took a couple of slow breaths.

Fred was an attorney and a friend. I was a priest. I worked at the Greek Orthodox Diocese of Chicago, where Fred served pro bono as legal counsel.[1] It was February 27, 1999.

A few days before, I had received a call at the diocese from a woman named Theodora, whom I had known since the earliest days of my ministry. It had been a pressure-filled morning—an afternoon deadline was looming—but when I recognized her voice, I leaned back in my chair, glad for a respite.

"Father Demetri," she said, "I'm wondering if you would be willing to meet with a man on death row?"

The question was so unexpected that I momentarily forgot the paperwork on my desk.

"Of course," I said, pulling out a notepad. "Tell me about him."

Theodora had felt called to prison ministry two years before, she said, and a priest had suggested she visit a man in the Pontiac Correctional Center, not too far from where she lived. "He's on death row," the priest had cautioned. "Are you okay with that?"

Death row? she had thought, but aloud she said, "Okay." The priest had given her the man's name, Andrew Kokoraleis.

Theodora had arranged to visit Andrew. She was used to rolling up her sleeves and getting things done, but she had never visited a prison, much less death row. She'd been a little uneasy, she told me. Andrew didn't know her—what would he think? Yet there she was a few days later, sitting across the table from a man in shackles. Theodora introduced herself, speaking English with a warm Greek accent. She told Andrew that God had not given up on him. She asked him about himself. Andrew answered, but the hardness on his face did not yield.

"It didn't go very well," she admitted to me. The awkward visit had lasted only fifteen minutes.

She was discouraged as she stood up to go, but she asked Andrew, "Would you like me to come again?"

A pause. "Yes," he answered.

"I'll be here next week," she promised.

She kept her word. Little by little, Andrew came to trust this kind weekly visitor. She urged him to pray. She spoke of faith and reassured Andrew that God loved him. His life had purpose, she told him, even on death row.

He gradually let down his defenses, and over the next two years they established a genuine relationship, she said. His bitterness seemed to lessen and then disappear. He started to pray. She gave him a gold cross necklace, and he wore it all the time. He asked Theodora if he could call her "Ma," and she said yes. She witnessed his change of heart and the profound difference it made in him.

"What do you think caused that?" I asked.

"He met God," she said.

∾

Andrew was one of six children. It had been hard for his parents, Costas and Wanda, to provide for a family of eight, and the children grew up poor in Chicago. Costas worked at a restaurant, and he could be severe with his children. One son recounted the day one of his sisters discovered drugs on him. When their father learned of this, he flew into an angry rage, made his son take off his shirt and lean forward over a table, and administered fifteen lashes to his back with a belt.[2] Some of Andrew's older siblings left home when they turned eighteen.

Andrew had been close to his mother, Wanda, who was a softer presence. A server at a restaurant, she fell ill with a medical condition that weakened her and finally proved fatal. She died when Andrew was only twelve; her early death left him adrift. Andrew's father, overwhelmed and struggling to provide for his family, was often at work, leaving his children at home to cope as best they could in the absence of either parent.

Andrew left home while still in high school. An acquaintance named Eddie Spreitzer, who had also dropped out of high school, later introduced him to a local contractor for whom Eddie sometimes worked. The contractor, named Robin Gecht, hired Andrew. One of Andrew's older brothers, Thomas, occasionally helped out on Gecht's contracting jobs as well.

But Gecht had a dark side. By day he led the three men in their work at construction jobs in and around Chicago, and after hours, he directed this same team to kidnap, rape, mutilate, and kill women. The men had attacked—and in some cases, killed—as many as seventeen women.

"It happened almost twenty years ago," Theodora said to me. "Do you remember? All four were arrested. They were known as the 'Ripper Crew.'" Andrew had been convicted of murdering a young woman named Lorraine ("Lorry") Ann Borowski and had been sentenced to death.

Theodora said that Andrew admitted he had been part of the terrible gang, but he insisted he had not killed Ms. Borowski. Theodora had listened, guardedly at first, but as she came to know Andrew better, her skepticism about his version of events softened. She believed he was telling the truth.

"Why do you want me to visit Andrew now?" I asked Theodora.

"They just scheduled his execution," she said, her voice catching.

"For what date?" I asked.

"March 17," she said—only three weeks away.

∾

At home that evening, I kept thinking about what Theodora had said during our phone call.

"Meet him and see what you think, Father," she had implored me. "You are the chancellor[3] of the diocese. Can you do anything to save his life?"

"I'll do my best," I'd promised her. Now I thought, *Someone she loves is going to be executed.*

Executed—standing in my living room, looking out at the dark expanse of Lake Michigan, a glass of scotch in my hand, the stark finality of it hit me.

In Illinois, I knew, being executed meant you would be accompanied to a room, strapped down to a table with leather belts, and have lethal drugs pumped into your veins. The execution would be carried out by the state on behalf of the people of Illinois, and visitors would be allowed to watch your agonizing last minutes through a window.

This was the first time that the death penalty touched me in any direct way. I had never really thought about it. Theodora had asked me to intervene, if possible, because I was a Greek Orthodox priest and the man on death row was Greek Orthodox. The church opposed capital punishment on theological grounds, of course, because every human life is sacred;[4] now, at a gut level, I was starting to understand why.

Looking out at the night, I tried to imagine how the parents of the young woman who had been murdered might feel about Andrew and his upcoming execution. Perhaps it would seem to them that justice had been served to know that the person convicted of killing their daughter would in turn be required to give up his own life.

I also had to wonder how I would feel if my own sister had been murdered. It was hard to imagine that Christian forgiveness would have been my first response. But all that I had ever learned at seminary and beyond affirmed that every human life, no matter how tarnished, is of infinite value and worth, including Andrew's.

I finished my drink, read a little, and went to bed, these thoughts still weighing on my mind.

※

The next morning, I arrived at work and headed downstairs from my second-floor office to the diocese kitchen. My boss of nearly twenty years, Bishop Iakovos of Chicago, was sitting at the kitchen table having a cup of coffee. Now in his seventies, Bishop Iakovos had a face framed with a neatly trimmed white beard. His white hair, also neatly groomed, was receding.

He had been born Michael Garmatis in Athens on April 4, 1928. The young man who would become Bishop Iakovos was twelve years old when Italian leader Benito Mussolini surprised everyone, including his ally Adolf Hitler, by invading Greece on October 28, 1940. The Greek army, despite being outnumbered, successfully counterattacked and within a month had forced the Italian army to retreat.

Six months later, on April 6, 1941, Germany invaded Greece. The Greek army could not withstand the onslaught. A punishing three-year occupation followed. In Athens, starvation stalked the streets, taking the lives of more than 300,000 people. Greek partisans were killed trying to defend the country. The Germans forcibly rounded up Greek Jews for deportation. Michael's parents took in a Jewish man and woman, hiding them in plain sight and claiming they were relatives until Michael's uncle, a priest, whisked them away to safety a few days later. For three years, Michael saw the hated Nazi flag dominate the landscape of his city. A swastika marked the uniforms and vehicles of the merciless occupying force.

Michael was seventeen years old when World War II ended and the Germans fled. Through courage and fortitude, the teen had survived two invasions, a war, and starvation. He had witnessed Nazis brutalizing and killing his countrymen. Yet he saw his parents and uncle maintain their moral bearings at a time of chaos and risk their lives to save others. Those experiences had forged his character.

A sociable man who enjoyed meeting people, Bishop Iakovos was also a private person with deep inner resources. He had an easy smile and could laugh at himself. Wise, compassionate, deeply faithful, he led the diocese with uncompromising commitment to living out the gospel message of love.

I poured myself a cup of coffee and took a seat facing him. We went over our schedules for the coming day, and then I related my conversation with Theodora. I told the bishop I was planning to visit Andrew. I described the violence of Andrew's past. The bishop listened, his face grim. He expressed compassion for the victims and their families. He had never been to death row and suggested that before I visit Andrew, I learn as much as I could about Andrew's involvement in those crimes. I promised I would.

He looked thoughtful. He asked when I planned to visit Andrew, and I told him I hoped to see him that weekend.

"Remember that all human beings are made in the image and likeness of God," he said. "All of us, no matter what we may or may not have done, are precious children of God."

I returned to my office with a full cup of coffee and did some research on the history of executions in the state. I learned that capital punishment in Illinois was older than the state itself.[5]

Then I called my friend Fred, an attorney. I wanted to tell him about my plan to visit Andrew and to ask for any legal recommendations he might have. In the small world of Greek Orthodox people in Chicagoland,[6] it turned out that Theodora had called Fred first for legal guidance, and Fred had recommended that she reach out to me.

Fred was familiar with Andrew's case and had even done a little digging. He had turned up two critical facts.

First, he told me, Andrew had been convicted of murdering Lorraine Borowski despite the absence of any physical evidence proving his guilt; there was no weapon and no DNA. The prosecution's only "evidence" against Andrew was his confession, a confession that Andrew claimed was wrung out of him by police and that he immediately recanted.

Second, all legal appeals had already been exhausted. As a result, Fred said, the best option to try to save Andrew's life was to reach out to the governor and try to persuade him to grant Andrew clemency.

This conversation was sobering. The new governor, George H. Ryan, had been sworn in only a month before. He had campaigned as a pro–capital punishment candidate. At this point, the odds were stacked against Andrew.

I thanked Fred for his thoughtful assessment. That's when he asked if I would like some company on my travel to death row.

A day later, Theodora offered to meet Fred and me at the restaurant that she and her husband owned in Pontiac. From there, she would guide us to the prison as well as accompany us inside.

※

The Pontiac Correctional Center was built in the Progressive Era that followed the Civil War. Originally established as the Illinois Boys Reformatory School, it embodied a hopeful vision popular among Illinois lawmakers at the time that child and teenage offenders, boys ages eight to sixteen, shouldn't be imprisoned with adult criminals, who could victimize and further corrupt them. Instead, juvenile offenders should be given a chance for rehabilitation. In 1871, the newly constructed youth facility in Pontiac received its first six boys, convicted of stealing horses in Peoria. The boys likely envisioned serving hard time in a cell block, but when they stepped out of the secure transport vehicle and onto the grounds of the Pontiac facility, they found themselves on a broad campus with a farm, orchards, school, dormitories, vocational school, baseball diamond, chapel, and hospital. They would attend school four hours a day, Monday through Saturday. They would also be taught a trade, such as electrical engineering, masonry, or tailoring, to help them become productive citizens and instill in them a solid work ethic. It was intended that they and the hundreds of boys who followed them would be released back into the world, reformed and able to earn a livelihood.

But the original dream of a place of rehabilitation for wayward boys had faded over the decades as the need grew for more cells to hold a swelling adult prison population. The ages of the inmates increased, and the rehabilitative aspect of work gradually disappeared as the facility became overcrowded and the inmates increasingly violent. The orchard vanished, then the farm. In 1978, the prison was the scene of one of the deadliest prison riots in Illinois history. Renamed the Pontiac Correctional Center, by 1999 it included a large maximum-security section. Part of that section housed a special category of inmates: convicted murderers sentenced to be executed by the State of Illinois. The hopeful vision of an agricultural campus rehabilitating up to four hundred boys at a time had given way to a heavily guarded facility that now held around two thousand of Illinois's most dangerous prisoners.

That's where Fred and I were going.

The sun was higher in the sky and our coffee cups empty when the gates of the Pontiac Correctional Center came into view. The exterior of the facility was bland, but the fence, guard towers, and concertina wire were persuasive evidence of the state's intention to contain thousands of male inmates in the secure facility. I felt an overwhelming sense of foreboding.

We followed Theodora's car as it turned into the parking lot. Fred found a spot and parked. We left both cars unlocked, as required, and Fred and I joined Theodora. Together, we walked to the prison entrance. My stomach was churning. I had visited prisoners before but never anyone on death row.

To my surprise, the entrance to the prison was a set of regular doors designed for use by everyday visitors. We walked past people sitting on drab couches and benches in a reception area. The room was institutional and dreary. Fred took a seat. Theodora and I approached the reception desk. When it was our turn, the attendant seated behind the desk asked us, "How many visitors?"

"Two," Theodora answered. The attendant asked us for identification. We each presented it and told him the time of our appointments and that we were visiting Andrew Kokoraleis. Theodora would see Andrew briefly in a large visiting room, and then I would see him privately in a smaller visiting room. The man confirmed our visits, gave each of us a lanyard with a plastic tag that read VISITOR, and directed us to hang our overcoats in nearby lockers and take a seat. We did and sat down beside Fred.

Minutes passed. Other visitors were summoned one by one. They were led into a room and emerged a little while later, only to disappear down a hallway.

Theodora's name was called. She smiled at me reassuringly as she got up. "I'll tell Andrew you are here," she said.

"Demetri Kantzavelos?" a guard called out. I stood, and it was my turn to enter a small room and endure a body search. I was asked to remove my suit jacket and was given a pat down, front and back. When I came out of the room, I was directed down a hallway to a window behind which a guard was seated. The guard had me extend my right hand through the cutout in the glass, and he stamped the back of my hand with ultraviolet ink. The prison seemed to reduce everyone, even the guards and the visitors, from human beings to objects to be processed. It was uncomfortable.

Once my hand had been stamped, I walked farther down the hallway to a desk outside the visiting area, where another guard scanned my hand, then buzzed me through a gray metal door. As the door swung closed behind me, I saw another closed metal door a few feet ahead of me. For a startling moment, I was boxed in. Then the metal door ahead of me buzzed open, and I was met by a polite guard. Each door I passed through seemed to shut out the world behind a little more.

I followed the guard down a long hallway, aware that I was going deeper into the building. The sound of our footsteps echoed. Soon he opened the door of a visiting room. It was a cold, concrete room, brightly illuminated by fluorescent ceiling lights. It felt sterile and unwelcoming. Several square metal tables were bolted to the floor, and around each table, four metal chairs were also anchored to the floor. One of the chairs had the word INMATE stenciled on it in black letters. VISITOR appeared on the other three. I sat down in a visitor chair opposite a chair marked INMATE. I thought, *This is where Theodora comes to see Andrew every week*, and that realization made the bleak room a little less forbidding.

As I waited for Andrew, I went over in my mind's eye what I had learned about him. I had searched for past media coverage of Andrew's case. It didn't take long to find. Soon I was reading a slew of lurid descriptions of what the "Ripper Crew" had done to at least seventeen women. The faces of the women, frozen in time, looked out at me from the newspaper. It was frankly shocking. No wonder people wanted Andrew dead.

It had started eighteen years ago, on June 1, 1981. A passerby came upon a body near the Brer Rabbit Motel in Villa Park, a suburb west of Chicago. It was the body of Linda Sutton. The twenty-six-year-old mother of two had been missing for a week and had last been seen twenty-two miles away in downtown Chicago near Wrigley Field. At the time her body was examined, investigators noted that her breasts were missing and chalked it up to scavenging animals. Her body showed evidence of having been beaten.

Nearly a year passed with no other victims. Then on the morning of May 15, 1982, Lorraine "Lorry" Ann Borowski, twenty-one, had left her apartment at 8:15 a.m. in Elmhurst, a suburb west of Chicago. She'd walked the three blocks to her job at a real estate office as she did every Saturday.

When Lorry's boss arrived at 9:00 a.m., he found the pavement outside the office littered with cosmetics, a set of keys, a pair of women's shoes, and a purse. The office door was locked, and Lorry was nowhere to be seen. He called the police. Police filed a report but had no leads. They couldn't find any witnesses to confirm what the terrifying evidence silently conveyed, that Lorry had been abducted. Where was she?

On Saturday, May 29, two weeks after Lorraine Borowski's abduction, thirty-year-old Shui Mak was driving home at 1:00 a.m. with her brother after helping close their family's restaurant in suburban Streamwood, northwest of Chicago. The two siblings were arguing fiercely. Only a few miles into their trip, near Hanover Park, her brother angrily pulled over, and Shui stormed out of the car. Her brother later said he had expected their parents, who were minutes behind them, to pick up Shui and drive her home, but Shui's parents never saw her again.

Two women were now missing in the space of two weeks. Were the cases linked?

Fifteen days after Shui Mak's disappearance, on Sunday, June 13, 1982, a passerby saw a woman bleeding by the side of the road and stopped to help her. Angel York, a professional sex worker, recounted to police that she had been on Chicago's North Side when she was approached by a customer driving a van. When she stepped into the van, she was surprised to see four men inside. They quickly overpowered her. The men forced her to mutilate her own breast with a knife. They threw the bleeding, traumatized woman out of the van, left her for dead, and sped away. York was able to describe her attackers to police.

On Saturday, August 28, 1982, two months after Angel York was attacked, someone discovered the body of eighteen-year-old Sandra Delaware. Stabbed, mutilated, and strangled, she had been left on the bank of the Chicago River under the noisy Fullerton Avenue Bridge, a multilane bridge on the North Side of Chicago. Her left breast was gone.

Another body was found on Wednesday, September 8, 1982. Rose Beck Davis was a thirty-year-old marketing executive. Her body was abandoned in the historic, well-heeled Gold Coast neighborhood of Chicago, deposited in an alleyway only a number of blocks from the diocese. Investigators observed that she had been raped, beaten with an ax, and fatally stabbed. Her breasts, too, had been slashed, confirming an emerging pattern of breast fixation and mutilation.

Around this time, the media announced that Carole Pappas, wife of Chicago Cubs pitcher Milt Pappas, was missing. She was last seen on September 11, 1982. Chicago braced itself. How many women were going to be victimized before police found the perpetrator?[7]

∞

In late September, one mystery was grimly solved. The remains of Shui Mak, who had vanished in May, were found in a field in South Barrington, a suburb northeast of Chicago. The medical examiner saw evidence that she had been attacked and, in a now familiar finding, that she, too, had experienced breast mutilation.

The pattern of mutilation prompted investigators to reexamine photographs of Linda Sutton, whose remains had been found more than a year before near the motel. They now understood what they were seeing. The injuries to her body, initially blamed on scavenging animals, were consistent with intentional amputation of her breasts. This opened investigators' eyes to the startling realization that the killing spree had begun a year earlier than previously believed.

On October 6, 1982, Rafael Tirado, twenty-eight, and his friend were standing in a Chicago phone booth when someone opened fire on them. Tirado did not survive. Police wondered if perhaps there was a connection to the abductions and killing of women, although it did not fit the pattern.

The day that Rafael Tirado and his friend were shot, eighteen-year-old Denise Gardner[8] was raped, mutilated, and left for dead near some railroad tracks in Humboldt Park, a suburb northwest of Chicago. Her left breast was gone, amputated, and her right breast had been severely slashed. In the hospital, she described her attackers to the police. Crucially, she was the first victim who was also able to provide a detailed description of the reddish-orange Dodge van they had used to abduct her. It featured a plywood wall between the front seats and the back of the van, she said. Once in the back, there was no way to escape, she noted, because the interior door handles had all been removed. Police were now on the lookout for the distinctive van.

On October 10, four days after Denise Gardner was attacked and Rafael Tirado was shot and killed, someone walking in an unused portion of a cemetery in Clarendon Hills, eighteen miles northwest of Chicago, came upon skeletal human remains and called the police. The victim,

Lorraine Borowski, was identified by her clothing. She had been missing for five months.

Attacks on the women had taken place in different sections of the city. The victims were women of different ages, races, employment, and economic background. The only thing they had in common was that each woman was alone when she was abducted. Police were stumped. Pressure was building on them to do something.

∞

Police finally had a break in the case on October 20, 1982, ten days after Lorraine Borowski's body was found. Based on the description of the van provided by Denise Gardner, an officer pulled over Edward Spreitzer, who was driving a van of the same description. Spreitzer led police to the owner of the van, Robin Gecht. Spreitzer and Gecht were taken in for questioning. In a police lineup, Denise Gardner positively identified Gecht as her assailant, and he was arrested for the October 6 attack. Gecht posted bond and was released. Spreitzer was not charged with anything and was allowed to go.

Now that Gecht was in the spotlight, the police turned up new information about him. He and three other men had rented rooms in the Brer Rabbit Motel in Villa Park, where the body of Linda Sutton had been found the previous summer. The motel manager told police he had suspected the men of being involved in a cult. Suddenly, the investigation was gaining momentum.

On November 5, Gecht was again arrested by police. This time, he was held in custody. Spreitzer was also brought in and held overnight.

Two days later, on November 7, police picked up Andrew Kokoraleis, nineteen, identified as one of the other three men at the motel, for questioning. The newspapers reported that he and Edward Spreitzer confessed to having murdered up to seventeen women. Gecht admitted nothing. Authorities began to refer to the group of men as the "Ripper Crew," a reference to Jack the Ripper, a serial killer who had mutilated and murdered women in London in the fall of 1888.

On November 7, acting on a tip from the former roommate of one of the suspects, police dug in a wooded area near railroad tracks in LaBagh Woods, northwest of Chicago, searching for the bodies of more victims. They did not turn up any evidence.

Five days later, on November 12, police picked up Thomas Kokoraleis. Andrew's brother had been identified as a suspect based on information obtained from the other three men. All four suspects were now in police custody.

Robin Gecht, Thomas Kokoraleis, Edward Spreitzer, and Andrew Kokoraleis, mug shots, November 1982. Chicago Police Department

The newspaper accounts detailed the gruesome crimes of which Gecht, Spreitzer, and the Kokoraleis brothers were accused.[9] The men didn't just murder women, it was reported; they tortured them, mutilated them, and then killed them or left them for dead. The amputated breasts were used for ritualistic sexual pleasure. The wounds on the women's chests from amputations were perversely used for sexual intercourse. The women's bodies were discarded.

I saw mug shots of the Ripper Crew in the newspaper. They were all young men. Robin Gecht, twenty-eight, seemed confident; Thomas Kokoraleis, thirty, was unguarded in his appearance; Edward Spreitzer, twenty-one, appeared frightened, wary; and Andrew, nineteen, was thin, with light brown hair, his face impassive.

∞

As I sat in my visitor chair waiting for Andrew, I wondered, *How can I understand, love, and identify with a person convicted of heinous crimes against helpless victims?* I did not know. I just knew that, as a person of faith and a servant of redemption, a priest, that was the challenge before me. I was nervous.

I heard a buzz and a lock released. I looked up. A prison guard had opened the door and was bringing a man into the room. I could hear the clinking of shackles.

I was about to meet Andrew.

2

✣

"Please Don't Do This"

November 1979

My father wanted his oldest child to be a success, not a priest. He was an ambitious man. A civil engineer turned entrepreneur, he loved Chicago, the brash city in which he had grown up and where he chose to raise his family. He was polished and urbane, a man of appetites who dealt well with the city's sharp-elbowed realities, proud of his Greek American heritage. He was also proud of my mother, who had been a teenage model, a girl from Chicago who attended the same Greek Orthodox parish that he did. Being an Orthodox Christian and having his family attend church was important to him. My father served on the parish council, too, sharing his practical knowledge and expertise for the benefit of our parish.

My mother, a homemaker, was also a beautician who worked from an adjacent room attached to our house and frequently traveled to nursing homes to provide on-site salon services to their residents. In agreement with my father, she raised us to be observant Greek Orthodox believers in a home where Greek was spoken more often than not. Considering my mother's background, this was no surprise. Her mother, my Yiayia (Grandmother) Maria, was one of the first Greek-language schoolteachers in Chicago. For thirty-eight years, she taught weekday, afternoon, and Saturday Greek school classes at our home parish of the Assumption and at St. Basil's Church in Chicago.

My mother tells me that when I was six years old, I would wake up on Sundays, get dressed, and bicycle several blocks to our church to serve as a junior altar boy, sometimes while the rest of the family was still asleep.

Merope and Christ Kantzavelos. Private collection of Bishop Demetrios C. Kantzavelos

She saw the first evidence of something that was already stirring. For me, the calling to be a priest was always present in a quiet way, an unspoken but familiar longing.

I remember walking into the church and up the side aisle, then pushing open a side door in the icon screen and stepping into the area where the altar stood. When I put on my altar boy's robes and stood near the altar, I felt at home. I loved the beautiful garments worn by those who served at the altar, especially the priests', made of fabric shot through with gold thread and trimmed with an ornamental strip of fabric on every edge.

Each item the priest put on conveyed deep meaning, from the cuffs he laced up onto each wrist, signifying the power of God's grace, to the stole around his neck, symbolizing the spiritual yoke of the priesthood, without which he could not conduct a liturgical service. During the service, I happily breathed in the reassuring fragrance of incense, which represented prayers to God and filled the church. Then at one moment, the other altar boys and I and finally the priest himself emerged through a side door of the icon screen and walked down the side aisle of the church and up its central aisle, moving among the congregation as surely as Christ had walked on the earth. The priest carried the gifts of bread and wine. He chanted a prayer as he went; then the chanters sang, too, and the choir joined in. This felt like my world.

I was inspired by the priests in our parish, the historic Assumption Greek Orthodox Church, who radiated joy in their work. Our parish was a vibrant spiritual greenhouse. (As of today, it has produced forty-two priests and three bishops, including me.) At the time, it was the largest Greek Orthodox parish in the United States, with 1,500 people attending services each Sunday, four priests, nearly one hundred altar boys, five hundred children in Sunday school, and a fully accredited elementary school, the Plato School. This busy, thriving parish demanded a lot of its priests, and they led it lovingly.

I grew up in Chicago in the 1960s and 1970s. Our parents raised the four of us—me, my two brothers, and my sister—with two guiding principles: "Whatever you do, we want you to be the best at it" and "We want you to do whatever would make you happy." One demanded excellence; the other urged us to trust ourselves. Underpinning it all was the strong message that we were loved.

I attended a small neighborhood elementary public school from the time I was in kindergarten through third grade, and I loved school. Then I moved up to the much larger elementary school for fourth through eighth grades.

Somehow, it was too much, and instead of excelling, I began to fall through the cracks. I didn't complain, and no one but my teacher seemed to notice. At a parent–teacher conference, my fourth-grade teacher warned my parents that I was underperforming. A few days later, my worried parents told me we were going to tour a different school. The school was in a nearby suburb, a forty-five-minute school bus ride away. It was smaller. During our tour, the teachers there made it clear that they loved their students and expected them to work hard. This suited my parents, so in fifth grade, I began riding the bus and attending a Missouri Synod Lutheran school that embodied conservative Lutheran values.

My new school was a welcoming place, and my teachers summoned my best academic efforts. I found I liked school again. When positive report cards and glowing teacher conferences confirmed I was doing well, my parents liked it too.

My teachers, while teaching us math, reading, and science, modeled the idea that God (like my teachers) loved us all—Lutherans, Christians of other traditions, and non-Christians—and quietly shaped an expectation in us that we were to try to love and get along with everyone else in the world, just as we did in class. Every Wednesday, we walked down the corridors to attend a prayer service in St. John's Lutheran Church. I asked my new Lutheran friends questions about their faith, and I answered their questions about why Orthodox Christians sometimes celebrate Easter on a different day, why we call it "Pascha"[1] instead of "Easter," and what an icon is.[2] My teachers and friends accepted me, and I felt loved. In this supportive environment, I happily spent four years. The fact that my Greek Orthodox parents had entrusted me to a conservative Lutheran school was not lost on me either. For me, this "ecumenical" world became a new normal.

As a high school freshman, I began attending the Missouri Synod Lutheran high school in north Chicago. One day during my freshman year, I stayed after school to audition for the school play. I was nervous and excited, and when I emerged from the school building later that afternoon headed for home, the crisp snap of autumn was in the air. The next morning, with butterflies in my stomach, I headed straight for the drama classroom, where a piece of paper was taped to the door: the cast list. I ran my eye down the list, and there was my name. I had a part in the play! I had been cast as Thomas Diafoirus in *The Imaginary Invalid* by Molière. The whole day I felt a tingle of excitement. I was going to be in the play!

For the next six weeks, each school day was brightened by the anticipation of my after-school rehearsals. It was another world. The other actors were becoming my friends, and the stage and my role in the play began to feel familiar.

When the day we had all worked toward, opening night, finally arrived, my whole family—parents, siblings, and grandparents—came to see me perform in *The Imaginary Invalid*. The costumes, the greasepaint, and the applause—the experience was intoxicating. I was hooked. I had discovered an unexpected talent for theater, and I became known as one of the school's thespians. We even had our own space in the school, a room behind the stage, where we sometimes hung out during part of the school day.

The man who orchestrated all our efforts and coaxed the best from us was the school's drama teacher, Bill Wallace. He was hip, young, and full of energy. His upbeat, confident bearing gave him stature in our eyes. He stood out among the school staff because of his chic glasses and Fu Manchu mustache—and also because he allowed us to call him "Wallace" instead of "Mr. Wallace," a noteworthy exception in our buttoned-down parochial school.

Wallace's enthusiasm for theater was contagious. He believed in his students, and we felt it. Twice a year, the school produced a play. A few behind-the-scenes students wanted to help with lights and direction, but most of us dreamed of being onstage, in costume, before a live audience. Wallace taught us that to be good actors, we had to "practice, practice, practice" being in touch with our emotions. "Share your feelings with the audience and with each other," he urged us daily.

Wallace's words began to sink in. When the final school bell rang each afternoon, hundreds of students slammed their locker doors shut, and among them a dozen thespians headed to the stage. The stage was built into the school cafeteria, and there we dropped our backpacks and jackets; we sat in a circle and read through the script together. Under the spell that Wallace cast, we talked about emotion as part of what makes theater so powerful. Wallace encouraged us to empathize with our characters by asking us questions: "What do you think your character is feeling?" and "Why do you think she said that?" When we rehearsed, Wallace challenged us to dive into whatever the character was experiencing: exhilaration, confusion, anger, or joy. "Share your feelings!" he said. Each time we stepped on stage, we practiced letting go of our inhibitions and channeling our characters' emotions.

Little by little, this liberated something in me. I encountered a kind of love and connection with the other actors that was new to me. It energized our performances onstage and connected us offstage. It stirred my heart, my imagination. For four years of high school, I poured myself into the plays, learning my lines, staying late for rehearsals, and soaking up all I could of the theater. I was even inducted into the prestigious International Thespian Society.

Only many years later did I realize the great gift Wallace had shared with the huddle of hopeful teenagers who gathered daily for play practice. He created a space for us—away from the noisy hallways and classrooms, where we felt the pressure to conform—a place where we were encouraged to trust ourselves, to cultivate empathy, and to practice being brave. He taught us to build up those qualities inside ourselves, to walk around with them. He did this so we would become better actors. There is little doubt that he helped us become better people. I'd learned those remarkable lessons on the stage in high school, thanks to my parents. My parents, whose plans for me I was about to throw to the four winds.

My parents' love of education, especially my father's, had prompted them to pack me off each morning to a school across town. This was done on my parents' nickel to provide me with every opportunity available. It was an investment in me and my future so that I could get into a good college, get a good job, raise a good family, and become a success.

That's why my parents had high hopes for me and my university prospects when the fall of my senior year came around. Their hopes were rewarded. For months, a table at home was awash in letters and brochures from universities. They saw I had my pick of schools. They knew that all their work, their sacrifices, were finally going to bear fruit. It was wonderful to see my mother and father so happy.

One night over dinner, my mother asked, "When are you going to apply to other colleges?" For despite the many glossy offers on the mail table, I had applied to only one college. Apparently, my parents had noticed. I had known it was only a matter of time.

Our family dinner table was a lively place, where loud differences of opinion were welcomed and competing views often jostled for dominance. My parents encouraged us to think, to speak our minds, to test our ideas in animated exchanges. We were not a shy family. So if I spoke boldly at the dinner table that evening, I could perhaps be forgiven for following family tradition.

"I'm not sure I am going to apply to any other colleges," I responded, looking at my mother. My heart began to pound.

A split second of silence. A loaded silence.

"What?" boomed my father, confused. He looked first at me, then at my mother; did she know what was going on? But her face, staring at me, was a stunned question mark.

"What do you mean, you're not sure you're going to apply to any other colleges?" my father demanded. "And where *did* you apply?"

"I applied to Hellenic College," I said. This Greek Orthodox Christian college, though popular among many Greek American students, was not even on my parents' fallback list.

"Hellenic College—?" my mother's tone rose as she said it, turning it into a question. "Why?"

My bewildered parents looked at me, pain on their faces.

It was now or never. I felt courage well up in me.

"Because I want to become a priest," I said.

My words hung in the air. No one spoke. My family grasped that I wanted to attend Hellenic College because it shared a campus with a seminary—Holy Cross Greek Orthodox School of Theology.

My mother looked at my father. My father took a deep breath. I went to my room.

Around the time my father, Christ (pronounced Chris), and my mother, Merope (pronounced Meh-ROPE-ee), became engaged, in December 1959, freeways were sprouting around Chicago. Many Chicagoans, weary of the noise, congestion, and growing social unrest of America's second city, fled the city on the newly built off-ramps that led to suburbs with quiet streets, lawns, and brand-new schools. By contrast, my parents, young and just starting out, rented an apartment in the city and later bought a house there for their growing family. All four of my Greek grandparents also lived in the city, so my siblings—George, Maria-Magdalene (Maria for short), and Michael—and I grew up in an imperfect but loving circle of family. It was a family known for strong opinions; views on topics from politics to religion to the state of the economy were enthusiastically shared, sometimes heatedly. Of course, everyone had an opinion about my wanting to be a priest.

My father's mother, Magdaline, whom we called Yiayia Lynn, was a widow and the most religiously faithful member of our family. From the time I was an infant, I had often sat with her at church, learning when to cross myself and when to kneel. When I was twelve, Yiayia Lynn helped me memorize the Nicene Creed in the original Greek. She was part of the reason I loved the Church, and I loved her dearly. She let me know she loved me too. Surely, she would agree that becoming a priest was a wonderful calling.

The day I told her I wanted to become a priest, she looked at me with sad eyes and took my hands in hers.

"Please don't do this, Demetri," she begged me. She had seen me on the stage at school plays. She knew I loved to dance. She was afraid that I would no longer be able to live a free life if I became a priest. I looked at her loving face, and I was at a loss for words.

"Wouldn't it make you happy to be a doctor or a lawyer?" suggested my clever mother, quietly telegraphing her dreams while trying to be supportive. "You could study premed or prelaw somewhere else," she counseled casually, "and then go to seminary later." She was playing the long game; she probably hoped this "priest phase" would pass before I graduated from college.

My father was unhappy. Not only was I putting all my academic eggs in one basket by applying to one college; he had enough experience in parish life to know that my expectations about being a priest were unreasonably rosy, that my idealized image of the priesthood probably didn't include the politics, difficult personalities, and financial stresses that confront priests daily. He understood that I was captivated by the pageantry of the services, the incense, the ancient chants and prayers written by believers almost two thousand years before, the transcendent, timeless quality of the liturgy. He didn't want me to suffer. He strongly urged me to reconsider.

Of course, he was right. What did I know about the priesthood? Not much more than beautiful church services. I understood little of the heavy lifting involved in administering a parish budget, raising money, overseeing staff, and working with a sometimes-argumentative parish council. I didn't understand the frustrating church politics up and down the hierarchy that priests had to negotiate. I hadn't witnessed priests bent with sorrow after hearing confessions or brokenhearted at the bedsides of the sick and the dying in fluorescent-lit hospital rooms. All of this was the work of priests.

My father was aware of this; I was oblivious to most of it.

In my imagination, the day-to-day realities of leading a parish were vague and manageable. My youthful experience in worship services as an altar boy favored the "there and then" over the practical demands of the "here and now." The events of the distant and ancient past—of the apostles, saints, and martyrs—and of the promised future—the Kingdom of Heaven—fascinated me. That's what I thought it meant to be a priest!

None of my faithful family's opinions changed my mind. In fact, the chorus of disapproval from them only strengthened my resolve. I knew they loved the Church. I knew they loved me. I knew I was called to be a priest.

I didn't apply to any other colleges.

※

During my senior year of high school, I told the head priest at our parish, Father Demetrios N. Treantafeles, that I wanted to go to seminary. He was pleased; he had known me for years as an altar boy. He also knew that for me to be accepted into the seminary-track program at Hellenic College, I would need a letter of reference from our new bishop, Bishop Iakovos of Chicago, to supplement the application I had already submitted.

Fortunately for me, one of the years-long traditions of our parish was that on Holy Thursday—the Thursday before Easter (Pascha)—the bishop of Chicago visited our parish. Our new bishop planned to continue that tradition; he would be at our parish in a few days.

Bishop Iakovos had served as the bishop of Chicago for less than a year, but he had already served as a bishop for eleven years. He was fifty-two years old. He was deeply familiar with the Greek Orthodox seminary—Holy Cross Greek Orthodox School of Theology—and the college affiliated with it—Hellenic College, in the Boston suburb of Brookline. He had been president of both institutions from 1971 to 1976 and had wrapped up his work there four years earlier.

I counted the days, and Holy Thursday evening finally arrived. Shortly before services began, I stood nervously in my altar boy's robes near the altar beside Father Gerasimos Annas, the second priest at our parish. Bishop Iakovos was sitting in a chair, waiting for the service to begin.

Father Gerasimos addressed the bishop, "Your Grace, Demetri would like to attend seminary."

Bishop Iakovos didn't miss a beat. "Well, Father, if Demetri would like to go to seminary, he should pick up the telephone and make an appointment to see me."

His words were like a splash of cold water. At first, I was taken aback, embarrassed for Father Gerasimos, but then I realized he was teaching me something: if I wanted to be taken seriously, I would need to start doing things for myself. He was challenging me to be an adult, which felt both good and a little scary. I found myself fearing and admiring our new bishop for the rest of the evening.

And so, the week after Pascha (known as Bright Week), I called the Greek Orthodox Diocese of Chicago and scheduled an appointment to meet with Bishop Iakovos. Father Treantafeles graciously accompanied me there. We were invited to take a seat in the diocese's comfortable reception area and were treated to traditional red Pascha eggs,[3] cookies, and coffee. Bishop Iakovos joined us. After some minutes of conversation, Father Treantafeles excused himself so the bishop could speak with me privately.

I was apprehensive. It was my first private meeting with a bishop. Would he ask me why I wanted to be a priest? Would he grill me? Would he like me?

The bishop gave me his blessing to pursue the priesthood and promised to write me a letter of recommendation. That was all. I kissed his hand and left, surprised and relieved. Only later did I come to understand that he had already received and read Father Treantefeles's thorough assessment of me and my suitability for the priesthood. It was reassuring that Father Treantafeles believed I was a good candidate for the seminary. Apparently, in our brief exchange, I had not given Bishop Iakovos any reason to think otherwise.

Bishop Iakovos's letter of recommendation was mailed to Hellenic College. Then I waited.

The days passed. Friends received hefty acceptance letters or thin rejection letters from their prospective colleges. "I got in!" they would announce in the hallways at school. Still, I waited. Finally, a thick envelope with my name on it arrived from Hellenic College. I had been accepted!

My father was probably disappointed, but he never said that to me. To his credit, although he didn't agree with my choice, he trusted me to make it. Like most Greek American fathers, he wanted me to be happy and to prosper. He looked forward to the day that, priest or not, I would marry (you can be a married priest in the Greek Orthodox church) and have a son, whom I would name after my father, and a daughter, whom I would name after my mother. My father would then be called Papou—Grandfather—and my mother, Yiayia—Grandmother. This was what he had done and what his father before him had done. After all, it was Greek tradition.

3

✝

Meeting Andrew

February 27, 1999

My first thought on seeing Andrew enter the visitor's room was surprise. He didn't look anything like the cocky, youthful person in the photographs I had seen in the newspapers. The middle-aged man who shuffled toward me in leg shackles wore glasses with square, chunky frames. He was bald. The muscles of his arms were defined but did not strain against the shackles that bound his wrists. His beige prison-issue scrubs accentuated a life-lived-mostly-indoors paleness.

My second thought was relief. I had expected Andrew to be physically intimidating, possibly bristling with anger. He had been described as a monster. The man approaching me under the bright lights was considerably shorter than me, and he exhibited no defiance or hostility toward the guard who accompanied him. The crispness of his garments and neatly trimmed Vandyke beard suggested tidiness. Around his neck was a gold chain with the cross that Theodora had given him.

When he reached the table, I stood.

"I'm Father Demetri," I said and reached out to shake his hand.

"It's nice to meet you; I'm Andrew," he said as he shook my hand, a bit awkwardly because of the shackles.

I glanced down at the hand I was shaking, a small hand with squared fingers. *Did he use those hands to murder someone?* The surreal thought momentarily disoriented me. I broke into a cold sweat as I released his hand.

Andrew sat down on the INMATE chair opposite me and placed his shackled hands on the metal table between us. As I sat down, I glanced

Andrew Kokoraleis, circa 1999. Chicago Police Department

over Andrew's shoulder and saw the guard withdraw, closing the door behind him and locking it. When I heard the lock engage, my brain instantly sent a shock wave through me—*I am trapped in a locked room with a man accused of murder*—and my heart started pounding.

But another part of me countered, *Theodora assured me he is safe, and guards are watching us.* With an effort of will, I focused on Andrew.

The man facing me had been convicted by a jury of torturing, mutilating, and killing two women, and he was going to be executed for the murder of one of them. More than a dozen other Chicago women had suffered the same fate. I saw their faces in my mind's eye and recalled disturbing descriptions of crime scenes. Autopsy results had revealed a callous disregard for the victims, even a perverse enjoyment of their suffering. The crimes committed by the Ripper Crew were repulsive, heinous. Had Andrew been part of this gruesome murder spree? Was he guilty?

I paused and reminded myself of the reason for my visit. I was not here to be judge or jury. I was here in the hope that I could help prevent his being executed by the State of Illinois.

"Theodora asked me to come see you," I said.

"Thank you for coming," he said. He regarded me calmly through the lenses.

I looked at him across the table. Shackles aside, Andrew seemed like a person I might see in the aisle of my neighborhood grocery store or walking a dog in the park. Theodora had said he was a good soul. In fact, he radiated a sense of calm. This helped me feel more relaxed.

"Andrew, I need you to know that no matter what, you are a precious child of God, a member of the body of Christ. The Church, your Church, is here for you." I wanted to reassure him with this message above all.

"Thank you, Father, and thank you for being here," he said, after which he hesitated. "I'm grateful, but I want you to know that I've come to terms with the idea that I'm probably going to be executed on March 17th."

It was as if he were telling me that I was powerless to do anything. Somehow that provoked me. It made me want to try harder.

"I understand," I said. "Still, I'm hoping that perhaps I can help get your execution vacated. I can't promise anything, of course, but I'd like to try, if that's okay with you."

"Of course, that would be great," he said. "I just hope you understand if I say I'm not going to get my hopes up."

I nodded and said we could talk about whatever he wanted.

∞

We talked a little about the legal side of things. It was disheartening. Over the past seventeen years, Andrew's lawyers had exhausted most of his legal appeals. He said his attorneys had recently turned up some new evidence that supported his claim of innocence and were hoping it could be introduced. It was a long shot, but, if allowed, the new evidence could help set the record straight and might even help prove that Andrew was innocent of the murder of Lorraine Borowski as he claimed. His attorneys were already scheduled to stand before a judge and argue the merits of holding a hearing to assess the relevance of the new evidence; of course, the prosecution would oppose it.

Andrew added that the Illinois Prisoner Review Board would soon hold a hearing on his case. His lawyers hoped that the new evidence might sway the board to view Andrew more sympathetically. Andrew knew the board had no legal power to change his fate, but a favorable recommendation from them to the governor could make a difference. Governor George Ryan had the power to delay Andrew's execution—or even to grant him clemency—if only he could be persuaded.

I offered to speak on his behalf at the Prisoner Review Board hearing.

"I would appreciate that," he said. "I will tell my lawyer."

Andrew's attorneys had also told him that the idea of a moratorium on executions in Illinois was being publicly discussed. Depending on the timing, a declaration of a moratorium by the governor could result in Andrew's execution being delayed. If his attorneys could just buy him some more time, maybe they could prevent his being executed on March 17. For his part, if his life could be spared, Andrew seemed ready and willing to spend the rest of his life in prison.

"It sounds like there's a lot going on in the next couple of weeks," I said.

"Yes," he agreed with a smile. "I don't have a lot of hope it will change anything, though. At this point, it seems that it's all politics." Unlike me—I was too naive at the time to see the powerful political machinations influencing his fate—he correctly understood that his case was one small element in a much larger political debate over capital punishment in Illinois.

"Father, I was convicted of murder, but I am innocent," Andrew said. "The only evidence they offered at my trial was my own confession"—a confession that Andrew told me had been beaten out of him after hours of physical abuse at the hands of police and one that he had immediately recanted.[1] Other people on Illinois's death row had been released when their confessions were later shown to have been coerced by authorities. Andrew had once hoped that perhaps he would likewise be proven innocent, but over time, those hopes had faded.

"Years ago, I took a lie detector test," Andrew said. The result of the polygraph test affirmed that Andrew had told the truth when he claimed that he was beaten into giving a false confession. However, such tests are generally inadmissible in court because they are not considered scientifically reliable.

I listened and wondered, *Is he telling me the truth?*

∞

Andrew told me a little about his childhood, his parents and five siblings, about living in an apartment on North Avenue in Chicago. He'd liked school and said, "I dreamed of becoming a teacher." He told me that he and his family had gone to church at the Assumption.

"The Assumption!" I said, surprised. "You went there too?"

"Yes," he said, "you too?"

We figured out we were about the same age, but neither of us remembered ever having met at our enormous parish. This unexpected connection opened a warm channel between us. He told me his father had emigrated from Greece and was a cook. His mother, a server, was not Greek. She had died very young, when Andrew was twelve. Andrew's family had been financially strapped when he was growing up. He'd left home before finishing high school, and despite his love of learning, he hadn't graduated.

Andrew told me about his arrest, which was consistent with his court testimony.[2] He said that police questioned him about three murders and he had claimed innocence concerning all of them. He said he had been interrogated all night, until five o'clock the next morning. He had been allowed to take a short nap on four plastic chairs in an interrogation room, then was awakened and questioned again. On that second day in custody, he had been intermittently beaten by police over the course of about three hours. Then a blanket was placed over his head, and he was struck again several times. To stop the beating, Andrew led police to a site where he said some bodies had been buried—Schiller Woods. There, police gave him a shovel and told him to dig. He did, but no bodies were found. An officer ordered him to lie down in one of the holes, and officers shoveled dirt on him. One of the officers kneeled on Andrew's chest, pointed a pistol at him, and said something like, "We should just blow this guy's head off." Two shots were fired, but neither hit Andrew. He said he was taken back for questioning and interrogated until midnight. He had not had anything to eat all day. That night, he slept in an interrogation room, handcuffed to a ring in the wall. He said he was questioned again the next morning. During his three days in custody, police supplied him with information about three murders and made him include that information in his statements.

Andrew told me he had been sent to jail in November 1982 when he was nineteen. He learned how to survive in Cook County Jail and DuPage County Jail. On February 11, 1985, a jury convicted him of the rape, murder, and aggravated kidnapping of Rose Beck Davis;[3] one month later, he was sentenced to life in prison for her murder. The judge's gavel went down, and Andrew was led out of the courtroom in handcuffs. Two years later, on March 18, 1987, he stood beside his defense attorney to hear another jury convict him of murder and aggravated kidnapping in the death of Lorraine Borowski, and on April 30, 1987, he was sentenced to death for her murder. He was taken to death row in Pontiac. From that point on, he had lived in solitary confinement, locked in his small cell for twenty-three hours a day.

Andrew eventually learned what had happened to the other three men. Edward Spreitzer was convicted of the murders of Linda Sutton, Shui Mak, Rose Beck Davis, Sandra Delaware, and Raphael Tirado and was sentenced to death and sent to death row. Andrew's brother Thomas was convicted of murder based on an accountability theory (he was held accountable for the acts committed by other individuals that resulted in Lorraine Borowski's death) and sentenced to seventy years in prison. Only Robin Gecht was never charged with murder. He was sentenced to

120 years for rape, attempted murder, aggravated kidnapping, and deviate sexual assault.[4]

Of the four men, Andrew alone faced imminent execution—this, despite their all having been accused and Gecht's being the acknowledged leader of the group. To Andrew, it seemed particularly unfair that Gecht, who had masterminded and perpetrated multiple horrors, had fared so much better than he had.[5]

Andrew told me that his anger simmered within him for a long time. Then an unexpected opportunity presented itself: Gecht was transferred to Pontiac. When Andrew found out, he asked around and learned which cell block Gecht was in. He lay on his bed and contemplated "in-house" revenge, wanting to make his former boss pay for the fact that he was languishing on death row and would eventually be executed while Gecht was not. Andrew weighed his options, how to get back at Gecht and how to let Gecht know that it was he, Andrew, who was exacting vengeance. But in the end, Andrew decided to let it go.

It took years, Andrew said, but he finally released his anger. He was helped in this by Theodora, who spoke of God's forgiveness for all (including Andrew) and radiated God's love during her prison visits with him. He told me he no longer held anything against Gecht, Spreitzer, his brother, or anyone else. He had been forgiven, and he forgave in turn. Hope was reborn in him. He began to redirect his energies to improving his life. He lifted weights to condition his body and read and prayed to condition his mind and soul.

∽

"Has your family visited you much?" I asked Andrew.

"No," he replied. His mother had died in 1975, and his father in 1996. His brother Thomas was in prison, and his other siblings lived in various states. The only support he had came from the Greek Orthodox Church. A priest, Father Kallinikos Zacharapoulos, had visited him at times, Andrew said, and he had recommended that Theodora visit Andrew.

It was Theodora who had reawakened his faith in God, Andrew said. "I call her 'Ma,'" he added, and his face broke into a wide smile.

I surprised myself by smiling back. For despite everything, I found the man sitting before me to be a likable, articulate person. This was confusing, for as he talked, the haunting articles I had read about the Ripper Crew victims—their pain, humiliation, terror, and in most cases, deaths—kept running through my head. Their photographs and gruesome deaths, their lives, could not easily be forgotten. I struggled to reconcile the grim stories about the Ripper Crew with the man seated before me. *Had he been involved in those awful events, as charged?* I couldn't help but wonder.

Perhaps in his late teens, Andrew had been a hapless misfit, adrift and desperately looking for somewhere to belong, and had attached himself to the wrong people. Perhaps he had become a criminal. I would never know the whole truth of his life. Yet whatever he had once been, and whatever he had once been capable of—as awful as it might have been—the thirty-five-year-old man in shackles seemed a different person now. He appeared to have done the hard work of taking stock of his life and taking responsibility for all of it, acknowledging the beautiful chapters and owning the darker passages as well.

There in the crucible of death row, Andrew had encountered faith and wrestled with the meaning of his life. I listened as he shared what he had learned on that lonely journey. In the tiny prison cell, isolated from others and encouraged by Theodora each week, he had to face himself and his choices. All the fear and shame he had experienced—wanting to die after his mother died, sad and scared; fleeing his father and a troubled home; struggling to survive on the streets of Chicago; befriending Eddie Spreitzer; working for Robin Gecht and being implicated in his twisted, unspeakable atrocities; and winding up in jail and, later, on death row—so much was dark and shameful. Yet for all the brokenness and pain of his journey, it had brought him, finally, to repentance, to a land of tears, a place of unexpected love and healing. He had encountered God's grace and mercy and had been transformed despite everything. He was at peace with himself and his accusers, he said. For all the years he spent on death row for the murder of Lorraine Borowski, Andrew had maintained his claim of innocence, and he did again that day.

I listened and was deeply moved. I had not expected this. It seemed to me that he had come to terms with it all: the transience and profound beauty of life, the transformative nature of love, and the mercy of God for everyone, however broken.

By the end of our visit, I believed that this polite, mild-mannered man was being honest with me. I believed his claim that he was innocent of the one crime for which he was to be executed.

※

It was time for me to go. I told Andrew that the diocese would do what it could to help and that a lot of people were working together behind the scenes to assist him. I told him Bishop Iakovos knew I was visiting with him and was also supportive. I promised that we would tap every resource we could on his behalf. I think Andrew was surprised and touched to hear that a group of Greek Orthodox faithful who didn't even know him cared about him and were advocating and praying for him.

I alerted the guard that we were done. The visit seemed to go by quickly, although it had probably lasted a little over an hour.

"Thank you for visiting me," Andrew said.

"Thanks for welcoming me," I answered.

"It's unlikely that you can prevent my execution, but I appreciate you trying," Andrew said, then added, "Perhaps God can use my execution to finally end all executions in Illinois."

We both stood up, and I spontaneously hugged him goodbye, kissing him on both cheeks in traditional Greek fashion. *Am I embracing a murderer?* Again, a surreal thought disoriented me, and I released Andrew. The guard let me out into the hallway and pointed me toward the exit. I heard the heavy metal door of the visiting room close behind me.

∞

I started down the sterile institutional hallway, reeling from the intensity of my visit with Andrew. I put a weary hand to my forehead and tried to process what had just happened. A whirlwind of questions descended on me, each demanding an answer. Had I really visited a convicted murderer? Yes. Was he a monster? No, he was a person. Was he guilty? I had no way of knowing. He assured me he was innocent, but the legal system assured me equally that he was guilty. Was he really going to be executed? Yes, this flesh-and-blood person, a human just like me, had his name on an executioner's calendar. What gives us the right to kill him? As far as I could see, nothing. Even if he is guilty, why should he be killed? There in the hallway, that question stopped me. *Why should he be killed?*

I had heard justifications for capital punishment: fulfilling the demands of justice, deterrence of murder, desire for revenge, concern for victims' families, "an eye for an eye." I put those arguments on one side of a pair of scales. I had heard reasons for opposing the death penalty: the possibility of executing the innocent, prosecutorial misconduct, incompetent defense attorneys, corrupt judges, forced confessions extracted by police, political motivations, and costs. I placed those competing claims on the other side. From my perspective as a person of faith, the scales came down on the side opposed to capital punishment.

Now, though, there was something more: I had met Andrew face-to-face. He had become a real person to me. Everything I had learned in seminary, read, and discussed with Bishop Iakovos or attorneys; every argument by death penalty opponents and advocates; everything I understood concerning the death penalty—all of it had coalesced there, in that visiting room with Andrew, when he and I sat together and looked into one another's eyes. In that moment, I realized that every argument had been silenced by the irresistible, overarching claim that is placed upon us—that each and every life matters.

Even Andrew's.

∽

I continued down the corridor and vividly recalled a conversation I had with my father years before, when I was a teenager. A strong proponent of the death penalty, he told me there were some crimes so abhorrent that justice demanded that the criminal forfeit their life. Yet it was from my tough-talking, pro–capital punishment father that I learned to be an opponent of capital punishment. For all his macho talk, my father was a man guided by a deep sense of fairness. When he spoke to me about execution, he cautioned, "This is one place we have to be certain that a person is guilty—*we have to be damn sure*—because you can't go back and correct that mistake."

Was Andrew guilty? He had been convicted without evidence, based solely on his confession, a confession he claimed had been beaten out of him. Could we be "damn sure" he was guilty?

The teachings of my faith took it even further: life is sacred, a profound gift given by God. It is not ours to take away, period. Why should Andrew be killed? He shouldn't, because his life is sacred.

Lorraine Borowski's life was sacred, too, and it had been viciously taken from her. Would the horror of her awful murder—and it truly was horrible—be changed by the horror of the state murdering Andrew, a man who claimed he was innocent of the crime? I did not believe so. We would have two murders instead of one and perhaps the execution of an innocent man. All the people of Illinois, including me, would be complicit in that act of premeditated murder.

The state—faceless, bureaucratic, impersonal, rife with political intrigue, powerful—wanted Andrew dead, and it planned to kill him in less than three weeks. In the face of this potent system, how could I possibly make a difference? Even I had to admit that Andrew's case looked hopeless. Yet how could I not fight for the sanctity of life, for his life? I couldn't just give up. I had to do something. We had to do something. The state should not be in the business of killing people.

What am I going to do? What can I do? I wondered. We had already started discussing advocacy for Andrew at the diocese. I had reached out to an anti–capital punishment group. It was not nearly enough, though; we would have to do a great deal more than that to sway the new governor, known for his pro–capital punishment views. I felt a growing sense of resolve, of determination. Could we exert enough influence to delay the execution, perhaps to prevent it? Maybe not, but we had to try.

I was buzzed through a door and found myself momentarily boxed in (no panic this time). Then a second door buzzed open ahead of me, and I was again in a long corridor leading to the visitor desk, where I signed out. I proceeded down the next hallway and soon found myself back in the reception area. Ahead of me, I spotted the familiar welcome desk, the institutional furniture, and finally the reassuring figures of Fred and Theodora. I was flooded by a sense of relief. When I saw my friends' faces, tears sprang into my eyes and rolled down my cheeks. I was suddenly overcome by love and exhaustion.

Fred stood up and began to cross the space between us. "How did it go?" he called out. As he got closer, he saw my sweaty, tear-stained face. I must have looked like a wreck because his own face registered concern, and he asked, "What happened?"

I answered him, my voice choked by emotion. "I went to minister to Andrew, and he wound up ministering to me," I said, covering my eyes and face with both hands and inhaling sharply. I slid my hands down my damp face and exhaled. Theodora joined us.

"Father," she said gently, and in her face I saw understanding. We had both met Andrew now.

I signed out at the reception desk, turned in my visitor lanyard, and retrieved my coat from the locker. My friends knew that what Andrew and I had discussed was confidential so they didn't expect me to share it. Together, the three of us walked out the exit doors into the cold winter sunlight. It was a physical relief to escape the oppressiveness of the prison, a relief to be in the fresh air—no doors, no locks, no guards!—and feel cool air fill my lungs. In silence, we made our way across the parking lot toward the cars. Fred and I thanked Theodora and said goodbye to her, then walked to his car.

As I got into Fred's car, I spotted our stained, empty coffee cups in the cupholders. Had it only been this morning that we had left Chicago? I sank heavily into the passenger seat and pulled the door closed, relieved to be in a safe, familiar space. I was trying to hold my feelings in check, and the walk to the car in the cool air had helped.

"Are you okay?" Fred asked.

"I feel worn out," I said.

I told him about the second waiting room as well as the grim, locked visitor room with its furniture bolted to the floor. I choked up when I began to describe Andrew—in his chunky glasses, noisy shackles, and trim goatee—and then I quietly began to sob, my shoulders shaking, as a rush of feelings swept over me. I felt despair. Despair at the jarring, dehumanizing elements of the prison that I had just encountered: the invasive body search, the sharp buzzes, the stamping of hands, the locked doors, the guards' sidearms, the sterile visitor room, and the shackles. I also felt profound sadness for the depersonalization that seemed to descend on everyone in the facility: visitors, prisoners, and staff alike. I was outraged by the macabre reality that Andrew, this surprisingly likeable man whom I had just met, lived in a place intended to keep a person alive (and healthy) long enough to be executed. I had a heavy sense of hopelessness and was keenly aware of my own helplessness to do anything. I sat in Fred's reassuring presence until the flood of feelings washed out of me and a sense of stillness came over me.

In that stillness, a peaceful clarity emerged. *This is why I became a priest*, I suddenly understood. It felt like an awakening. A calm relief filled me, and hope rose in my chest. I felt a strengthening of resolve that I would do all I could to help Andrew.

Fred put the car in gear and pulled out of the prison parking lot, and we made our way back to Chicago.

4
✢
It Isn't for Everybody

August 1980

It was a steamy day in Chicago in August 1980 when I got into the car with my mother and a dear family friend, Jeannie Antonopoulos, and we headed east. We were bound for Brookline, Massachusetts, a suburb of Boston, where I was about to begin my freshman year at Hellenic College. Left behind were the heat and humidity of Chicago and its midwestern sensibilities. The twenty-hour road trip ended on a leafy, winding, uphill road that brought us to the shared campus of Hellenic College and Holy Cross Greek Orthodox School of Theology, where we pulled up to the curb and parked. It was hot and sticky here too. The two women helped me unload the car, then stood waiting at the curb as I carried my things into the mostly empty lobby of a dorm where other freshmen were checking in. They, too, were hauling suitcases, carts, and pillows.

Among the many items I carried that day was one of particular significance: a black cassock. Hellenic College undergraduates like me who had applied for and been accepted into the seminary-track program were given "seminarian status" and were required to wear a cassock to daily chapel services and to religious and formal events.

Months before, when I'd gone with Father Treantafeles to meet with Bishop Iakovos at the diocese after Pascha and the three of us had sat together talking, I'd mentioned in passing that I would be visiting Greece with a classmate after my high school graduation. "Call me when you get to Athens," the bishop had said, and he had given me a telephone number.

Chapter 4

After I arrived in Athens that June, I remembered this and repeatedly tried calling the number the bishop had given me. When I finally managed to reach him by phone, he suggested that I meet him at the shop of the Athenian tailor who made his priestly garments so that I could order the cassock I would need for college. Two months later, here I was, carrying it into the dorm.

I left the cassock draped over my pile of belongings in the lobby and rejoined my mother and Jeannie at the car. I looked at the two women and felt a pang: it was time for them to go. Our parting was no surprise—it was the point of the whole trip, really—but I felt suddenly unprepared for it. We said our emotional farewells, and, after a final hug, I watched them drive off.

∞

To say I was green when I arrived at Hellenic College was an understatement. Moments after saying goodbye to Jeannie and my mother, I returned to the dormitory building, where I met the acting dean of student life, Allen Poulos,[1] who was receiving incoming freshmen. It was hot, and I was looking forward to cooling off.

"Where's the pool?" I asked peremptorily.

He looked at me, rolled his eyes, and laughed. "You're going to have a long seven years here," he said.

∞

Not many days later, during freshman orientation, the pay phone on the wall of our dormitory hallway rang, and I heard someone answer it. A moment later, one of my dormmates, Manny Burdusi,[2] appeared at the open door of my room, where I was lounging on my bed.

"You have an important phone call," he said.

I emerged from my dorm room, and Manny handed me the receiver.

"Hello?" I said.

My father's familiar voice broke as he told me that his mother, my Yiayia Lynn, had died unexpectedly. I could still hear other freshmen down the hallway, laughing and horsing around, but my focus shifted inward and far from Brookline, as I tried to wrap my mind around the impossible words my father had just spoken. I'd seen Yiayia Lynn only days ago, just before I'd left for college, and now she was dead. Stunned, I made arrangements with my father to return to Chicago. I spoke with Allen Poulos, and soon I was flying home.

The funeral was held in the Assumption, the church where so many joyful events had been celebrated. Near the end of the service, after everyone else in the church had respectfully filed past the coffin to say their goodbyes, my grief-stricken father and mother stepped forward and stood before the open casket. For the first time I saw my parents, who had always seemed so strong, appear vulnerable. They kissed Yiayia Lynn and stepped back. The priest anointed my grandmother's body, pouring a small amount of oil on her in the form of a cross, saying, "Wash me with hyssop and I shall be pure; cleanse me and I shall be whiter than snow." Sprinkling some earth on her body, he said, "The earth is the Lord's and the fullness thereof, the world and those who dwell therein; you are earth, and to earth shall you return." Then the priest closed the casket lid.

Familiar prayers and hymns surrounded us that day, and when the funeral concluded, my family processed behind the casket, which other pallbearers and I carried to the hearse. In the cars, following the hearse to the cemetery, we exchanged stories about Yiayia Lynn, and laughter blended with the salty taste of tears.

Two days later, for the second time in as many weeks, I said farewell to my family and headed to Massachusetts.

My first year went well. As my parents intended, my Lutheran high school had provided me with a solid academic foundation for college. I recall crossing the campus, looking with some envy at the older seminarians who sported black cassocks and beards.

※

The summer after my freshman year, I was at home, padding around the house barefoot, when the phone rang. It was the receptionist from the Greek Orthodox Diocese of Chicago. Was I available to drive Bishop Iakovos to and from the elementary school graduation at my home parish that day? *What an honor!* I thought.

"Yes!" I answered. I put on a suit and tie, jumped in the family car, and drove to the diocese to pick up the bishop at the appointed time.

Decades earlier, my grandparents had come to the United States with thousands of other immigrants, spilling out onto the new land with scarcely any knowledge of English, their minds full of dreams. On the noisy streets of Chicago, they were attracted to the strange newness of things—crowded streetcars moving past, paperboys shouting out headlines to sell their papers—even as they clung to familiar elements of their old life. They straddled two worlds; when they had children, they passed on this duality of cultures. It showed up in my life too. I grew up bilingual, speaking Greek in our home and at church (at the insistence of my father) and English everywhere else. My brothers, sister, and I, beyond learning two languages, learned two cultures, Greek and American. Our parents raised us to value being Americans, Chicagoans, and part of an ethnic community with roots stretching back to antiquity.

That upbringing helped me that day with the bishop. Our conversation was in Greek (although he spoke English fluently) because he was originally from Greece.

To my surprise, a couple of weeks later, the diocese offered me a summer job. I happily accepted.

I learned a great deal that summer. As in the early church, a bishop today is responsible for the well-being of the parishes, priests, and faithful living in a large geographic area (in this case, Illinois, Iowa, Minnesota, Wisconsin, northern Indiana, and southeastern Missouri). I assisted the chancellor and registrar—clergymen whose administrative work helped the bishop tend to the needs and well-being of fifty-eight parishes—doing everything from helping maintain accurate baptismal records to sending out correspondence. But by far most meaningful to me were the opportunities to accompany Bishop Iakovos to some of his meetings and liturgical services throughout the Midwest. With each trip, I came to know and admire this wise, thoughtful gentleman a little more.

At summer's end, I was invited to work at the diocese whenever I was home for Christmas, Pascha, or summer break. I thanked them and promised to be back, and each time I was home I took them up on their offer.

The next few years passed quickly, and in 1984, I graduated from Hellenic College with my bachelor's degree and a beard that I had grown at the start of my sophomore year and maintained ever since. My proud family was there to see me graduate. I showed them around the Brookline campus. Then we all returned to Chicago, where I again worked at the diocese for the summer.

The next fall, I returned to Brookline to begin my studies at Holy Cross Greek Orthodox School of Theology.

∞

During my seven years of study at Brookline, my father let me know that if I ever wanted to change course, he would happily support that decision. Any time I called home and vented frustrations I was experiencing at school, he unabashedly suggested, "Why don't you just come home?"

That was not really what I wanted to hear. Still, he supported me and allowed me to follow my own path.

∞

A long-standing rite of passage at Holy Cross Greek Orthodox School of Theology is held every fall for students in their final year of seminary. This ceremony is held annually on September 14, the feast day of the theological school. The archbishop, who is based in New York City, makes a special visit, both to celebrate the seminary's feast day and to participate in this annual tradition.

On September 14, 1986, it was my turn to be part of this ceremony. I woke up that morning full of anticipation and walked to the chapel to attend the early morning service (which we call Orthros and Roman Catholics call Matins) and the Divine Liturgy (which Roman Catholics call the Mass).[3] Like every seminarian who would graduate the following spring, I carried a neatly folded new garment, an *exorasson*, with me. This garment is meaningful to seminarians because it is worn by clergy, which we were all aiming to become.[4]

When the Divine Liturgy ended, there was a low buzz of excitement in the chapel. The archbishop called my class forward, and we stood before him, each of us with a folded *exorasson* in our hands. He delivered a brief pastoral message and prayed over us. Then, one by one, each seminarian approached the archbishop, presented his *exorasson*, then turned so his back faced the archbishop, who draped the *exorasson* over the seminarian's shoulders and called out the traditional exclamation, "Axios!" ["Worthy!"]. Everyone in the chapel responded, "Axios!" It was thrilling.

From that point on, each of us was required to wear the *exorasson* over our cassock for daily chapel services and other formal occasions. It was a great honor.

This ceremony was a sign to us that we were nearly done with our studies and a vote of confidence that we would one day be ordained. The idea of leaving a campus that had been my home for so many years—six years, going on seven—was exciting. I was ready for more than studying theology. I was looking forward to applying it.

Fall soon turned to winter, and winter, to spring. I finished my spring midterms and started packing my suitcase for Chicago. It was time for spring break, Holy Week, and what I knew would probably be a difficult visit home.

Graduation was approaching. I would soon have to answer a question that came up frequently among students like me who were in their final year of seminary and weren't engaged or married: was I planning to remain unmarried or to marry? I was almost twenty-five years old. Some of my friends were already married; most weren't. I had dated a little but nothing serious. Now, the pressure was on. My parents knew this as well.

For the first thousand years of Christianity—before the Christian Church was divided between the Orthodox Church in the East and the Roman Catholic Church in the West[5]—priests were allowed to be married, just as St. Peter the Apostle, the first bishop of Rome, was. In the Orthodox Christian tradition, priests are still able to be married; that is, a man may marry *before* he is ordained a deacon. If he is later ordained a priest, he will be a married priest.

A candidate for ordination also has the option to delay his ordination; he does not have to be ordained right after graduating from seminary, so he can take his time in deciding about marriage. Of course, this also delays his progress in becoming a deacon and then a priest.

Finally, some seminary graduates choose not to marry and are ordained unmarried. They cannot then enter into marriage. That option is closed to them.

In the Orthodox Church, it is from this last group, known as the monastic clergy, that bishops are traditionally selected.

Thinking about the monastic clergy brought Bishop Iakovos to mind. In the six years I had worked for him, he had spoken with me about his journey of faith and his decision to serve God by remaining unmarried. He had made a good choice, he told me, and I believed him. I could see the positive influence that his leadership of our church made, and I could see his satisfaction in his life's work for the sake of the gospel. On a more personal level, I held him in high esteem. He was a true gentleman, elegant in his manner, speech, and bearing. He was poised, generous, and hospitable. He was genuinely full of faith and laughed easily, sometimes even at himself. The idea of mirroring his life by making the same decision he had held a lot of appeal. Was that my path?

I thought about my parents. I was their oldest child, and I knew they wanted grandchildren, but I hadn't really talked to them about whether or not I would marry. They had modeled a loving marriage. Even after twenty-seven years of marriage, the warm affection between them was evident and genuine. I thought especially of my father. I still longed for his approval. I could see how thoroughly he enjoyed his family and his work. He had made a good choice by marrying my mother. Was that my path?

This question—"To marry, or not to marry?"—may seem like a curious anachronism, but to Orthodox seminarians, it is the choice of a lifetime, a decisive fork in the road leading to the priesthood, a significant aspect of one's calling. I witnessed some of my fellow unmarried seminarians wrestling with this question: should they marry, or should they not? Some argued the pros and cons. Others were torn, undecided, struggling. For those who decided they *would* like to be married, should they marry the person they were currently dating, or should they wait for someone else? How long might it take to find the "right" person—an Orthodox Christian woman who would want to serve God in a parish by being married to a priest, which was its own kind of calling? These are important questions, and complicated. The need to answer them added an intensity to the last year of seminary as day by day we moved toward graduation.

But in my own life, I found that these were not questions I needed to answer. In my experience, there was no struggle. The choice to be a member of the monastic clergy was, somehow, a natural thing—as natural as the calling to be a priest had been. Deep down, I knew I would never marry and have children. I had sensed this years before, when I started seminary, and I had been comfortable with it ever since. When I spoke with others who decided to remain unmarried, I found that they had experienced something similar: a peaceful contentment with the idea of serving as one of the monastic clergy.

Graduation from seminary was only a couple of months away, so I knew that my parents were probably wondering about my plans. I knew that at some point soon, I would need to break the news to them. I wasn't looking forward to it.

My mind occupied with these thoughts, I closed my suitcase and took one last glance around my dorm room. Then I headed back to Chicago for Holy Week and spring break.

∞

A few days later, I was having dinner in Chicago with my family, enjoying our evening together and catching up on everyone's lives. At some point, my siblings excused themselves, and my parents and I were left alone, empty plates still on the table. The topic of conversation shifted. My mother reflectively said they'd noticed that I wasn't dating and hadn't mentioned anyone special in my life, and they knew that I would soon be graduating from seminary.

My father was more blunt.

"Are you planning on getting married or not?" he asked me candidly.

"No—no, I'm not," I answered, my heart in my throat.

"Are you sure?" he asked, clearly hoping I wasn't. He leaned forward and spoke passionately about his own life: the rewards of marriage, the fulfillment of having children, the satisfaction of family. He made a persuasive case, trying to change the mind of his misguided son. *Perhaps it is not too late?* his eyes seemed to plead. I listened, looking at his face, a face dear to me since childhood, and realized with a sudden stab of emotion how much I loved him.

"I am sure," I answered. "Marriage isn't for everybody."

My father, his face full of emotion, silently got up from the table and went outside to the backyard patio.

My mother, still in her chair, looked wistfully after her husband of twenty-seven years.

"You know, he's out there crying," she said.

I looked at her and sighed. No words came to my aid.

After spring break, I returned to Brookline. The excitement of the final semester steadily increased. I heard classmates talking about their ordination plans, their faces flushed with happy anticipation. Most people knew I had been working at the Diocese of Chicago over the summer and winter holidays for six years, and they probably guessed that I might end up there. I hoped I might, too, but nothing was formalized. When asked, I said truthfully that I didn't have any concrete plans for ordination yet.

Graduation day arrived. After a summer holiday, I returned to Chicago, Master of Divinity diploma in hand. After six years of trying to prove myself, I was offered a two-part position at the diocese, to be the registrar and to serve as Bishop Iakovos's assistant. It was an outstanding opportunity for someone who had just graduated from seminary, and I knew it. In this way, in August 1987, I began working full-time for the Greek Orthodox Archdiocese of America through the Diocese of Chicago.[6]

Even though I'd told my parents that I planned not to marry, I'd never said this to Bishop Iakovos, my bishop and mentor. But somehow, it seems, he had known. He never even asked if I planned to marry or not.

One day at the diocese, as we were meeting about work matters, the topic of my ordination came up. He advised me to wait awhile before being ordained a deacon. Taking his fatherly advice into consideration, I decided to postpone my ordination.

In the meantime, I was glad that at least I had a job working for the Church.

※

I was twenty-five, working hard to establish myself in my new role at the diocese, but I still lived at home. That needed to change. A year into my new job, I started looking for an apartment.

My parents strongly advised me, however, not to rent but to purchase a condominium, then surprised me with a generous financial gift that helped make it possible.

"We would have given this to you for your wedding if you had married," my mother said, "but this seems like a perfect moment to help you establish your new life." This gesture was profoundly meaningful to me. My parents were affirming the path I had chosen, a path they had not wanted; it touched me deeply. My mother even helped me select furniture and housewares—dishes, pots and pans, and more—for my new home.

One of the unexpected joys of my new building was my octogenarian neighbor, Helen Doppelt, who lived a few doors down the hall from me. This friendly Jewish woman, diminutive and quick-witted, soon learned I was pursuing ordination to the priesthood. Whenever we bumped into each other, she would ask me, with a thick Yiddish accent, "So, did you get the title yet?"

"No, not yet!" I always chuckled. Her encouraging smile reminded me that my goal was in sight.

Helen's confidence was proven right. On October 21, 1989, two years after graduating from seminary, I was ordained a deacon of the Greek Orthodox Church at my home parish, the Assumption Church.

It was a beautiful ceremony. Bishop Iakovos celebrated the liturgy; Bishop Isaiah of Aspendos,[7] who was the chancellor at the diocese, was also prayerfully in attendance. They were joined by many brother priests in praying for me to be blessed in my service as a deacon. It was very moving. My godparents had presented me with a new set of deacon's vestments, with which I was newly clothed during the ceremony.

As part of the ordination rite, I was brought forward to give my testimony as to why I was seeking ordination. Consistent with tradition, I

Newly ordained Deacon Demetri being led out from behind the icon screen by Bishop Iakovos of Chicago, October 21, 1989. © Gus Psichogios, photographer

did not face the congregation but the bishop, who, when celebrating the liturgy, represents Christ Himself. I spoke of my grateful journey, my experience of faith.

"The call to the priesthood is the call to follow Jesus Christ," I said as part of that testimony. "It is a call to Love and to be loved. It is a call to see Truth and to live in and with the Truth. It is this call that I am answering." I felt the emotion in my voice as I spoke.

The highpoint of the ordination was when I was led behind the icon screen and I bent down on one knee before the altar. Bishop Iakovos put the end of his stole on my head and his hand on the stole (the traditional laying on of hands), and he prayed the prayer of ordination for a deacon. Then the bishop lifted me up by my right hand and brought me out from behind the icon screen to face the congregation. He proclaimed, "Axios!" The congregation thunderously responded, "Axios!"

The many priests and clergy who participated in the ordination—including people I had met in my role as registrar of the diocese—and their supportive presence were deeply appreciated. Most meaningful of all, of course, was that my family was there that day to celebrate with me. I could see on their faces that they were proud of me. Their loving support meant the world to me.

It was an amazing feeling to be a deacon—and a relief. I realized that I had been holding my breath nearly a decade for just this moment: I was an ordained servant of Jesus Christ, consecrated to serve His Church.

I finally exhaled.

⚜

My nephew, Nick Kantzavelos, is a gifted pitcher who was awarded a full scholarship to play for East Georgia State College Baseball. One day when we were talking, he taught me the meaning of a sports term, "utility player." In baseball, a utility player is an athlete who can play several different positions on the field. He added that from the perspective of a team manager, it helps to have a player that versatile who can step in wherever needed.

I soon discovered that deacons are (and have always been) the utility players of the Orthodox Church. They have a specific role to play in church services, but the rest of the time, they do whatever work a parish priest assigns them. They helpfully lighten the load of one or more priests, and in this hands-on way, they gain practical experience in the day-to-day work of the priesthood, such as leading Bible studies, teaching catechism classes, and running youth programs.

In my case, once I was ordained a deacon, I was assigned to serve not at a parish but as Bishop Iakovos's deacon. This was an extraordinary honor. My new role was to lighten the load of the bishop, who was both the spiritual and administrative leader of fifty-eight parishes, and to learn all I could along the way. In addition, I had to learn a new, very specific liturgical role—assisting a bishop during church services—which was demanding in its own right. During church services, the pressure to "perform" well was intense, for I had to serve in front of congregations of Greek Orthodox faithful who were used to a seasoned bishop being accompanied by a capable deacon. I couldn't afford a misstep.

I was also still working as the registrar, so while trying to master my new role as bishop's deacon, I scrambled to meet every administrative deadline at the diocese and keep up with office correspondence; often, I was burning the candle at both ends, assisted by caffeine and a strong desire to prove myself. That said, the next two and a half years were the experience of a lifetime.

※

The liturgical services of the Orthodox Church are highly scripted, like a play or an opera, reflecting the Jewish liturgical roots of Christianity. I practiced the deacon's liturgical role over and over, learning the words, music, and actions for each type of service (for there are many different services). I put these rehearsed efforts into action whenever I accompanied the bishop to a service.

The need to follow a script is especially true of the Divine Liturgy. The Orthodox Church has been using the same liturgical text for nearly 1,800 years. Like a theater company performing Shakespeare's *The Tempest*, everyone needs to know their part and follow the director—in my case, the bishop. Unlike a play, the Divine Liturgy was designed so that certain elements change daily, weekly, or seasonally. To be ready for a given day's liturgy, I always needed to prepare ahead of time.

Beyond a desire not to embarrass myself was a deep sense of responsibility, the importance of getting it right for the sake of our faith. The celebration of the Divine Liturgy, unchanged, across time, distance, and in different languages, has helped the Church survive for approximately two millennia as one continuous, unchanged community of faith despite hundreds of years of persecution and the movement of peoples around the globe. The Divine Liturgy is both evidence of the Church's continuity and a means of maintaining that continuity. Entrusted as a caretaker of this work in my role as deacon, I was determined to do it right.

Sometimes I stumbled. Since I was accompanying a bishop, my mistakes were inevitably public, witnessed by priests, deacons, laypeople, and, at times, other bishops. Bishop Iakovos was patient, but he also wanted things done "decently and in order," and my gaffes reflected poorly on him. When I would slip up during a service, he would correct me later—never in public—so that I would get it right next time. He commented on small and large errors of language and action. "You've got to be careful!" he would remind me, for he cherished serving God through worship. But he was a gentle teacher.

One Sunday, Bishop Iakovos's schedule was particularly full. We drove to a parish where he celebrated Orthros and the Divine Liturgy. That was followed by a luncheon at the parish, an afternoon rest, and then an evening service and dinner at another parish miles away. Between the services, the meals, and the driving between Chicago and two other cities, it was a long day. It was nearly midnight when we pulled up to the diocese where the bishop resided, my last stop before heading home.

Weary from the day, I followed the bishop into the diocese, carrying his bulky liturgical luggage in each hand, a piece or two under each arm, and up the stairs toward his residence.

"Deacon!" he said, stopping on the steps and turning to me.

"Yes," I answered, my arms aching.

"*Epi ti*—the ending is *ti*. You said *tin*. It was wrong."

It took me a moment to realize that he was referring to words from the service that morning; I had mispronounced a Greek word, which resulted in a grammatical mistake. No one in the congregation heard it, and none of the priests or altar boys would have noticed, because it was in a brief liturgical exchange between a bishop and a deacon. Yet it was important enough to the bishop that he corrected me thirteen hours later so that I would learn to say this word correctly, even if no one else was listening. I was so tired I almost laughed. But it also reminded me of St. Paul's first letter to the Corinthians, where he writes, "But all things should be done decently and in order" (1 Corinthians 14:40).

I never made that mistake again.

∞

Serving the bishop as his deacon went well beyond church services. The experience of being at his side deepened my understanding and educated me in the ways of the Church. Many days, from 7:00 a.m. until midnight, the bishop went to services, meetings, luncheons, and dinners, and I accompanied him. We met people from all faiths, all walks of life; my early ecumenical experience at Missouri Synod Lutheran schools had prepared me to get along with believers from other faith traditions in my work as a deacon. Although I had assisted the bishop in the past and seen slivers of his life, now I saw up close how he oversaw nearly sixty parishes in a manner consistent with the gospel message.

For example, in conjunction with the women's philanthropic group of the diocese, the Ladies Philoptochos Society (Philoptochos for short),[8] Bishop Iakovos had launched a Feed the Hungry program at the Annunciation Greek Orthodox Cathedral in Chicago. Every two weeks, a group of dedicated women from one of several Chicago parishes would take a turn in the kitchen at the cathedral, serving a free lunch to hungry people who flocked to the cathedral's social hall. It was a successful biweekly outreach, and guests were served healthy food and treated to a warm welcome.

Bishop Iakovos related a story about the dean of the cathedral, who once complained to him about the Feed the Hungry program. Homeless people dirtied the chairs, the dean had said, and it was always a mess to pick up after them. The bishop had listened attentively. Then he reminded the dean that the cathedral had been allocated extra funds specifically to hire someone to clean the social hall and the restrooms after each Feed the Hungry luncheon; new chairs could be purchased if needed. Bishop Iakovos had ended the conversation with an observation. "Father, I would rather *you* leave the parish than that we remove the homeless people that our cathedral hosts."

From this and other examples, I learned that the bishop was unapologetically devoted to the gospel, and he expected the same of his priests. I also understood that he did not readily bend his principles, although it would have been easier simply for the sake of getting along or being a popular leader. In leading the church, he exhibited severity or mercy as circumstances required, but I recall him most often with a warm smile on his face.

One day in the diocese kitchen, I discovered a loaf of bread with some mold on it, and I was about to throw it away when the bishop stopped me.

"No," he said, lifting the loaf from my hand, "you don't know what it's like not to have these things." He cut away the moldy portion, sliced up the remainder of the loaf, and put the slices in the oven to toast them. Then he stored the cooled toast in a plastic container.

"You've never lived through an occupation," he added, as he put the container away.

Of course, I haven't lived through an occupation, I thought. *This is the United States of America in the twentieth century.* Only then did it strike me that in his war-torn youth he had probably gone hungry. I thought back to the Feed the Hungry program, and I now grasped the source of his deep compassion for the people at the cathedral. He himself had known hunger. He wanted to make sure that the hungry people of Chicago had something to eat.

I loved my work, but after two and a half years of becoming a seasoned deacon, I was finding it hard to make ends meet financially on my salary. I was nearly thirty years old. Both my years-long desire to be a priest and the modest state of my bank account prompted me to ask Bishop Iakovos if I could soon be ordained a priest. He considered my request and finally gave his blessing for my ordination to the holy priesthood.

The day I had dreamed of since childhood took place at the Annunciation Cathedral of Chicago on that parish's one-hundred-year anniversary and feast day celebration, on March 25, 1992. Because the day celebrated the centennial of the parish, every pew was full. Bishop Iakovos celebrated the Divine Liturgy accompanied by several priests, deacons, and altar boys. My parents, sister, brothers, and cousins were there. My godparents were there. Friends from all walks of life came to show their support, too, including other Orthodox clergy and believers of many different faiths whom I had come to know in my work as a deacon.

When it was my turn to speak, my speech included words of gratitude for the many people who had guided me in my journey, especially my parents. Then I singled out one person who had played such an important role in my development as a person of faith and, finally, as a priest, my *geronta*, my spiritual elder, Bishop Iakovos.

"I will never forget when I first met Your Grace. I was seventeen years old and an altar boy at the Assumption Church in Chicago. It was Holy Thursday, and then, as the new Bishop of Chicago, you made a pastoral visit to our community. Before the service began, Father Gerasimos Annas expressed to Your Grace my interest in attending Hellenic College and Holy Cross. It was from that moment on that you encouraged me and became my mentor." I went on to thank him for his support and the many opportunities to serve and to learn that he had made possible.

As I knelt on two knees before the altar, Bishop Iakovos placed the end of his stole on my head and his hand on his stole and prayed the prayers of ordination to the priesthood. Then, in front of the congregation, my fellow priests dressed me for the first time in my new priestly garments—an affirming, brotherly gesture to initiate a new priest, a traditional part of the ordination ceremony. After so many years of longing, it felt wonderfully natural to be wearing these vestments. I looked at my parents, and they were beaming.

After decades of dreaming and hard work, I was thrilled to be standing before the congregation, a priest.

The service ended, and it was announced to the congregation that I was being assigned to that very parish as a new associate pastor, a tremendous honor.

The celebration that followed with my family and friends lasted well into the night. I couldn't stop smiling. My parents let me know that they loved me for who I was, an unmarried priest, and that they were proud of me. They embraced the success that I had sought for twelve years, and when other people congratulated them on the ordination of their son, I could see the pleasure written on their faces.

I imagine it is how a bride and groom must feel on their wedding day, having made a lifetime commitment and looking forward to all that is to come, full of hope. I returned home exhilarated. I was finally a priest!

⚭

A few days later, my neighbor Helen and I saw each other in the hallway.

"So, did you get the title yet?"

"Actually, I did!"

"Mazel tov!" Helen exclaimed. "What's the title? What should I call you?"

"Well, it's actually Father Demetri, but since you're my neighbor, just keep calling me Demetri," I said.

"No, no, no—listen to me!" she said, finger in the air, chin lifted. "You worked hard for the title and earned it. So use it!" Then, leaning in conspiratorially, she tested me, "So *what* should I call you?"

"*Father* Demetri," I said, acceding to her admonition.

I walked into my apartment, thinking of what my kind neighbor had said. It was nice to know that the hard work was behind me. Of course, I knew I had much to learn about being a priest, just as I had had to learn to be a deacon.

But still basking in the afterglow of ordination, I saw only a smooth path ahead.

5

✣

Even the Dogs

March 1999

Nothing ever happens in a political vacuum, and Andrew's upcoming execution was no exception.

In the days after I met Andrew, I digested as much recent history as I could find about the death penalty debate in Illinois. I had a lot of catching up to do. I found myself rereading old news stories and understanding them in a new light, and I became increasingly aware that a handful of significant events over the course of the previous six years had set the stage for a clash over capital punishment.

※

In 1993, the case of Chicago police area commander Jon Burge was front-page news when abundant evidence proved that for twenty years, Burge and the detectives he worked with had systematically beaten and tortured people they had rounded up as suspects—for instance, putting gun barrels in mouths; plastic bags over heads; cigarette burns to arms, legs, and chests; and electrical shocks to lips, ears, and genitals—for the purpose of extracting false confessions. The forced "confessions" were then given to prosecutors and used as evidence to send defendants, whether innocent or guilty, to death row. In early 1993, the disgraced Burge was fired by the Chicago Police Board.[1]

Only two months later, a retired judge, Cook County Circuit Court Judge Thomas Maloney, was himself on trial. Maloney was convicted on four charges of having accepted bribes to acquit guilty defendants, three of them defendants in murder cases.[2] Wanting to avoid the impression that he was going easy on those defendants, Maloney had engaged in compensatory bias. He treated at least one defendant who had not bribed him even more severely.[3]

Four years later, a stinging critique of the death penalty came from an unexpected source, the American Bar Association (ABA), an organization that had never taken a position on the death penalty.[4] Two groups within the ABA jointly prepared a report that concluded that "efforts to forge a fair capital punishment jurisprudence have failed. Today, administration of the death penalty . . . is . . . a haphazard maze of unfair practices with no internal consistency."[5]

On February 3, 1997, the ABA's policymaking House of Delegates passed a resolution calling for an end to federal and state executions until policies were adopted to ensure greater fairness and due process[6]: competent counsel for defendants in capital cases, more power for federal courts to review capital cases from state courts, improved efforts to eliminate racial discrimination in capital sentencing, and a ban on executing persons with intellectual disabilities or those who were under eighteen at the time they committed their crime.

Not long after, the Death Penalty Information Center issued a report on the problem of innocent people being sentenced to death. In the report's opening paragraph, the State of Illinois was singled out for a dubious distinction: of the twenty-one condemned inmates wrongfully sentenced to death and then released in the United States between 1993 and July 1997, seven of them—one out of three exonerees—had been sentenced in Illinois courts.[7] Two other innocent men had been exonerated in Illinois in 1987, making a total of nine since the death penalty was reintroduced in the state in 1977.

The stories of how those nine death row inmates in Illinois were set free range from the merely surprising to the nearly unbelievable.

A young prosecutor, Michael Falconer, was reading an article in the investigative journal *Chicago Lawyer* that revisited the case of the murder of a Chicago hot dog stand owner and one of his employees. Two men, Perry Cobb and Darby (Williams) Tillis, had been convicted for the murders ten years earlier. As Falconer read the testimony of the prosecution's key witness, Phyllis Santini, he recalled having worked in a factory years before with Santini. At the time, she had confided to Falconer that her boyfriend had killed somebody and that he and she were working with the police and the prosecution to try to frame someone else for the crime. Falconer realized with a start that he had information about the identity of the actual murderer. He reached out to the defense and subsequently testified for them, which helped the two innocent men serving on death row to be set free in 1987.[8,9]

William Dulin, an eighty-eight-year-old farmer in Iroquois County, was robbed and murdered in 1988. Police arrested Joe Burrows, a housepainter from a small town in Illinois. Burrows was convicted of armed robbery and murder. The story piqued the interest of Peter Rooney, an investigative journalist from the *Champaign News-Gazette*, who began interviewing people about the case. As a result, one of the two principal witnesses who had testified against Burrows, Gayle Potter, confessed that she was the murderer. This led to Burrows's release in 1994.[10]

A little girl, ten-year-old Jeanine Nicarico, was kidnapped, raped, and murdered in 1983. Prosecutors convicted Rolando Cruz and Alejandro Hernandez. Meanwhile, a sociopathic killer named Brian Dugan, who had already pleaded guilty to two rapes and two murders, admitted to authorities that he was responsible for the girl's murder.[11] Police wondered whether the three men had jointly committed the crime. Finally, a high-ranking police officer acknowledged that he had given false testimony; Cruz had never incriminated himself as detectives claimed. Proven innocent, Cruz and Hernandez were set free in 1995.[12]

Dennis Williams and Verneal Jimerson were convicted of abduction, rape, and murder in 1978 and sentenced to death. Years later, the two men were exonerated by an emerging technology, DNA evidence from a vaginal swab. Simultaneously, three journalism students at Northwestern University, assigned to investigate the case in a class taught by Professor David Protess, managed to identify the true perpetrators. Three murderers were convicted based on detailed confessions, corroborated by DNA evidence. Williams and Jimerson were released in 1996.[13]

In 1993, Gary Gauger, an organic farmer, arrived at his parents' farm in Illinois to find them dead. Police accused him of murder, and he was convicted. Later, two members of a motorcycle gang, James Schneider and Randall Miller, were indicted in Wisconsin for multiple counts of racketeering and the murder of Gauger's parents. At Miller's trial, prosecutors played a recorded conversation in which Miller bragged that authorities would not be able to link him to the murder because he had been careful to leave no physical evidence at the scene.[14] Gary Gauger was released in 1996.

Carl Lawson was convicted of killing his former girlfriend's eight-year-old son, Terrence Jones, in 1989. On appeal, the Illinois Supreme Court allowed what the trial court had not—forensic testing of some of the evidence, which ultimately demonstrated Lawson's innocence—and granted him a new trial in 1994. This led to two retrials, at the second of which Lawson was acquitted, in 1996.[15]

In all, these nine men spent a cumulative sixty-eight years on death row in Illinois for murders they did not commit.

One of the people involved in advocacy for five of the nine men was a law professor at Northwestern University, Lawrence C. Marshall. His passionate advocacy for innocent people on death row was immense. In November 1998, Marshall organized the first-of-its-kind National Conference on Wrongful Convictions and the Death Penalty. Held at the Northwestern University School of Law, the three-day conference attracted more than one thousand lawyers, legal scholars, law students, death penalty opponents, and journalists. Panel discussions and presentations explored topics such as DNA evidence, investigative techniques, faulty forensics, the damage inflicted on the innocent by being wrongfully incarcerated, and other related issues.[16] The conference pushed back on the commonly held notion that wrongful convictions in capital cases are rare.

The highlight of the conference occurred when thirty-one men and women were seated on the stage before an auditorium full of conference attendees. The house lights dimmed, and the audience went quiet. One by one, the thirty-one guests walked to the podium and said some variation of "My name is ____. If the State of ____ had its way, I'd be dead today." The audience was transfixed. These were thirty-one of seventy-four people who had been wrongfully convicted of capital offenses and sent to death row and were later exonerated and released.[17] Each person's freedom usually came only after many years on death row, often after having lost their marriages, members of their families, their businesses, and their reputations. "It was a chilling flesh-and-blood reminder of the greatest fear of opponents and supporters of the death penalty—the execution of the innocent," wrote journalist Don Terry.[18] (As I was reading this article, my father's exhortation "you better be damn sure" came to mind.)

The landmark conference garnered national attention. Its message flew in the face of support for capital punishment, the view held by a majority of Americans at the time.[19] It opened up a fresh national discussion about the death penalty. Lawyers, academics, and law students heard—and journalists conveyed—the idea at its heart, that the death penalty system is too flawed and unjust to be maintained. It should be abolished.

∞

The same month Lawrence Marshall welcomed guests to the National Conference on Wrongful Convictions and the Death Penalty, the people of Illinois went to the polls and elected a new governor, George Ryan, a conservative downstate Republican. He was known for his pro–capital punishment stance (his Democratic opponent, Glenn Poshard, also supported the death penalty[20]). He had, as a state representative from Kankakee, voted in 1977 to reintroduce the death penalty in Illinois.

As George Ryan prepared to move into the governor's mansion in December 1998, a brewing crisis over capital punishment, six years in the making, was already waiting for him. It is unlikely that he was aware that from the very hour he was sworn in, his single term in office would be defined by this issue. Andrew Kokoraleis would play a part.

George Ryan took the oath of office on January 11, 1999. That morning, the *Chicago Tribune* published the first part of an explosive five-part series focused on the primary reason so many innocent people were ending up on death row: prosecutorial misconduct. The series began with a damning indictment:

> With impunity, prosecutors across the country have violated their oaths and the law, committing the worst kinds of deception in the most serious of cases. They have prosecuted black men, hiding evidence the real killers were white. They have prosecuted a wife, hiding evidence her husband committed suicide. They have prosecuted parents, hiding evidence their daughter was killed by wild dogs. They do it to win.
>
> They do it because they won't get punished.[21]

Two journalists, Ken Armstrong and Maurice Possley, took a deep dive, investigating cases dating back as far as 1963. They found that in 381 cases, prosecutors had knowingly obtained wrongful convictions in capital crimes against innocent people; when their misconduct was later proven, the innocent had been freed. For five successive days, readers followed the journalists as they delved into the sometimes scheming, underhanded, and unethical world of prosecutors. They revealed how prosecutors can cheat and noted that they are often rewarded for their misconduct—becoming judges or district attorneys—rather than punished, even though their misdeeds can send innocent people to death row. The series was a bombshell.

Only three weeks later, a seismic event occurred. A Chicago man named Anthony Porter, who had been scheduled to be executed by lethal injection on September 24, 1998, was instead released from death row on February 5, 1999.

Porter, convicted of a double murder committed in 1982, had served fifteen years on death row. Shortly before the scheduled execution, one of Porter's volunteer lawyers had him psychologically evaluated to determine if he was "losing his mind" under the stress of the anticipated execution. During that evaluation, Porter was accidentally given an IQ test, his first while incarcerated, to determine if he was competent enough to be executed. The test revealed that Porter's IQ was fifty-one.[22]

His lawyer requested an emergency stay of execution. The courts granted the stay out of concern that Porter might not be capable of understanding why he was being executed, which Illinois law requires.[23] Further testing and a hearing were scheduled to determine Porter's fitness for execution. In the meantime, Professor David Protess and journalism students from Northwestern University again stepped up, partnering with private investigator Paul Ciolino to look into Porter's original conviction.

Astonishingly, their investigation yielded a corroborated, videotaped confession from the actual murderer. Porter, proven innocent, walked out of prison a free man. He had come within forty-eight hours of being executed.[24]

Everyone was alarmed. The State of Illinois had very nearly executed an innocent man.

The new governor, George Ryan, was stunned that a team of journalism students had saved Porter's life. This case was fresh, damaging proof that the death penalty system in Illinois was dangerously broken. Ryan said, "I think there's got to be some kind of another [sic] check put into place. I'm just not sure yet what it is."[25] (His confused language reflected just how unsettling Porter's story was.) The former Cook County State's Attorney, whose office had wrongly convicted Porter of murder, was Richard M. Daley, who had since become mayor of Chicago. Mayor Daley issued a statement saying that he continued to support the death penalty but favored a moratorium on executions.[26] The *Chicago Tribune* ran a blistering editorial that called for a moratorium as well.[27]

Two weeks later, on February 19, the Illinois Supreme Court reversed the murder conviction of death row inmate Steven Smith. They concluded that the testimony against him was less reliable than the contradictory testimony of other witnesses. Smith was released after having served fourteen years.

Illinois had reinstated capital punishment in 1977. In the intervening twenty-two years, eleven men had been executed, and now, eleven men had been exonerated and released. Death penalty advocates in the state, including the new governor, were facing mounting evidence that the system they claimed was "fair and just" was not, and the public was paying attention. Pressure to end the death penalty, or at least temporarily suspend executions, was building. The widely publicized release first of Porter and then of Smith brought the matter to a crisis point just twenty-six days before Andrew's scheduled execution.

∽

When I began researching capital punishment, I was surprised to learn that in 1972, the US Supreme Court declared the death penalty unconstitutional under the Eighth Amendment in the case of *Furman v. Georgia*. This legal ruling effectively nullified all existing death sentences and halted all executions for a four-year period in the United States.[28] Opponents of the death penalty were pleased. Some jurists optimistically suggested that this ruling signified the end of capital punishment in the United States.

However, some state legislatures intent on capital punishment sought a workaround. They modified their laws, crafting them to accommodate the specific legal concerns raised by the US Supreme Court. In 1976, the Court ruled that the "careful and judicious" use of the death penalty may be appropriate under limited circumstances (*Gregg v. Georgia*).

One of the people paying attention to this legal back-and-forth with growing alarm was a former high school teacher in Illinois, Mary Alice Rankin, who was deeply opposed to the death penalty. A grandmother with a soft voice,[29] she founded the Illinois Coalition Against the Death Penalty (ICADP) in 1976 with the goal of preventing the state from adopting capital punishment. Rankin reached out to liberal and religious groups that might be willing to work together with her on this issue. The advocates jointly organized anti–capital punishment efforts.

Despite fervent advocacy, they didn't succeed, and in 1977, the General Assembly of Illinois voted to enact new death penalty legislation. The governor signed the bill into law. That same year, executions resumed in the United States.

Not to be defeated, Rankin and her dedicated organization regrouped and began to direct their efforts to abolishing the death penalty and educating the public about the flaws and injustices in the Illinois capital punishment system. Each time an execution was scheduled in the state, the ICADP went into high gear with public protests, letter-writing campaigns, and appeals to state senators and representatives and the governor.

By 1999, ICADP had been tirelessly working to bring about change for more than two decades. The organization was reinvigorated around that time by the introduction of DNA testing, which was proving some people's innocence, and by the slew of recent exonerations, proof of one of ICADP's key claims, that many people sentenced to die by state execution are, in fact, innocent.

A few days before I went to the Pontiac Correctional Center, I had made a cold call to the ICADP to discuss Andrew and his scheduled execution. I had never been involved in advocacy to end the death penalty, but I understood the importance of finding allies. I spoke with a volunteer who was receptive but somewhat cautious when I mentioned Andrew. Abolition of the death penalty and educating the public about injustices in the state's capital punishment system were always the organization's goals, but the disturbing facts surrounding the Ripper Crew weighed heavily on Andrew's case. Even those who advocated on behalf of death row inmates understood that Andrew was not a poster child for the abolition of capital punishment.

I told the volunteer I understood and appreciated it. I spoke passionately in support of Andrew, explaining the religious reasons that I was seeking clemency for him. I requested that whenever possible, the diocese and the ICADP coordinate our efforts in his case. I received a warm response to this suggestion by being invited to join the board of directors. I accepted and even had a brief meeting with representatives of the ICADP in the days before Fred and I had driven south to meet Andrew.

※

On Monday, March 1, after a meeting in downtown Chicago, I drove past one of the city's many architectural jewels, the Tribune Tower. The architects had graced the skyscraper with a soaring design and elegant details. Located in the heart of downtown Chicago, it had opened in 1925 to tremendous fanfare, its hundreds of windows glittering in the morning sunshine.

The same year the Tribune Tower opened, a more modest architectural feat was accomplished seven and a half miles west of it. A group of faithful Greek immigrants pooled their resources to purchase an eight-car wooden parking garage in a mostly German neighborhood and lovingly converted it into a church. It was named the Assumption Greek Orthodox Church (everyone called it the Assumption for short). A decade passed, and the thriving congregation outgrew their wooden building. They hired an architect; razed the old church; and in 1937, erected a large, beautiful, stone-and-steel church in its place. The parish continued to flourish. Some twenty-plus years later, a Greek immigrant and his non-Greek wife attended services there with their children. The Kokoraleis family considered the Assumption their parish. My family did too—my parents had met and married there, my siblings and I were all baptized there, and that is the parish at which I was ordained a deacon.

I pondered this coincidence as I parked outside the diocese offices. It had been surreal to discover that Andrew and I had attended the same parish as children and we were only a year apart in age.

I hung up my coat and sat down at my desk. Sixteen days remained until Andrew's scheduled execution. Sixteen days! That morning, I had opened the *Chicago Tribune* to find an op-ed article about capital punishment by columnist Eric Zorn, who was also pondering the issues raised by the upcoming execution. He wrestled with his gut feelings and a desire for retributive justice (which, he acknowledged, was "valid and not uncivilized"), on the one hand, and the lessons of innocent Anthony Porter, on the other, that justice administered by fallible human beings sometimes fails. In the end, he took a reluctant but considered stand against the death penalty.[30]

It was a fitting beginning to the day, a day I put my other work aside to finish sorting through the research I had gathered about Andrew's case. From my briefcase, I retrieved an assortment of papers, photocopies, and notes that had, until that morning, cluttered my dining room table. I was still piecing together what Theodora had told me, what Andrew had said, and what I had learned by reading through old newspaper coverage, documents, and other sources. I gazed at the photograph of Andrew that had been printed repeatedly in the newspapers and broadcast on the evening news in November 1982: a lanky, defiant nineteen-year-old youth. It didn't take a powerful imagination to conclude that he "looked" guilty.

What the picture couldn't show were moments that predated the photograph by several years, moments I now knew about. In fall 1975, twelve-year-old Andrew returned home to find his mother, Wanda, dead at age thirty-eight after a prolonged illness. Andrew and his siblings, some of them younger than he, shattered by their loving mother's death, looked to their grief-numbed father, Costas, for strength and direction when their stable world imploded. The overwhelmed, hapless father, pressed upon by the day-to-day responsibilities of two parents, bereft and suddenly alone, sometimes faltered. As often happens when one parent dies, much of the family cohesion vanished. The Kokoraleis family's homelife became untethered and less predictable. Life with a sometimes-volatile father could feel chaotic.

In fall 1978, Andrew was a fifteen-year-old sophomore at Steinmetz High School with a shy smile and glasses.

Andrew Kokoraleis, 15, sophomore at Steinmetz High School, fall 1978. Image used courtesy of Steinmetz College Preparatory School Alumni Association

Sometime after the beginning of his junior year, he stopped attending school and left home. When he left, his brother Thomas, who was three years older than Andrew, went with him. Thomas had an IQ of seventy-five.[31]

Together, sixteen-year-old Andrew and nineteen-year-old Thomas managed somehow to eke out a living for a little over a year. Around that time, Andrew met Eddie Spreitzer, whose ability to communicate verbally was impeded by a speech defect.[32] Eddie, two years older than Andrew, lived with his mother and stepfather.

In 1981, Andrew's father and some of Andrew's siblings moved to an apartment in the Villa Park suburb of Chicago. At that point, Andrew and Thomas were known to stay a couple of nights in the family home and spend the rest of the week living with friends in Chicago.[33] From the outside, it appears that Andrew's circumstances weren't particularly rosy or stable and his prospects were few.

One day in mid-1981, Eddie Spreitzer introduced Andrew to a contractor named Robin Gecht, for whom he worked. Concerning that work, Spreitzer would later testify that "the jobs that we did do, that was fun. I was learning."[34] A year before, in February 1980, Gecht had pleaded guilty to contributing to the delinquency of a minor in connection with a sex attack on a young girl, but it is unlikely that Andrew was aware of that.[35]

Gecht was not particularly tall, slight of build, with sandy-colored hair and large blue eyes. He ran his own construction business. For two and a half years, he had a storefront for his business "R & R Electric" on North Mason Avenue.[36] Gecht had a wife, Rosemary; a son; and two daughters.[37] He was evidently liked by many of his neighbors, to whom he would wave a friendly hello. A capable contractor and electrician, he made improvements to his rental home in the 2100 block of North McVicker Avenue, a quiet working-class neighborhood on Chicago's near Northwest Side. Gecht sometimes volunteered to help neighbors do home repair on their homes. He was known for high-quality work, and the family was known to be pleasant.[38]

However, Gecht proved adept at psychological manipulation, a behavior noted by police. "Gecht was the dominant personality, a skilled player of mind games who manipulated Spreitzer and the Kokoraleis brothers, who were classic followers," a west suburban police authority later commented.[39] Other observers noted that Gecht made a point of cultivating relationships with and hiring impressionable teenage boys—vulnerable kids, including Spreitzer—who, like Gecht, had dropped out of high school.[40]

Gecht offered Andrew work, which Andrew accepted. Andrew testified that he worked for Gecht from mid-1981, around the time he turned eighteen, until May 1982. Part of that time, Andrew said, he was a live-in babysitter for Gecht and his wife, looking after their three small children.[41] Other than that, it appeared he did low-wage construction work for Gecht.

I tried to imagine Andrew's experience of being welcomed by Robin Gecht. From the perspective of the rootless young Andrew, Gecht may have seemed like a godsend.[42] Gecht provided stability for Andrew. It probably felt good to have steady work, to learn new skills, to earn money, to earn respect. It may even have been reassuring to sleep in the same house day after day, feeling included, like part of the family. Andrew depended on Gecht for work and, for a time, for lodging, and this gave Gecht some leverage in the relationship. Andrew spent most of his waking hours in Gecht's orbit, either working with Gecht or in his home, and this, too, afforded Gecht time to influence Andrew. While Andrew's dependence on Gecht did not excuse any criminal behavior on Andrew's part—in the end, Andrew still chose to do whatever he did—it is also true that when you are eighteen and you depend on someone to provide a roof over your head and a paycheck and they ask you to do something, it is harder to say no.

The unraveling of the Ripper Crew began when one of Gecht's victims survived and was able to describe his distinctive van and later identify him in a police lineup in the hospital where she was recovering from her attack.[43] From that point, police focused on Gecht. The three other men were soon rounded up as well. Some wondered if Gecht was able to psychologically manipulate his three friends in a manner similar to Charles Manson.[44] Although the police were not able to confirm it, Gecht was said to have a disturbing fascination with women's breasts and was reported to have cut his own wife's breast in the midst of lovemaking.[45] By late November 1982, Gecht's wife filed for divorce, citing "extreme mental cruelty" and "inhuman treatment."[46]

It made for unsettling reading. I put these materials back in their files on my desk and thought about my next task: reaching out to those who might be allies in the effort to prevent Andrew from being executed. Only sixteen days left, and already, half of the day was gone.

※

That day I shared much of what I was learning with Bishop Iakovos. I also mentioned that Fred was drafting a letter to Governor Ryan on behalf of Bishop Iakovos and the diocese.

What was of greatest interest to Bishop Iakovos was my visit with Andrew. He asked for my impressions. What kind of a man was he? I told the bishop that he was articulate, friendly, and calm and seemed genuine in his faith. I also described what I had learned about Andrew's past. I noticed that he did not ask me if, having met Andrew, I thought he was guilty or innocent.

∞

One of my early responsibilities—and honors—as a priest was to assist Bishop Iakovos in representing the diocese on the Council of Religious Leaders of Metropolitan Chicago (CRLMC). I was not a voting member, but I was allowed to listen and offer support to the bishop.

Founded in 1984, the organization was the ingenious brainchild of Joseph Cardinal Bernardin of the Roman Catholic Archdiocese of Chicago. He had reached out to five other prominent religious leaders in Chicago with a vision. They would get to know each other, share perspectives about the challenges and opportunities facing Chicago, and cooperate in bringing the moral voice of religion to bear upon developments in their beloved city. Over time, the CRLMC came to include leaders of practically every major religious tradition in the broader Chicago area. It spoke with a unified moral voice on issues of the day and promoted a climate of interfaith understanding and cooperation.

When I first attended meetings, public statements from the CRLMC ranged from topics as diverse as public school funding in Chicago to the Gulf War. CRLMC members did not always agree on issues, reflecting the views of the communities they represented. Sometimes a member brought a difficult issue to the CRLMC seeking support, and discussion about the issue revealed deep disagreement around the table. In those instances, I (as a young priest) marveled at the CRLMC's commitment to interfaith dialogue, supporting one another as leaders and finding consensus. For, more often than not, the CRLMC managed to find a point of agreement, a common denominator, even if members could not fully agree. That allowed most of the CRLMC's public statements to be made with a united voice.

When the diocese had learned of Andrew's pending execution, the timeline was so short that we couldn't reasonably expect the CRLMC to gather and quickly hammer out a public statement on an issue as fraught as the death penalty. However, Bishop Iakovos and I agreed that it would be sensible to reach out to individual members of the CRLMC who opposed capital punishment to ask if they would support our effort to seek clemency for Andrew by writing a letter to Governor Ryan.

That afternoon, March 1, I reached out to some members of the CRLMC, and the response I received was heartening. Francis Cardinal George of Chicago; Bishop Vsevolod of Scopelos of the Ukrainian Orthodox Western Diocese; and Bishop Job of the Orthodox Church of America, Diocese of the Midwest, among others, agreed to send a letter. I was overwhelmingly grateful to them. I knew that they would be praying for Andrew, alone in his prison cell; that, too, was deeply meaningful. Several asked me to let them know if there was anything else they could do to assist. I promised that I would.

Beyond the CRLMC, two other towering religious figures promised to send Governor Ryan a letter: Archbishop Gabriel Montalvo Higuera, Papal Nuncio, and Archbishop Spyridon of the Greek Orthodox Archdiocese of America. Their influence would surely grab the attention of the governor.

Just weeks earlier, an unprecedented event had occurred in nearby Missouri that also fueled our hope. Pope John Paul II had visited St. Louis and personally appealed to Governor Mel Carnahan—a Southern Baptist and supporter of capital punishment—to show mercy to Darrell J. Mease, who was scheduled to be executed on February 10 for murdering Lloyd, Frankie, and William Lawrence.[47] The governor had yielded to the appeal for clemency and spared the man's life.

Perhaps the coordinated appeal for mercy from several of Chicago's religious leaders would similarly influence our new governor? It was worth a try. Together, we were adding a vibrant, religious voice to the increasingly loud public calls for a moratorium on executions in Illinois.

I was determined to use as many tools as I could find to delay—or even prevent—Andrew's execution.

The following morning, I received the draft of a letter to Governor Ryan, written by Fred and his law partner, Tina, on behalf of Bishop Iakovos. It laid out the facts related to Andrew's conviction, including the coerced confession and lack of evidence. The letter made the case for clemency and appealed to Governor Ryan to use the powers of his office to spare Andrew's life. I shared the letter with Bishop Iakovos. He read it over and agreed that it was good. I also updated him on the promises of support we had received so far from some leaders in the CRLMC, Archbishop Spyridon and Archbishop Gabriel Montalvo Higuera, Papal Nuncio.

I called Fred to let him know that the bishop approved of the letter. The letter was delivered to the governor's offices in Springfield and in Chicago that very day.

A couple of days later, a handful of people, including Fred, were gathered at the diocese for a meeting with Bishop Iakovos and me on a topic unrelated to Andrew. When the formal meeting concluded, someone brought up the fact that the infamous convicted murderer Andrew Kokoraleis was a Greek Orthodox Christian. His case was gaining more attention in the media as his execution date was approaching. It was bad enough that a Greek Orthodox man had been convicted of murder. Was it really necessary for the diocese to take a public position supporting him?

Someone else countered that the tradition of our faith meant that we should take a stand in support of Andrew, for life and against capital punishment, and not worry about how we, as a people, looked. We were talking about someone's *life*.

The first man opined that yes, yes, he understood that the Church is pro-life, but did the diocese really want to go on the record appealing for mercy for someone who may have been involved in some of the most obscene, gruesome attacks and murders in recent Chicago history? If the diocese did advocate for Andrew, it would come at a political cost . . . and was a convicted murderer really worth it?

This casual dismissiveness of the Church and its pro-life position frustrated me. I adamantly defended advocating for clemency for Andrew. It was the work of the Church since the Church is, indeed, pro-life—pro *all* life, from womb to tomb.

The first man now spoke directly to Bishop Iakovos.

"If you get behind this, you'll look bad, Your Grace," he warned the bishop. "Andrew Kokoraleis may be guilty of every crime they've accused him of."

The man who warned Bishop Iakovos was, I knew, a faithful layperson. He just wanted the bishop and the diocese to play it safe. From a purely political perspective, he was right. It *would* be safer for Bishop Iakovos not to get involved, to keep his head down and his hands clean of anything having to do with Andrew Kokoraleis and his messy, gruesome case. Advocacy for Andrew was risky. It would put the diocese in the crosshairs of critics and in the middle of a statewide controversy. It wasn't the kind of attention the layperson wanted for his Church or for himself.

The temperature in the room was rising, the arguments getting heated. Concerned faces reflected the tension, mine included. Everyone looked at Bishop Iakovos.

The bishop sat in thoughtful silence. He had been quietly listening as people exchanged their views. He sat calmly at the head of the conference table, hands folded on the table, leaning back in his chair, relaxed and confident. I had known him now for nineteen years. He was respected by those he led, among other reasons, because he was a careful listener and had gathered wisdom over the course of a lifetime. He was now seventy years old.

Bishop Iakovos looked at the first man and spoke with quiet authority.

"Yes, he may be guilty," he agreed, "but as the Canaanite woman said to Jesus, 'Even the dogs eat the crumbs that fall from their master's table.'"[48]

With that, everyone understood—the diocese would stand with Andrew Kokoraleis.

6

✤

Meeting Bob

March 1992

I had been a priest for only a couple of months when the telephone in my basement office at the diocese buzzed, and the receptionist transferred a call to me.

"Hello," I answered, "Father Demetri" (I was still getting used to saying that).

"Father, I'm hoping you can help me," the man at the other end of the phone began. "I'm calling the diocese because I'm sick and I'd like a priest to come see me. Can you arrange that?"

"I'll try to help," I said. "What's your name?"

"Bob," he answered. "I live here in Chicago."

"Bob, do you attend a parish? Have you called your parish priest?"

"Yes, I have. He—he won't visit me." He paused, then added bluntly, "I have AIDS."

A cold fear swirled in my chest. It was 1992, and the diagnosis of acquired immunodeficiency syndrome (AIDS) was as terrifying a diagnosis as existed. It was deadly. In the United States, a staggering 190,000 people had already died of it, most of them gay men. I had a basic knowledge of AIDS. It was caused by the human immunodeficiency virus (HIV), people contracted it mostly through unprotected sex or shared needles from intravenous drug use, it was not contagious but infectious, and it killed those it infected because there was no cure.

People were afraid of AIDS and those who had it. Bob's parish priest was no exception; he had made excuse after excuse not to see him, Bob said. The priest, who had known Bob since he was little, probably feared that if he visited him, he would contract the disease. Bob—sick, isolated, scared—longed to know that his church had not abandoned him, that God still loved him.

What should I do? I thought, gripping the receiver. I felt anger at the priest's unwitting ignorance as well as an overwhelming compassion for Bob, who was being hurt by that ignorance. Jesus's words came to mind, "I was sick, and you visited me."

"What's your address, Bob?" I asked. "I'll come see you." We set a date for a visit.

On the appointed day, I climbed into my car and put my priest's travel case on the seat beside me. I felt my stomach knot as I drove toward his home. This was my first time visiting someone diagnosed with AIDS, and I realized I was not sure what I was going to do. I prayed that my visit would make a difference to Bob. I was also keenly aware of how green I was as a priest. I hoped Bob wouldn't be disappointed by a visit from a rookie.

I parked outside the house, picked up my priest's case, and stepped into the warm spring air.

That March morning was so beautiful—the first warm spring day that hinted at the sultry summer to come—that I almost regretted stepping into the shade of the unfamiliar porch and ringing the doorbell. It was eleven o'clock in the morning. The front door was opened by a neatly dressed middle-aged woman, kind but hesitant. She welcomed me respectfully in Greek, lowered her eyes, and with a nervous gesture invited me in. I followed her quick steps and soon found myself passing through a living room in which each piece of furniture was covered with a translucent plastic drop cloth. The overall effect was unsettling. As we walked on through the modest, well-ordered home, I glimpsed the sheen of plastic in other rooms as well.

The woman led me into a sunny kitchen, and at her invitation, I took a seat at the kitchen table; I heard the crinkle of plastic as I sat on a chair swathed in plastic wrap. She sat down across from me, clasping and unclasping her hands on the table. When she looked at me, her eyes revealed hope and doubt.

"Father," she said quietly, almost whispering, "I ask just one thing. Please keep what happens here today a secret. Don't say anything to anyone."

"I promise," I said.

Of course, the fact that I am relating it to you now could rightly make you question if I kept that promise.

I heard footsteps and turned to see a man enter the sun-filled kitchen, where the woman and I sat. He was emaciated, sunken eyes resting in a gaunt face. The collar of his T-shirt sat loosely around his skinny neck, and the shirt hung from his bony shoulders. His arms were unnaturally thin. I kept my gaze level, trying not to stare or look away. I had read about the ravages of AIDS, of course, but the reality of Bob's suffering was a shock. It was difficult to grasp that the skeletal man before me was only twenty-six years old.

"Hi, I'm Father Demetri, the priest you spoke with on the phone," I said, standing and introducing myself. I extended my hand to him, prepared to shake his hand or to receive the traditional kiss given to a priest.

"I'm Bob—Haralambos,"[1] he said. "I'm glad you came." He took my hand in his and kissed it. Then he sat down in a chair that was also bound in plastic wrap. I sat down too. It appeared to me that he did not have long to live.

Bob looked at me evenly across the kitchen table. His eyes, though sunken, were clear.

"Father, I asked you to visit because I'm going to die soon," he said. His palms turned upward resignedly in silent appeal. "My priest won't come see me, and I can't go to church; I would terrify other people," he added, looking at his mother. "But I still believe in God."

I nodded. "I'm glad you called," I said. "You did the right thing."

He smiled. His mother excused herself and left us alone in the kitchen to talk.

Bob told me about himself. His parents had immigrated from Greece, and he had grown up in Chicago. He had an older, married brother. Not that long ago, Bob said, he had been muscular and brawny and he'd made a living loading and delivering mattresses for a mattress dealer. Then he began to lose weight and tire more easily. He didn't know what was wrong, so he went to see his doctor. They didn't find anything. Eventually, he was tested for HIV. The result came back positive.

Positive?!

That hit him hard. It was completely unexpected. He'd thought that HIV/AIDS was isolated to the gay community. He also wasn't sure when or how he had contracted the virus. He had no history of using needles or of receiving transfusions. He wasn't gay. His sexual activity had been very limited, he told me, but it appeared that that's how he had contracted HIV.

"I think I may have been infected by the girl I took to the high school prom," he said somewhat sheepishly.

"The *prom*?" I repeated.

"Yes," he said, rolling his eyes. I tried not to laugh, but I couldn't help it. He joined me, and the laughter lit up his face.

He asked me, "Did you go to prom?"

"Yes," I said, "twice."

At that moment, we were simply two friends talking about a high school dance.

※

Eleven years before Bob and I sat talking in the kitchen, doctors in Los Angeles encountered a handful of baffling medical cases. One by one, five patients with mystifying symptoms sought treatment and were treated between October 1980 and May 1981. Three hospitals received the sick patients, willing to heal them but unable to figure out how. The five patients were diagnosed with a rare pneumonia, *Pneumocystis carinii* pneumonia (PCP).

The disease that afflicted them, PCP, falls into the category of "opportunistic" diseases: a disease that is caused by an infection so mild that a healthy immune system has no trouble fighting it off. Like a protective wall around a city, a robust immune system is regularly preventing disease from invading, fending off would-be illness. It is so effective at its work that most of this happens without our being aware of it, but when that protective wall of defense collapses, even weak infections can invade and sicken us. The diagnosis of PCP is evidence that a patient's immune system is failing, and this was true of each of the five patients in Los Angeles.

Encountering a patient with PCP, a doctor would attempt to determine why the patient's immune system was failing. Usually, this was not difficult because a compromised immune system could easily be explained by one of a handful of known causes. A patient was asked some routine questions, and whichever one a patient answered yes to would determine the course of treatment.

"Have you had an organ transplant?" No.

"Do you take immunosuppressant drugs for any reason?" No.

"Do you have a previous history of a compromised immune system?" No.

This result—three noes—was puzzling; in fact, it was unheard of. All the known explanations for why a patient's immune system would stop working had been ruled out, but something was drastically undermining the patient's immune system, allowing disease to freely infiltrate the unprotected body. What was it? Doctors could not explain the condition; they had never seen anything like it before. Not knowing the cause, they could only treat the symptoms and hope for the best. This was true for all five patients.

At the time they were admitted to the hospitals, the five patients did not know each other, and they had no known shared contacts. What they had in common was that they were all young, sexually active gay men.

Despite physicians' best efforts, one patient, hospitalized in February, died in March. Another entered the hospital in March; he died in May. Of the five original patients, only three left the hospital alive.

An article documenting these five unusual cases was published the following month, on June 5, 1981, by the Centers for Disease Control (CDC).[2] Once that report came out, other vexing cases began to be reported, and a month later, on July 3, 1981, another CDC article was published describing clusters of cases in New York City and California that were strikingly similar to those seen in Los Angeles.[3] Over the previous thirty months, the article noted, doctors on both coasts had seen a sudden uptick in cases of an opportunistic skin cancer, Kaposi's sarcoma. Notable for causing purple skin lesions, this cancer was normally diagnosed in organ transplant recipients whose immune systems had intentionally been weakened by immunosuppressant drugs. Like the five patients diagnosed with PCP in Los Angeles, the twenty-six patients diagnosed with Kaposi's sarcoma did not have a history of organ transplants, and all of them were gay men.

The July report also noted that ten more cases of PCP in gay men had been identified in California, bringing to fifteen the total number of such patients since September 1979. Altogether, the report indicated that opportunistic diseases had affected forty-one gay men in two states.

The same day the CDC issued its report on Kaposi's sarcoma cases, the *New York Times* published the first mainstream news article about the emerging disease, "Rare Cancer Seen in 41 Homosexuals"[4]:

> Doctors in New York and California have diagnosed among homosexual men 41 cases of a rare and often rapidly fatal form of cancer. Eight of the victims died less than 24 months after the diagnosis was made.
>
> The cause of the outbreak is unknown.

The spike in the occurrence of PCP and Kaposi's sarcoma alarmed health officials, and the CDC established the Task Force on Kaposi's Sarcoma and Opportunistic Infections in the summer of 1981 to try to understand what was happening and why. They knew that most affected patients were gay men and that something was knocking out their immune systems wholesale. They didn't know the cause of this immune system failure or whether the cause was the same for patients suffering from PCP and from Kaposi's sarcoma. Was it an infectious agent passed through sexual contact from person to person (this was the favored explanation), or was it exposure to some noninfectious agent, such as recreational drugs?[5]

Whatever the cause, of the 337 cases of severe immune deficiency reported in the United States that year, 130 of those patients were already dead by year's end.[6]

※

In the kitchen of Bob's home, Bob and I continued to talk. He was a few years younger than me, and he was slowly dying. Sick and weak, he couldn't work. His friends didn't come see him anymore. He had assured them he was straight, but he guessed that some of them privately believed he was gay. He hadn't told more distant family members that he had AIDS out of fear that they would judge him and shun his parents. He had stayed away from church, and his priest had stayed away from him.

"The thing is, I understand my priest," Bob said. "He is afraid that he might get it." His compassion for the priest, whom he clearly loved, was moving. "But it still hurts," he said.

Even in his parents' loving home, Bob experienced isolation.

"My father and mother are terrified to touch me," he said, his skeletal face filled with unbearable sadness. I thought of their well-intended but misguided attempt to avoid infection by covering the house in plastic. It was heartbreaking, yet I understood. Bob's parents were immigrants. It was hard enough to obtain accurate information about AIDS in English, much less in Greek. They were scared. They were doing their best based on what they knew. Out of love for him, they continued to let their son live in their home—his home—they loved him, fed him, and took him to his medical appointments, but they kept their distance.

"What I miss most is my mother's embrace," he said, his eyes brimming despite himself. I listened, then asked if he wanted me to pray for his healing.

"Yes," he said.

I put on my priest's stole, then pulled out a small icon and set it on the table. I prayed with Bob and anointed him with holy oil on his forehead, chin, cheeks, palms, and the back of his hands. As he rubbed the glistening oil into his skin, I asked, "Would you like to receive Holy Communion?" He nodded. I retrieved the pyx (a special vessel designed to contain the eucharist) from my case. Bob had received Holy Communion since the time he was baptized as an infant, but his recent inability to attend church and his priest's unwillingness to visit him at home meant that he had not received this life-giving mystery for more than a year. He felt abandoned by his priest and cut off from the healing and reassuring rituals of his faith. By extension, he felt forgotten by God.

"The servant of God, Haralambos, receives the precious Body and Blood of our Lord, God, and Savior, Jesus Christ, unto the remission of sins and life everlasting," I said as I administered Holy Communion to him with a traditional Communion spoon.

Bob wiped a tear from his sunken cheek. His face, gaunt from illness, radiated peace. A kind of healing had just taken place, and witnessing it, I experienced an epiphany. *This is why I became a priest.*

∞

In 1982, the year after the CDC published its first two reports about the new disease, it was already spreading at a rapid clip. The terms used by some to describe it—"gay cancer," GRID (gay-related immune deficiency), or "gay flu"—mistakenly suggested an inherent link between homosexuality and the new disease. The CDC established a more accurate term, "acquired immune deficiency syndrome (AIDS)," in fall 1982. It also identified what it called four risk factors for AIDS: male homosexuality, intravenous drug use, Haitian origin, and hemophilia. Meanwhile, scattered cases of AIDS were also being reported in women and infants and in those who received blood transfusions during surgery or after an injury.

That year in New York City alone, 775 people were diagnosed with AIDS. Activists there founded the Gay Men's Health Crisis (GMHC), the first community-based AIDS service provider in the nation. One of its volunteers set up a GMHC information and counseling hotline on his home phone, and none too soon: the first night he received one hundred phone calls.

Two years after the initial CDC reports on AIDS, in 1983, researchers at the Pasteur Institute in France successfully isolated and identified a new retrovirus from a patient with AIDS, and the following year, scientists at the National Cancer Institute in Bethesda, Maryland, did likewise. This work constituted a breakthrough. After years of uncertainty, AIDS finally had an identifiable cause: a virus that eventually came to be known as the human immunodeficiency virus (HIV).

Having isolated the virus, researchers could now start the hard work of developing tests for HIV and a treatment for patients living with HIV/AIDS. Their work was fruitful, and in March 1985, the federal government licensed the first test to screen the nation's blood supply for exposure to HIV. This protected people with hemophilia, surgical patients, and others dependent on donated blood from becoming infected with HIV.

Developing a way to accurately test people for HIV infection proved more difficult, but in October 1985, the US Department of Defense was able to begin using an HIV-screening test for its new recruits. HIV testing would not be widely available to the public for some time, however.

In the meantime, medical staff faced new challenges because most did not know their patients' HIV status. In operating rooms and delivery rooms, in exam rooms when drawing blood, in emergency rooms, and when arriving by ambulance to attend to someone who was bleeding—that uncertainty meant everyone needed to take additional precautions. What should a school nurse do if a child ended up with a bloody nose on the playground?

Fear of becoming infected with the lethal virus swept through the nation, creating a panic. Parents wanted to protect their children, schools wanted to protect their students and staff, and employers wanted to protect their employees. The spread of wild rumors aggravated those fears, such as the wrongheaded idea that a person could become infected with HIV by touching a doorknob.

Fear also caused people to look for someone to blame. Sometimes people lashed out in a desperate attempt to draw a line between an infected "them" and an uninfected "us." Antigay sentiment bubbled up in the nation. Some professed Christians went so far as to claim that AIDS was a punishment from God for homosexuality, that it was not a medical condition but a moral condition. This view conveniently excused its self-righteous adherents from the Christian imperative of caring for the sick; after all, they could claim, AIDS patients had "brought it on themselves." Patients' families and friends were sometimes targeted for exclusion too.

The social stigma associated with HIV/AIDS multiplied the suffering of sick people already trying to cope with the medical and financial realities of being infected. AIDS patients often found themselves abandoned by those who would have stayed beside them had they had a different diagnosis. People like Bob were often isolated and alone. The stigma of having AIDS caused many to hide their diagnosis, and when it could not be hidden, the consequences could be heartbreaking.

∞

On December 6, 1971, a baby boy was born in Kokomo, Indiana. Three days later, when he was circumcised, the bleeding did not stop. Doctors told his concerned parents that he had severe hemophilia, a hereditary blood coagulation disease that causes even minor injuries to result in significant blood loss. His parents did not have it, nor did his older sister. The worried parents did as the doctor recommended, and their newborn baby began to receive weekly infusions of factor VIII, a blood product, as a treatment. It worked well, with only one hitch: it meant the little boy depended on blood donated by other people.

For years, the weekly transfusions allowed the boy, whose name was Ryan, to live a normal life. Soon after his thirteenth birthday, however, Ryan became quite ill and was diagnosed with pneumonia. A concerned physician ordered a lung biopsy. Pathologists returned scary results:

Ryan had AIDS. He had been infected by an HIV-tainted transfusion. It was December 1984, and his doctors gave the boy six months to live.

News of his diagnosis spread in the community. Like Americans elsewhere hearing of similar cases, many people in and around Kokomo were frightened of the boy and his diagnosis.

Astonishingly, Ryan started feeling better, and in early 1985, doctors confirmed that he could safely return to school because he was not a risk to other students or school staff since AIDS is not airborne. The day finally came for Ryan to return to school.

It is hard to imagine what he must have felt as he approached his familiar school in nearby Russiaville, Indiana, and encountered a hostile human barricade made up of teachers and parents who were loudly yelling at him and physically blocking him from entering his school. The protesters succeeded in keeping the boy out that day.

Local administrators sided with the protestors, who pulled together and held a community fundraiser in the school gym to raise money to prevent Ryan from returning to school. Ryan's mother, Jeanne, fought back through legal channels, aiming to secure an education for a child who had a diagnosis of AIDS but was not a threat to other students. Despite her dogged advocacy, on June 30, 1985, she was informed that Ryan was officially banned from his middle school.

∞

A few weeks later and 2,122 miles west of Kokomo, Hollywood icon Rock Hudson boarded a flight from Los Angeles to Paris.

Hudson was the definition of a leading man. Handsome, strong, and suave, he had been on the silver screen across three decades, paired with leading ladies from Elizabeth Taylor to Doris Day. An aging but elegant star, he was still a television celebrity on the series *McMillan & Wife*.

His flight touched down in Paris on July 21, 1985, and he checked into the Ritz Hotel. Soon after Hudson's arrival, the hotel physician received an urgent message: one of the guests had collapsed in his room. The doctor quickly assessed his patient, and Hudson was loaded onto a gurney and into an ambulance. The doors of the ambulance were closed, and he was rushed to the American Hospital of Paris, sirens blaring.

In the hospital, his condition stabilized. Conflicting explanations were offered to the press about the ailing celebrity, suggesting that he had liver cancer, fatigue, or anorexia. Days later, he disclosed his true diagnosis. The startling news flashed around the world that Rock Hudson had AIDS. Hudson's homosexuality, previously a private matter, was brought squarely into public view as part of his medical story. Many of his Hollywood friends, who had known he was gay, now surrounded him with vocal support.

To the public, the news that Rock Hudson was gay was a shock. Not only was he a Hollywood star, but also a friend of President Ronald Reagan, who, along with his wife, First Lady Nancy Reagan, had hosted Hudson at the White House. *He was gay?*

Sympathetic national media coverage of the beloved celebrity put a human face on AIDS for the first time, bringing Hudson's personal story to every television set and newspaper and heightening the visibility of the health crisis.

※

On the heels of Rock Hudson's stunning announcement, news out of Indiana came into the national spotlight that August: a teen who contracted AIDS from an HIV-infected blood transfusion had been banned from his middle school. The story of Ryan White captured the headlines and was often accompanied by a photograph of a friendly teenage boy with a cheerful smile.

Ryan's story created an uproar. On one hand, it forced people to rethink the simplistic position that AIDS was a plague visited on "immoral" people who "deserved" it. For some, his case allowed them to understand for the first time that AIDS was a medical problem. Ryan's experience also made it plain that someone living with HIV/AIDS could still participate in daily life without threatening the well-being of others. This challenged ideas that those living with HIV/AIDS should be isolated from others.

On the other hand, AIDS was affecting a growing number of people, and there was still no cure; 15,527 cases of AIDS were reported in the United States in 1985. The rapid spread of the incurable disease drove some panicked people to double down on the idea of staying away from anyone with AIDS, treating them as pariahs.

Rock Hudson died that fall, on October 2, 1985. Days later, the US Congress appropriated $221 million to develop a cure for AIDS. President Reagan promptly signed the bill into law. It had taken four years, but a shift in the national conversation about AIDS had begun, and significant resources were dedicated to finding a treatment. It was a win; but even then, many AIDS activists argued passionately that the government's efforts fell short because they were not driven by a sense of urgency, an urgency felt keenly by those living with HIV/AIDS and those who loved them. Many people were getting sick, and many were dying.

Back in Kokomo, Ryan White and his mother were steadfastly making the legal case to allow Ryan to return to school. In fall 1985, Ryan was allowed to attend his classes by telephone. After much legal back-and-forth,

Ryan was allowed to return to school on Friday, February 21, 1986. That day, 151 of 360 students stayed home; that afternoon, a judge granted a restraining order barring Ryan from school. In April 1986, he was again allowed to return to school. For the rest of the academic year, the school required Ryan to eat with disposable utensils, use separate bathrooms, and not attend gym class. Upon returning home one day, Ryan's family discovered a bullet had been fired into their living room window. At the end of the school year, the family pulled up stakes and moved to Cicero, Indiana.

In the fall of 1986, Ryan was welcomed to his new high school in nearby Arcadia, Indiana, by the principal, school superintendent, and several students who knew about AIDS and were not afraid to shake Ryan's hand. Education was starting to make a difference.

∞

The push-pull over the pandemic seen in Indiana was mirrored around the nation. Compassion for those living with HIV/AIDS competed with fear of the disease. As the deadly disease spread beyond gay men to the wider population, so did panic. It was clear: no one was immune. AIDS activism increased with the creation of the AIDS Coalition to Unleash Power (ACT UP) by Larry Kramer in 1987. Called "the most effective health activist [group] in history" by *Time* magazine, it successfully pressured drug companies and government agencies to speed up the efforts to find better treatments for people with AIDS.[7] It used a combination of highly visible public protests and science-informed negotiations with political and pharmaceutical leaders to push the cause of curing AIDS into the spotlight.

Simultaneously, political leaders played a role in shaping public views of AIDS. One particularly clear-eyed leader saw the need for Americans to understand AIDS better. The nation's top physician, Surgeon General C. Everett Koop, wrote the *Surgeon General's Report on Acquired Immune Deficiency Syndrome*. It explained what AIDS is, how it is transmitted, and how to avoid getting it. Prepared in pamphlet form, it featured bite-size nuggets of friendly, accurate information. In an unprecedented move, Dr. Koop had the pamphlet delivered to the mailbox of every American household in May 1988. It was the largest public health mailing in history. In a brief foreword, he expressed compassion for his readers:

> Some Americans have difficulties in dealing with the subjects of sex, sexual practices, and alternate lifestyles. Many Americans are opposed to homosexuality, promiscuity of any kind, and prostitution. This report must deal with all of these issues but does so with the intent that information and education

can change individual behavior, since this is the primary way to stop the epidemic of AIDS. This report deals with the positive and negative consequences of activities and behaviors from a health and medical point of view.

He also reassured his audience. In a brief section titled "You Won't Get AIDS From Insects—Or A Kiss," he wrote:

> No matter what you may have heard, the AIDS virus is hard to get and is easily avoided.
>
> You won't just "catch" AIDS like a cold or flu because the virus is a different type. The AIDS virus is transmitted through sexual intercourse, the sharing of drug needles, or to babies of infected mothers before or during birth.

He then listed ways one would *not* become infected: everyday contact at work or at school; swimming pools; mosquito bites; saliva; sweat; tears; urine; clothes; telephones; toilet seats; drinking glasses; eating utensils; or sharing a crowded bus, train, or elevator.[8] It was an extraordinary gesture of concern for the public and provided reliable, clear information.

Ryan White died in April 1990, a month shy of his high school graduation. That summer, Congress passed the Ryan White Comprehensive AIDS Resources Emergency (CARE) Act, which was signed into law in August 1990 by President George H. W. Bush. The largest federally funded program in the United States for people living with HIV/AIDS, it provided grants to improve the availability and quality of care for individuals and families affected by HIV. It has been renewed by Congress repeatedly.

∽

Bob and I were still talking in his family's kitchen when Bob's mother reappeared. She moved comfortably around the kitchen preparing each of us a snack, a ham sandwich on white bread.

We ate, and Bob told me he was as fearful of AIDS as his parents were. He knew he was probably to blame for making a foolish mistake on prom night. He was also sad and guilty to have been the cause of his parents' suffering. I reassured him that his family loved him; that God loved him; and that his life, however long or brief, had meaning and value. He looked at me, and I saw doubt written on his face. I told him that whatever had brought him to this place, he was still a beloved child of God, of infinite value and worth.

That afternoon, Bob, his parents, and I all sat together. We all knew Bob did not have long to live. This fact hovered over our conversation, creating a sense of sadness in the room. A fragment of an Orthodox Christian funeral hymn came to mind, "I lament and am pained when I contemplate death."

I saw their sadness and wanted to do more for this family. Many of the "safeguards" his parents had put in place to protect themselves from becoming infected with HIV were unnecessary, and they deserved to know that. I needed to demonstrate to his mother and father that they could embrace their own beloved son. So when it was time to go, I hugged Bob, and, as is customary in Greek culture, I kissed him on both cheeks as we said goodbye. Bob smiled at me. I promised we would see each other again soon.

I stepped off the porch into the afternoon sunshine with a mix of heavy heartedness and exhilaration. Bob had received a visit from a priest, and he and I had gotten to know each other. Maybe it encouraged him to believe that God truly loved him. Perhaps Bob's mother and father would be less afraid to touch their son. I hoped so. The knowledge that a priest would visit again and be there to pray with Bob at the end of his life, whenever that might be, had perhaps reassured them that they were not on this difficult journey alone.

But as I got into my car and started back to the office, the difficulty of their path settled on my heart and rested heavily there. It would be hard for them, and for Bob most of all. He would die in the near future. Beyond some visits, how could I help?

As I drove back to the office, it occurred to me that Bob was likely the tip of the iceberg. Other Greek Orthodox faithful living with HIV/AIDS were probably isolated, suffering privately, lacking medical information, and wanting to be visited by a priest. Their families, too, were probably in pain. I thought again of Bob's priest and his absence.

An idea began to take shape in my mind. By the time I reached the diocese office, I had a rough outline of a plan. I would do some research. Before I approached the bishop, I wanted to make sure I had enough information.

※

Bob had opened my eyes to a wider problem. As AIDS deaths had multiplied in Chicago, I had seen Roman Catholic, Episcopalian, Protestant, Jewish, Muslim, and Bahá'í believers, to name a few, reach out to people through organized AIDS ministries. They were already out there, raising money and providing services to help the hurting as a natural expression of their faith.

What were we doing? Aside from AIDS outreach undertaken by individual Greek Orthodox priests, we had no AIDS outreach or education for our own parishioners or others. We did not yet have a plan to educate our clergy about HIV/AIDS. We did not have any AIDS ministries. Parishioners like Bob were falling through the cracks.

It seemed to me we had to solve two problems: how to educate our clergy so they could visit and minister effectively to people living with HIV/AIDS, and how to let the Greek Orthodox faithful know that the Church continued to embrace and minister to everyone, HIV positive or not. This would involve changing people's minds about a deeply controversial issue, an enormous task.

But meeting Bob had changed me. Previously, I had sat at the edge of the AIDS pandemic. I didn't know anyone diagnosed with AIDS, or if I did, they didn't tell me their diagnosis. Encountering a lonely person suffering from the deadly illness, an outcast from his own family and his church, had made me care to a degree that I did not expect. Bob's tear-stained face had moved my heart in a way that suddenly made his cause my cause. Controversial or not, people living with HIV/AIDS were suffering, and it was part of our work to respond to their need.

I knew I had to bring this matter to the attention of Bishop Iakovos, who oversaw so many parishes. I suspected that Bob's priest was not the only one hesitant to visit a parishioner out of fear of contracting the virus. Still, I wasn't sure how receptive the bishop would be to the idea of asking his clergy to reach out to parishioners living with HIV/AIDS. But Bob was proof that the need was there. We couldn't just look away.

I came upstairs from my basement office and walked into the diocese kitchen, where I knew I would find the bishop at this hour.

"Good afternoon, Your Grace," I said.

"Good afternoon," he said. I took a seat.

In his mid-sixties, Bishop Iakovos was a traditional man leading a church steeped in almost twenty centuries of tradition. But he had often demonstrated a marked openness to new ideas and a gentle compassion for the people he shepherded. He was kind and dignified. We chatted a little about the day, and then I described my visit to Bob.

"The Church hasn't been there for Bob and his family," I said. Recalling it made me angry.

We talked about my visit—the plastic-draped furniture and Bob's parents' fear of touching him. I told the bishop I thought there might be a lot of people like Bob and a lot of priests like Bob's priest in our diocese. I also mentioned that the number of people living with HIV/AIDS was increasing.

"This is important, Your Grace," I said. I looked at him and then plunged in. "What would Your Grace think of starting an AIDS ministry?"

"You have an idea," he said with a wry smile, lifting his eyebrows.

Trying to contain my enthusiasm, I suggested that we initiate a two-part program. We could educate our clergy and lay leaders so they would know how to safely minister to people living with HIV/AIDS, I said. We could let parishioners know that if they or somebody they love is living with HIV/AIDS, the Church is there for them with support and information. The bishop listened. We talked about AIDS, how it spread, what it did to people, and how meaningful it had been to meet Bob. Talking about the idea, I became more and more convinced we should do it.

Of course, it was easy for me to recommend starting an AIDS ministry. I was a young, newly ordained priest and had little to lose. It was another thing for the bishop to agree. No one had to tell me that responding to the AIDS crisis by launching a ministry would be an enormous risk for Bishop Iakovos. If we started it, it would be the first diocese-wide Greek Orthodox AIDS ministry in the Western Hemisphere. The bishop would be sticking out his neck politically for the sake of people living with HIV/AIDS, including, for instance, men having sex with men, professional sex workers, drug users, and their families—people who had been written off by much of society, including by many of our faithful. What would the other eight bishops think, particularly the archbishop? What if the bishop's own priests, the diocesan priests, pushed back against the idea? Even I could anticipate that to many Greek Orthodox believers, having the church minister to those living with HIV/AIDS could be misunderstood as condoning human behaviors—homosexuality, promiscuity, intravenous use of illicit drugs—that they found objectionable.

The bishop, too, knew that creating an AIDS ministry could be controversial. He looked thoughtful. Was I sure about my medical facts? he asked. Did I know how many people were living with HIV/AIDS in our diocese? Was there a cure for AIDS? I assured him that my facts about AIDS transmission were correct and that priests would not be put at risk, and I confirmed that there was no cure for AIDS. I also said that I didn't know how many Greek Orthodox believers in our diocese might be infected with HIV. But I was certain that Bob was not the only one. I was sure that many believers did not have access to accurate information about HIV/AIDS, leaving them vulnerable.

Thinking of his clergy, the bishop said, "I think many of our priests feel the way Bob's priest does."

"Yes," I agreed. "They are making decisions based on what they know. But they need to learn the facts about the virus from a medical perspective and an Orthodox Christian perspective."

Then I added, "The Roman Catholics, the Episcopalians, and the Lutherans already have AIDS ministries." It was disappointing to realize just how far behind we were, but at the same time I suspected that the existence of other successful faith-based AIDS ministries might help persuade the bishop as he weighed the merits of beginning a new health-oriented ministry. He asked me to describe the other AIDS ministries. How did they work? I explained what I had read about and what I had seen.

For part of the afternoon, we talked about whom we could bring together to help formulate a plan. Greek Orthodox physicians? Other health professionals? I added that we could reach out to other Christian leaders in Chicago who were already running successful AIDS ministries who might be willing to share their expertise. Some of my friends were Roman Catholic and Episcopalian priests who might help us. The bishop encouraged me to see what I could come up with. The idea that had sprung from a visit to Bob began to take shape: we would create a committee charged with starting and overseeing a new AIDS ministry for the diocese, and we would figure out how to fund it.

That day, Bishop Iakovos gave his blessing to the idea, and he authorized me to coordinate a new task force. (In retrospect, it is probably good that I did not understand the enormous implications of this decision.) As it was, I thanked him and was thrilled as I stood up from the chair.

"Your Grace, it would help a great deal if people know you are behind this initiative," I said, treading on politically sensitive territory. "Perhaps it could be called the 'Bishop's Task Force on AIDS,'" I said.

He shrugged his shoulders. Such things were of little interest to him.

"That would give it Your Grace's seal of authority," I added.

"Okay," he assented.

"Thank you, Your Grace," I said excitedly. I had butterflies in my stomach. We were about to establish a new AIDS ministry.

7

✢

Lessons in Advocacy

March 3, 1999

The land we now know as Illinois recorded its first instance of capital punishment on June 15, 1779. The unfortunate man, named Manuel, was tied with rope to a stake, and the woodpile at his feet was then lit on fire. He went up in flames, the punishment for witchcraft. A handful of years later, when Illinois became part of the Northwest Territory, it was newly governed by the terms of the Northwest Ordinance of 1787, which allowed administering the death penalty for the crimes of treason, murder, arson, horse stealing, and rape, but not witchcraft. The mechanism of execution shifted too; hanging became the norm.

Illinois was declared a state in 1818, and the state's first execution occurred eight months later, on July 14, 1819. John Killduck was hanged for murder. Hanging as the means of execution by the state continued for more than one hundred years until 1928, when Illinois adopted the electric chair.

Electrocution remained the preferred method of execution in Illinois until 1989, but in the period from 1963 to 1989, the State of Illinois did not execute anyone. It would quickly make up for that merciful gap after adopting a new practice, execution by lethal injection, in 1990. That year, one man, Charles Walker, was executed, and between 1991 and 1998, Illinois executed ten more men.

Across that span of 219 years—from the burning of Manuel at the stake in 1779 until the execution of a man named Lloyd Hampton by lethal injection in 1998—a total of 359 people were convicted of capital crimes and executed in Illinois. Of them, 357 were men and two were women. It appeared unlikely to me that Manuel had been guilty of witchcraft. This begged the question: how many of the other 358 people who lost their lives were also innocent?

Two days after meeting Andrew, I sent him a letter and enclosed a small black knotted fiber cross necklace, a modest monetary gift, and a sermon I wrote that was inspired by our meeting, which I had delivered the Sunday after I met him. I hoped these things would encourage him as the seconds quietly ticked off the hours, moving him closer to his execution date. That same clock urged me to hurry. I was determined to prevent him from being the 360th person executed in Illinois.

※

It was now Wednesday, March 3, 1999, two weeks until Andrew's scheduled execution. Bishop Iakovos and I were strategizing, looking for any opportunity to advocate for clemency for Andrew. The bishop recalled that back in the spring of 1998, in the lead-up to the gubernatorial election, he had received a visit at the diocese from Bill J. Vranas. A Greek Orthodox supporter of candidate George Ryan, Mr. Vranas came on the candidate's behalf to request Bishop Iakovos's blessing for Ryan to attend the numerous Greek Orthodox church festivals that would soon brighten weekends throughout metro Chicago with Greek dancing, music, and authentic foods. These festivals draw thousands of people—a good reason for a candidate to visit them.

"Of course, Mr. Ryan can attend the festivals. No blessing is needed; everyone is welcome," Bishop Iakovos told him warmly.

"Thank you," said Mr. Vranas, adding that should George Ryan get elected, Bishop Iakovos and the Diocese of Chicago would have an open door to the governor's office. It was a simple exchange, a common promise made by any candidate running for office.

All these months later, Bishop Iakovos remembered that promise. I foolishly decided to take it seriously—or perhaps, realizing that a man's life was at stake, I was willing to try anything that offered hope that Andrew might live. Perhaps Mr. Vranas could gain us access to the new governor?

I called Mr. Vranas, and I asked if it might be possible to arrange a meeting with the governor about Andrew Kokoraleis. The person I needed to speak with was Tom Coutretsis, he advised. Originally from Greece, Mr. Coutretsis had done well in his adopted country. He was a well-known Chicago businessman, philanthropist, and civic leader who had the governor's ear. A meeting was arranged, and I was grateful that Mr. Coutretsis was able to see me so quickly. I hoped this was a good sign.

On the appointed day, I took a cab downtown to Mr. Coutretsis's office. I knew a lot was riding on this meeting; this man could open the door to the governor's office. I had rehearsed what I was going to say. In my briefcase was a sealed manila envelope with copies of letters to Governor Ryan from the Greek Orthodox Archbishop of America, the Roman Catholic Papal Nuncio, and many Chicago religious leaders. I hoped it would be enough. I arrived early.

I took the elevator to the second floor, spotted Mr. Coutretsis's office as I stepped out, and knocked on the door precisely on time. Mr. Coutretsis opened the door and welcomed me into his office, and we introduced ourselves. He invited me to take the seat facing his desk, and he sat down behind his desk. He exuded the bold confidence of a man who knew how to get things done.

"What can I do for you, Father?" Mr. Coutretsis asked obligingly.

I thanked him for meeting with me, then said I was there on behalf of Bishop Iakovos. He listened politely. I told him that the diocese had appealed to Governor Ryan to grant clemency to Andrew Kokoraleis, whose execution was scheduled for March 17. I added that several other religious hierarchs in Chicago, including Francis Cardinal George, had supported our appeal, as did the Papal Nuncio and Archbishop Spyridon of America. I placed the manila envelope of letters on the desk in front of him. "Copies of their letters to the governor are in this envelope," I said, gesturing to the packet on his desk, "as are our arguments for clemency." He did not look at the envelope but continued to look at me. He said nothing. Uncomfortable seconds passed in silence. He was clearly waiting for me to ask for what I wanted, and he was not going to make it easy.

"I'm here to ask for a face-to-face meeting with Governor Ryan to appeal for the life of Andrew Kokoraleis," I said.

From across the desk, Mr. Coutretsis considered me in silence, his face impassive. Then he told me he had lived in this city for many years. In that time, he had seen a lot and had supported a number of causes in Chicago. As far as Andrew Kokoraleis was concerned, however, everything he'd read and heard about him confirmed that this man was an animal and part of a depraved gang. Many people believed that he deserved to be executed for what he had done to many women, he said. Without his needing to say it, it was evident that Mr. Coutretsis was of this opinion as well.

I thought of Andrew, his years in solitary confinement and what he had told me about being beaten by police until he had given a false confession. Instead of disagreeing with Mr. Coutretsis about Andrew's likely innocence or arguing about the morality of the death penalty, I held my tongue. Was there some other appeal I could make that might sway him?

He paused as if willing to entertain any rebuttal I might offer.

"Mr. Coutretsis," I said, "we know that Andrew is not a choirboy. We are seeking clemency not because Andrew is without fault but because our faith teaches that all life is sacred—even Andrew's. Governor Ryan has the power to show mercy and spare a man's life. Please, intervene with the governor for a face-to-face meeting with him so that we can appeal for Andrew's life."

"I'll see what I can do," he said noncommittally and stood up. The meeting was over.

"Thank you for your time," I said and shook his hand.

I left his office with a glimmer of hope. At least he hadn't said no.

∞

Days passed, and I didn't hear from Mr. Coutretsis or the governor's office. I had naively believed that Mr. Coutretsis would let me know if anything developed one way or another. I again contacted Mr. Vranas, who said the ball was in Mr. Coutretsis's court. I reached out to the offices of the religious leaders who had sent letters to the governor to see if any of them had received a response. No one had.

I was a newcomer to the world of Illinois politics, but in the deafening silence that followed my meeting with Mr. Coutretsis and the coordinated letter campaign by religious leaders, it became clear even to me that the door to the governor's office was closed.

∞

Governor Ryan had many things on his mind that winter, including education. On March 5, 1999, twelve days before the scheduled execution, he traveled to Murphysboro High School in southern Illinois to learn about the school's innovative use of technology in the classroom. It was impressive, and a media entourage followed him on his visit to the school. While there, the governor was confronted by six peaceful anti–death penalty advocates carrying signs near the school. To his credit, he approached them. Elsie Speck and others from the Southern Illinois Death Penalty Moratorium Committee had been joined by Catholics Against Capital Punishment. Speck requested that Governor Ryan declare a moratorium on executions.

Governor Ryan responded by acknowledging that the state's record of having imprisoned eleven innocent men on death row was unacceptable. He was going to prevent that from happening again, he told them, by having a "double review" of the evidence against Andrew. "My obligation is to make sure this guy is completely guilty," he said. As for a moratorium, he added, after Andrew, there were no executions scheduled for at least another six months, meaning there would be a de facto moratorium. The demonstrators said they had gathered to let the governor know that "down here in Southern Illinois we're concerned about the people who end up on death row. We care."[1]

The next day, March 6, the *Chicago Tribune* opinion page printed a letter suggesting that the public push for a moratorium on executions was creating new alliances:

> The Chicago Council of Lawyers has joined with Rep. Coy Pugh (D-Chicago) to draft a bill, House Bill 723, to stop executions for one year while the state attempts to reform the system to prevent more innocent people from being sentenced to death.[2]

(The measure, introduced to the Illinois House Judiciary Committee the previous week, had passed, 9-2.[3]) The letter also recommended that while the legislature deliberated Representative Pugh's bill, either the governor should grant a temporary reprieve to Andrew or the Illinois Supreme Court should postpone his execution. The logic was straightforward: the death penalty system had proven to be dangerously flawed, and Andrew's execution should be stopped in its tracks until capital punishment in Illinois could be assessed and improved.

Aviva Futorian, a defense attorney in capital cases and a member of the Illinois Coalition Against the Death Penalty (ICADP), also weighed in: "Governor Ryan should stay this execution, at least until the pending legislation on a moratorium is resolved."[4]

∞

I received a neat typewritten letter from Andrew postmarked March 7, 1999. He thanked me for my letter, my small gifts, and my sermon. He continued:

> At the time of this writing, I'm 10 days away from execution. One way or the other, this time of anxiety will be past soon. As the day gets closer, I feel like a laboratory mouse under a microscope. Everybody has been watching me. I've heard the expression "living in a fishbowl" before, but I didn't really appreciate its meaning until now!

I imagined Andrew sitting alone in a his six-foot by nine-foot cell, counting down the days and hours until his execution. I could only imagine how anxious he must feel. I decided to make another trip to Pontiac.

This time, I went alone. I was familiar with the visiting process and no longer shocked by it. When I entered the visitor room and saw Andrew there, I was genuinely glad. I asked how he was doing, and he told me. I caught him up on our advocacy efforts. I told him the governor had so far ignored the appeal from religious leaders but that we weren't giving up: we were planning a press conference the following Sunday. He thanked me. When I said goodbye to him, I felt confident that we would succeed. In the back of my mind, however, I recognized the real possibility that this would be the last time I would see him alive.

The idea of an interfaith press conference had emerged because none of the religious leaders who had asked the governor to have mercy on Andrew had heard from the governor's office, not even a form letter. We decided to make a public case to the governor for sparing Andrew's life. The press conference would be held on Sunday, March 14. Should the governor change his mind by that date, we would cancel the press conference.

∽

The week before Andrew's scheduled execution was packed with decisive developments.

On Tuesday, March 9, in the Chicago suburb of Wheaton, DuPage County Judge Ann Jorgensen donned her judicial robes and took her place at the bench. She was the presiding judge of the Criminal Division. One of the questions before the court that day was whether newly discovered evidence about Andrew's case could be introduced.

Andrew's legal team had only recently become aware of a promising piece of information. According to the book *Deadly Thrills* (written by former Chicago police officer Jaye Slade Fletcher), Edward Spreitzer and Thomas Kokoraleis had originally pinned the guilt for Lorraine Borowski's murder on Robin Gecht; only later, fearing retaliation by Gecht, did they flip-flop and tell police that Andrew, not Gecht, was guilty.[5] Andrew's attorney, Alan Freedman of the Midwest Center for Justice, requested an evidentiary hearing to allow the court to assess the new evidence, which, he argued, might prove that Andrew was innocent as he claimed. Everyone understood that granting a new evidentiary hearing would delay Andrew's execution. Freedman also asked the judge to allow him to conduct legal depositions of some of the detectives involved in the investigation as well as Andrew's brother and two friends.

John Kinsella, DuPage County Assistant State's Attorney prosecuting the case, was unimpressed.

"This motion is basically a request for more public debate on the death penalty," he said.

Judge Jorgensen heard the arguments from both attorneys. She decided that the evidence did not merit a new hearing.[6]

Lessons in Advocacy

The same day that Judge Jorgensen made her ruling, the Illinois State Bar Association's Board of Governors was meeting in Chicago. Initially, they considered a proposal supporting a moratorium on executions in Illinois in response to increasing calls for a moratorium, some of which came from among their 35,000 members. However, they voted instead to support the expanded review of death penalty cases that had been announced the previous month by Illinois Attorney General Jim Ryan. His office would now plan to meet with prosecutors and defense attorneys in capital cases before deciding whether to ask the Illinois Supreme Court for a final execution date. Andrew's case, too, would be reviewed, he'd said.[7]

Only four avenues remained open to prevent or delay Andrew's execution, and most of them were long shots. Andrew could be spared by a reprieve from Governor George Ryan, which was unlikely. The Illinois Supreme Court could either grant an emergency stay of execution or rule in favor of an appeal for a new evidentiary hearing to assess the value of the new evidence in Andrew's case; to that end, Andrew's attorney had already filed petitions with the court. Neither petition had much likelihood of success, however. The Illinois General Assembly might succeed in passing a bill to assess the death penalty and could request a moratorium. But the governor could veto the bill; the legislature didn't have the authority to impose a moratorium, only the governor did; and movement on the bill seemed to have stalled, in any case. Finally, the least likely option was that the US Supreme Court might be persuaded to stay Andrew's execution.

It was around that time that Andrew's lawyers sent a clemency petition directly to the governor's office.[8] In it they described the new evidence. They reiterated that the only evidence of Andrew's guilt offered by the prosecution in the murder of Lorraine Borowski was a coerced confession that Andrew had immediately recanted. Other death row inmates, wrongfully convicted based on coerced confessions, had been exonerated. Andrew's attorneys appealed to the governor on behalf of their client, who, they argued, might actually be innocent of the one crime for which he had been sentenced to death.

※

On Wednesday, March 10, a week before the scheduled execution, a letter signed by 322 Chicago-area lawyers landed heavily on the governor's desk. Signed by both supporters and opponents of the death penalty, the letter urgently advised Governor Ryan to establish a special commission to assess the state's death penalty and make recommendations to improve it. The lawyers lamented:

The system we care deeply about suffers with every new accusation that possible police misconduct, prosecutorial abuse or inept defense has produced the wrongful conviction and death sentence of an innocent person. We shudder at such charges.

The letter further counseled the governor that it would be "unseemly and inappropriate" to carry on with executions while the death penalty was being reviewed and recommended instead that Governor Ryan grant reprieves to all condemned inmates with scheduled executions. The letter was written by the legal director of the MacArthur Justice Center at the University of Chicago Law School, Locke Bowman. Among the attorneys who signed it were heavy hitters from major Chicago law firms.

The governor's spokesman, John Torre, publicly responded to the letter by saying that the governor did not support a moratorium, that he would consider each capital case separately, and that his attorney general had already added an extra layer of review for capital cases.[9]

⁂

It was now Thursday, March 11. With only six days remaining before the scheduled execution, the Illinois Prisoner Review Board was meeting and would consider Andrew's case for clemency. Andrew's lawyer, Alan Freedman, hoped that the new evidence from Fletcher's book, *Deadly Thrills*, might make a difference. I knew that the family of Lorraine Borowski would probably be at the hearing. I planned to be there to add my voice in support of clemency for Andrew.

I walked into the dark auditorium and took a seat facing the illuminated stage. The board, which provides confidential, nonbinding recommendations to the governor, was hearing the cases of several inmates that day. None of the inmates were present. Members of the board were seated at a table on the stage. As each case came up, the defense attorneys and prosecutors took turns making their arguments. Additional petitioners (like me) were called by name to make a statement but were not allowed to carry any papers or notes with them when it was their turn to speak to the board.

Finally, it was time for Andrew's hearing.

The hearing was uncomfortably tense. The prosecution laid out the terrible murder case against Andrew. Then Alan Freedman spoke, and I couldn't tell if the Prisoner Review Board was convinced by his argument that new evidence of Andrew's innocence had been uncovered and was significant.

When my name was called, I walked to a podium facing the stage and introduced myself as the Chancellor of the Greek Orthodox Diocese of Chicago. I appealed to the board for mercy for Andrew, noting his troubled upbringing, his consistent claim of innocence of the murder, and his claim that his confession had been coerced from him and was immediately recanted. I spoke of the sacredness of life. I asked the board not to execute Andrew but to allow him to live in prison for the rest of his life with no possibility of parole.

When I was done, I left the auditorium. I did not hear Lorraine Borowski's father, Raymond, make his own impassioned plea. He believed that Andrew had participated in torturing and killing his daughter. Based on that understanding, it is not surprising that he said of Andrew that day, "It's his turn to take that final walk—a walk more humane than the one which was afforded Lorry. He wants clemency? Ha! Did Lorry get clemency? Absolutely not. Will Andrew suffer the tortuous pain and humiliation she suffered at his hands?"[10] I had considered staying and speaking with the Borowski family, but in the end I did not. I knew they would hear me make a plea for mercy for Andrew that day and would feel offended by what I had to say. No matter what my intentions, it would add insult to injury for me to approach them on a day in which the horror of their daughter's ghastly murder was vividly revisited. I headed back to the office.

That evening, Attorney General Jim Ryan announced that his office had again reviewed Andrew's case, as promised. Not surprisingly, they concluded that no further investigation was needed.[11] The execution would proceed as scheduled.

∞

Friday, March 12, was a flurry of activity. I was in touch with Chicago clergy and the ICADP throughout the day. We finalized details for Sunday afternoon's press conference and reached out to the media. A handful of speakers would present arguments for opposing the death penalty. A lawyer and faithful Greek Orthodox Christian by the name of Carol Mavrakis would speak on behalf of the diocese and would address the legal side of things. I would be the emcee. We invited laypeople to attend.

This planning was a meaningful distraction as we awaited the results of an important appeal taking place that day. On the heels of Judge Jorgensen's recent dismissal of his petition, Alan Freedman was now arguing before the Illinois Supreme Court that the newly discovered evidence supporting Andrew's innocence did merit an evidentiary hearing, as it might finally help prove his client's innocence. He also appealed to the court for a delay of execution. Surely, no one wanted to execute an innocent man.

In the middle of the afternoon, the diocese receptionist, Faye Peponis, transferred a call to my office. The news wasn't good: the court denied the motion for a delay and dismissed the appeal for consideration of new evidence.[12] Justices Moses Harrison II, James D. Heiple, and S. Louis Rathje dissented. In his dissent, Justice Harrison lashed out at his colleagues on the bench:

> The court cannot pretend that it has made even cursory assessment of the merits. An appeal under these circumstances is no appeal at all. The most important check in our justice system has been lost.

He also wrote:

> There has been nearly universal recognition by this State's legal community that our system of capital punishment is in dire need of change. . . . Until we have a better understanding of where the system is failing and how, if at all, it can be remedied, the State of Illinois has no business continuing to send defendants to their deaths. It must be stopped from executing Kokoraleis and every other defendant sentenced under the existing capital punishment system.[13]

He also noted that the governor possesses the constitutional authority to grant a reprieve.

I remember hanging up the phone and sitting in my office, numb and staring into space. Andrew! How much time did he have left? *Saturday, Sunday, Monday.* On Tuesday morning, they would airlift Andrew from Pontiac Correctional Center to Tamms Correctional Center, where he was scheduled to be executed shortly after midnight, in the first minutes of Wednesday, March 17—St. Patrick's Day. A day beloved by many Chicagoans, full of celebration and a joyous parade, would begin with an execution.

Gravely disappointed and angry, I spoke with Bishop Iakovos. Then I called Fred, who confirmed what I already knew. A decision by Governor Ryan was the only viable option left. The General Assembly didn't have the authority to impose a moratorium, and the US Supreme Court was unlikely to stay Andrew's execution. I imagined that the ruling by the Illinois Supreme Court must have been received with mixed feelings in the governor's office; for now, the choice whether Andrew would live or die was the governor's alone. Whatever happened, Governor Ryan would have to own it. I became even more resolute in getting the governor's attention with our upcoming press conference

One bright spot illuminated that dark Friday. Bishop-Elect William Persell, who would be consecrated the new Episcopal bishop of Chicago the following day, held a press conference to introduce himself. Standing before the microphones, cameras, and reporters, he proclaimed, "The Episcopal Church is on the record opposing the death penalty, and I am very opposed to it personally." Bishop-Elect Persell stated that he had written a letter to Governor George Ryan seeking clemency for death row inmate Andrew Kokoraleis. He also said that he planned to join fellow religious leaders at a press conference opposing the death penalty to be held on Sunday.[14] He had supported Andrew's cause as he introduced himself to Chicago and beyond, and I was inexpressibly grateful.

The press conference the bishop-elect mentioned was now our religious coalition's best chance to capture the governor's attention. Changing the governor's mind was paramount; if only he would agree to meet with us. My fellow clerics and I had our work cut out for us. Sunday would soon be upon us.

8

✢

Empathy in Action

March 1993

The conference room was comfortable and well lit. The speaker at the podium looked out on rows of attentive listeners, priests from every parish in our diocese. I sat among them. Despite weeks of private worry about how the controversial topic of HIV/AIDS would be received this morning, ninety minutes in, I had to admit that the opening session of our annual clergy retreat seemed to be going well.

The presenter, a brilliant scientist and physician, described HIV and its stealthy, uncanny ability to invade the body and render the human immune system defenseless, eventually resulting in AIDS, which, at the time, was a virtual death sentence. She moved on to a discussion of how HIV is transmitted. The stakes were high, she told the priests. Becoming infected with HIV all but guaranteed eventual death from one or more opportunistic diseases that the defenseless body could not fight. She stressed that abstinence was the only foolproof way to prevent HIV transmission; however, using condoms during sexual relations would greatly reduce the risk of its transmission. She then described sexual behaviors that leave people vulnerable to HIV infection, candidly and appropriately referring to human genitalia and other anatomy as she did.

A man's voice abruptly interrupted the speaker. "Do you realize that you are speaking to the Greek Orthodox clergy of the Diocese of Chicago?" he spat out contemptuously.

Dear God, who is that? I thought. Everyone turned to see who was speaking. Standing tall in an arrogant posture, his face red with anger and eyes blazing, a priest was glaring accusingly at the speaker. My heart sank in sudden recognition. He was one of the diocese's most prominent and highly respected clergymen.

I gritted my teeth as a thought flashed like a warning light across my mind: *The Task Force is going to fail before it has even had a chance to get off the ground.*

The room fell into a strained silence as priest and scientist squared off.

∽

One Year Earlier, March 1992

The very day Bishop Iakovos agreed to give his blessing to start a new AIDS ministry in March 1992, I had begun calling Orthodox Christians who might be willing to be part of a new task force, both priests and laypeople: doctors, infectious disease specialists, dentists, social workers, and philanthropic leaders. Almost everyone I asked said yes.

Compared to other faith communities in Chicago, we were latecomers to the world of AIDS ministry, so in the days before we had our first Task Force meeting, I reached out to more experienced groups for help. I met with other faith leaders to learn how they had educated their leadership and congregations about HIV/AIDS and how they did outreach. People were overwhelmingly generous in relating their own experiences, both heartwarming successes and bitter failures. The knowledge and wisdom these faithful leaders shared with me was immense, and I brought it back to the Task Force. Our late arrival to the world of AIDS ministry proved to have one tremendous benefit: we stood on the shoulders of others and learned from their mistakes.

Keenly aware that we were newcomers, the Task Force sought allies from outside the Orthodox Christian world. One was Steven Montgomery, who served on the Episcopal Diocese of Chicago's AIDS ministry board. He was pleased to learn about the new Task Force, and when I asked him, he agreed to join our board. Ernest Vasseur, a liaison who was graciously sent from the AIDS Pastoral Care Network (APCN) of Chicago to help the Task Force get its ministry up and running, also agreed to serve on our board. They added a much-valued ecumenical dimension to the Task Force's discussions. Over the years, as our board members changed, the Task Force always sought to include an ecumenical participant and perspective.

∽

One rainy Chicago morning, I stepped into a crowded café to meet my friend Christian Schutte for coffee. Sitting at a table beside the rain-streaked window, I told him that the diocese was starting an outreach ministry to people living with HIV/AIDS. A smile lit up his face.

We talked about it, and he recommended that "If you really want to know how AIDS is affecting the gay community, you should start reading *Gay Chicago* and *Windy City Times*." I raised my eyebrows at this.

"You're suggesting a Greek Orthodox priest should pick up copies of gay magazines and newspapers and read them at the diocese?" I asked.

He nodded.

I told him I already had.

We shared a laugh. It was more proof that AIDS had turned the world upside down.

∞

The Bishop's Task Force on AIDS numbered about twenty-five people, all from the Chicago area. We gathered for the first time in April 1992, a little over a month after I met Bob. We knew the stark statistics. Between 1981 and 1990, health departments around the United States had reported 100,777 deaths among persons with AIDS; almost a third of those were reported in 1990 alone.[1] Only two years later, by the end of 1992, that number would more than double, to a total of 229,205 deaths among persons with AIDS.[2] Eleven years after first identifying the deadly new disease, there was still no cure in sight.

AIDS activists—many of whom were scared for their own lives or the lives of those they loved—were frustrated that the urgency they felt to find an effective treatment for HIV infection and AIDS wasn't mirrored by policy makers and others in the United States. "We've tried all the quiet negotiations. We tried to be good little boys and girls. We've tried to work within the system. There's a new AIDS death every half hour.... At this point, we just want to raise the issues. We are dying," said Larry Kramer, the founder of the AIDS Coalition to Unleash Power (ACT UP).[3] ACT UP New York and others resorted to staging public demonstrations to put pressure on the government and the pharmaceutical industry to do more and at a more rapid pace.

On April 25, 1989, four ACT UP activists, dressed in business suits and carrying power tools in their briefcases, arrived at the headquarters of Burroughs Wellcome, a pharmaceutical company in Research Triangle Park, North Carolina. The company was the sole manufacturer of azidothymidine (AZT), the only government-approved drug to treat AIDS. The four men entered an unoccupied office and barricaded themselves in, bolting small metal plates to the door and doorframe to seal the door. They demanded that the company reduce the price of AZT.[4] Why, the activists argued, was the price for this life-saving drug so high—$8,000 to

$10,000 per year, making it unaffordable for many—when public dollars had paid to research and develop it? "Either they knock down the cost or they knock down their own walls to get us out," said protester Peter Staley. (Officers did cut through the wall and led the protestors away in handcuffs.) This action garnered press attention but did not impact the price of AZT.

Five months later, ACT UP activists, dressed in suits and bearing fake credentials, entered the New York Stock Exchange and chained or handcuffed themselves to the VIP balcony. They disrupted the opening bell by blowing miniature air horns, then unfurled a banner that read "Sell Wellcome!"[5] In the pandemonium, trading couldn't begin. It was the only time in history that the New York Stock Exchange opening was delayed. Activists dropped fake $100 bills onto the traders below. The bills read "F--- Your Profiteering. People are dying while you play business" and "White Heterosexual men can't get AIDS . . . Don't bank on it." Meanwhile, on the street outside, an estimated 1,500 protestors carried signs depicting bloody hands and passed out fake bills. Within days, Burroughs Wellcome reduced the price of AZT by 20 percent.[6]

ACT UP activists and others went even further a few months later. On December 11, 1989, during a Mass being celebrated by John Cardinal O'Connor at St. Patrick's Cathedral, activists chained themselves to pews, while others were shouting or lying down in the aisles, disrupting the Mass to protest the cardinal's recent statements on homosexuality and AIDS.[7] Outside, protestors blocked Fifth Avenue traffic in front of the cathedral by lying down on the street. This provocative, highly controversial action propelled the topic of AIDS to headlines in newspapers well beyond New York City. However, even some AIDS activists questioned it.

On May 21, 1990, more than one thousand protestors swarmed the National Institutes of Health (NIH) campus in Bethesda, Maryland, to demand that the NIH accelerate the pace of HIV/AIDS research, include AIDS activists and community members in committees overseeing AIDS research, expand its investigations beyond research on AZT, and include research on HIV-related diseases that affected women (since women with AIDS develop different opportunistic diseases than men), children, and people of color.[8]

Closer to home, ACT UP Chicago sponsored a march in downtown Chicago on April 23, 1990, snarling traffic at eight o'clock on a Monday morning. One thousand protestors, many with signs, decried inadequate health care for people living with HIV/AIDS. Police tried to keep demonstrators on the sidewalks, but they soon flooded the street. Demonstrators marched from the Prudential Building to Blue Cross Blue Shield Association offices to the American Medical Association (AMA) and held a "die-in," drawing chalk lines around their bodies and demanding fair health coverage from health insurance companies for people living with HIV/AIDS and protesting the AMA's opposition to national health insurance.[9]

Outside the Cook County Building, activists deployed fifteen mattresses in the middle of the street, and women donned hospital gowns over their clothes and sat down on the mattresses, surrounded by two defensive rings of other activists, creating a human wall that faced off with police, some of whom were on horseback. Protestors were calling attention to the lack of beds for female AIDS patients at Cook County Hospital. (Soon after, a women's AIDS ward was opened at the hospital.) Other activists slipped into the nearby County Building and unfurled a banner from a second-floor balcony that read, "We Demand Equal Healthcare Now." Many arrests were made that day.[10]

In this charged environment, our Task Force had its work cut out for it. We shared a sense of urgency. We knew the Greek Orthodox Church rightly had a role in reaching out to those living with HIV/AIDS, and we knew we needed to start with our own community so that people like Bob and his family would be embraced and ministered to by their church. We also wanted everyone, clergy and the laity, to be armed with accurate information in the midst of a medical crisis that continued to expand.

Our Task Force determined that its aims were, as expressed in our mission statement, to:

- educate and sensitize clergy and laity as to the medical and pastoral issues surrounding HIV/AIDS;
- help meet the needs of diverse Orthodox faithful and others who are living with HIV/AIDS; and
- offer advocacy on behalf of and comfort to those faithful who live with HIV/AIDS, those who care for them and about them, and those who have sustained the loss of a loved one due to HIV/AIDS.

As we considered how to achieve these aims, the Task Force drew inspiration from the best practices of more established faith-based AIDS ministries in Chicago. We agreed to start with three goals. First, we would send each of our priests an AIDS ministry packet with easily digested information about HIV/AIDS and materials to help him minister to those living with HIV/AIDS. Second, we would launch an Orthodox Christian HIV/AIDS speakers' bureau whose representatives would travel to parishes in all six states of the diocese. Third, we would ask Bishop Iakovos if the Task Force could invite guest speakers to share information about HIV/AIDS at the next diocese-wide gathering of clergy.

We began our work with these three goals in the hope that they would help us bring about change in the Greek Orthodox culture of our diocese on the topic of HIV/AIDS. We wanted our priests to minister lovingly to their flocks, and we wanted to keep people from becoming infected with HIV—aiming to save lives. We hoped to enhance both medical knowledge and compassion in the diocese concerning HIV/AIDS.

∞

One morning Bishop Iakovos asked if I'd seen the newspaper clippings he'd left for me. He had taken to cutting out articles about AIDS from the *Chicago Tribune* and Greek-language newspapers. I said I had and thanked him. He made his way to the diocese kitchen, where I joined him several minutes later.

The day before, I told him, I'd gone to a home meeting to hear someone talk about what it's like to live with HIV/AIDS. I'd heard about the meeting from an AIDS activist friend of mine who attended the Dutch Reformed Church. (We didn't think of ourselves as "activists" at the time. We were just interested in compassionate ministry.) The meeting was open to the public and advertised in the gay media.

I had left my clerical collar at home to attend the meeting. I was one of perhaps ten people who gathered in someone's living room to hear an HIV-positive individual share personal experiences and provide HIV information. The meeting was arranged by Test Positive Aware (TPA),[11] an organization founded five years before by seventeen Chicagoans who tested positive for HIV but were not diagnosed with AIDS. They had banded together to share their stories, support one another, and find out as much as they could about the deadly virus. Over time, their peer-led group expanded. They met in small groups, warmly welcoming people who were HIV positive and others, like me, who wanted to know more about HIV.

That afternoon, the speaker talked about the importance of safer sex practices, including how to use a condom correctly and then remove it safely so the semen doesn't leak; he demonstrated this by placing a condom over a banana and removing it. I related this to Bishop Iakovos, and he laughed. He had lived in the United States since 1954 and was still a keen observer of American society. He enjoyed hearing anecdotes that provided insights into his adopted country.

I told him that hearing someone's personal story about being HIV positive had been a moving experience. Toward the end of the home meeting, everyone had introduced themselves. People were shocked and delighted when they discovered that a Greek Orthodox priest had wanted to learn more about HIV.

The Task Force was constantly bumping up against challenges. One of them was language. We knew we would need to prepare printed materials in both English and Greek and be ready to speak to our priests and their congregations in both languages. At the time, there was little or nothing available about HIV/AIDS for people in the United States who spoke only Greek. We knew that the best way to do AIDS education and outreach to Greeks and Greek Americans was through the Church.

The Task Force prepared bilingual HIV/AIDS ministry packets for our priests. Since this was the first time they would receive formal guidance from the diocese about AIDS, we had to make certain we met priests where they were, recognizing that—however much they desired to serve the sick—most were probably frightened of HIV/AIDS. We wanted to provide them with a "tool kit" that would enable them to minister effectively to their flock without fear of contracting HIV. We knew that if our parish priests were moved to compassion for those living with HIV/AIDS, it was likely that their parishes would follow their loving example.

First, the Task Force developed bilingual fact sheets. They explained key facts about HIV/AIDS, HIV transmission, and HIV prevention.

Next, we created Orthodox Christian materials that would be meaningful to our priests and the faithful they visited. These included an icon card[12] for priests to give to those living with HIV/AIDS. On one side was a beautiful detail of an icon, showing Jesus being held by his mother and others after being brought down from the cross. Many hands are touching his body, a reminder that people living with HIV/AIDS could and needed to be touched without fear.

On the other side was a new prayer that could be prayed by those living with HIV/AIDS; it was composed by a member of the Task Force, Father Kyprianos Elias Bouboutsis.[13]

We also provided a priest's version of the new prayer that clergy could pray when visiting a person living with HIV/AIDS.

Serendipitously, we were able to include the work of a leader from the Orthodox Church of Greece—a wonderful and unexpected addition to our ministry packets.

One afternoon, I opened my mail to find a pastoral booklet written in Greek about HIV/AIDS. It had been sent to me by a Chicago-area priest, Father George Kaloudis.[14] I read it and was deeply moved. Both factually accurate and compassionate, the booklet included compelling

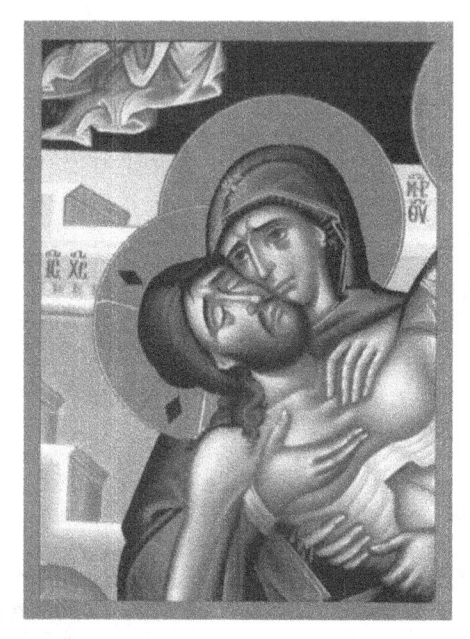

A Prayer of Comfort for People Living with AIDS

Holy Father, Physician of our souls and bodies, who knows the strength of the spirit and the weakness of the body of each of us, You, who out of love for Your creation condescended to take on flesh and the suffering of humanity, bring peace, which comes only from You, to me, Your child, who is in need.

Comfort me in this moment of seeming loneliness, and make Your presence known to me, that I may not despair but grow in the knowledge of Your salvation as I endure the trials of this illness.

Stretch forth Your ever healing hand and bring calm to the physical and spiritual infirmities from which I suffer.

Enlighten and bless the physicians and caregivers ministering to my infirmity, so that they might, with sensitivity and love, carry out diligently the tasks necessary to relieve the present pain and uncertainty caused by this disease.

Guide, support, strengthen, and console those who share in the pain of my suffering. Allow them, through their love for me, to shed tears, which are a gift from You, for the cleansing and regeneration of our souls.

O You, who reach out to the lonely, the suffering, and those in need, hear my prayer and bring comfort to me, Your servant. Through the prayers of Your holy Mother, our blessed and glorious Lady, the Theotokos and Ever-Virgin Mary, and of all the Holy Unmercenaries, have mercy upon me and save me. Amen.

Icon: Apokathelosis, detail.
    St. Basil Greek Orthodox Church, Chicago, Illinois.
    Mr. Tom Clark, Iconographer.

THE BISHOP'S TASK FORCE ON AIDS

Bishop's Task Force on AIDS icon card. Detail from the Icon of "Apokathelosis" ["Descent from the Cross"], St. Basil Greek Orthodox Church, Chicago, Illinois. Iconographer Tom Clark.

photographs that evoked empathy in the reader, such as that of a man with the purple lesions of Kaposi's sarcoma. The booklet had been prepared and published by Metropolitan[15] Christodoulos of the Metropolis of Demetrias and Almyros in Greece, an outspoken advocate of the need to serve rather than condemn those living with HIV/AIDS.[16]

I reached out to Metropolitan Christodoulos and told him about the Task Force. I asked him if he would provide us with copies of the booklet for our priests. He sent us hundreds of them! We inserted one into each packet. The booklet further legitimized the Task Force's efforts in the eyes of our priests: a metropolitan in Greece was teaching the same thing, namely, that the Church, her priests, and her laypeople are called to be merciful and to minister to those living with HIV/AIDS. This was a boon to us.

∞

Once the packets were assembled, we added a cover letter signed by me as chair of the Task Force, with the blessing and approval of Bishop Iakovos. The bishop's support was crucial to the legitimacy of the mailing. We slid the packets into nine- by twelve-inch envelopes addressed to our priests throughout the diocese, sealed them, and added postage.

I drove to the post office with cardboard boxes full of these envelopes, each of which bore a return address label that read "Bishop's Task Force on AIDS." The truth is that none of us knew how this material would be received. I dropped off the packets, hoping as I drove away that our clergy would read the contents and be moved by compassion.

We had accomplished our first goal. It was a start.

∞

Members of the Task Force had heard curious rumors about HIV/AIDS circulating in the Greek community. Some immigrant Greeks and Greek Americans were in denial, believing they couldn't become infected with HIV, that AIDS wasn't an issue "in our community." This attitude was common in some other ethnic communities as well. At the other end of the spectrum, some faithful had stopped receiving Holy Communion, terrified that they might become infected with HIV by sharing the Communion spoon with an HIV-infected person. Both ideas were patently false. But it was evidence of the lack of knowledge that was causing needless suffering in our community. We needed to provide people with accurate information.

The Task Force set up an Orthodox Christian HIV/AIDS speakers' bureau to offer presentations at parishes throughout the diocese. Whenever a priest or a group from a parish, such as a youth group, invited us to come and speak, we happily sent a trio of volunteers: a priest, a social worker, and a medical professional. We were mindful of our audience and tailored our message accordingly. Was it mostly a Greek immigrant community? Mostly Greeks born in America? Mostly Greeks who were married to non-Greeks and less ethnically oriented? Was it a youth group, a philanthropic women's group, a men's group? Was it Sunday school teachers ("What do we do if a kid cuts himself in class?")? Was it solely clergy? Would we speak in Greek, English, or both?

AIDS was a topic on everyone's mind. Since the Task Force was approved by the bishop and the presenters were other Orthodox Christians (rather than "outsiders"), we could be trusted. As a result, our traveling outreach teams were invited to speak at many parishes. We gave straightforward presentations about HIV/AIDS, answered questions, brought along bilingual health materials to distribute, and let the audience know about the work of the Bishop's Task Force on AIDS. We welcomed donations for the ministry. Our visits established the topic of HIV/AIDS as something that could be discussed more easily, without embarrassment.

During those visits, we encountered another challenge: how to talk to our audience about the very sensitive issue of human sexual behavior. The truth is that HIV is primarily spread by sexual contact, so we needed to educate people accordingly.

We told our listeners that abstinence was the only way to guarantee that a person would not contract HIV. This accorded with the teaching of the Church that sexual abstinence is the Christian ideal unless one is married, and then sexual relations are only with one's spouse.

Yet we also realized that many Christians—even among the sincerely devout—fall short of the ideal or stray from this path. So we discussed "risk-reducing behaviors"—use of condoms, no unprotected sex, and no sharing of needles. These were uncomfortable subjects. We understood the discomfort our listeners experienced, including priests, but we forged ahead. Our aim was to educate and advocate, not to judge.

That very thing—the human tendency to judge others—was yet another challenge. To help our listeners empathize with, rather than judge, those living with HIV/AIDS, we led them through a guided meditation that another AIDS activist friend of mine, Jack Rosenberger—at the time, a Jesuit scholastic at Loyola University of Chicago—shared with me. Rather than focusing on factual knowledge, the goal of the meditation was to experience a *felt* knowledge of the deep losses experienced by someone living with HIV/AIDS.

We gave participants four notecards and a pen and asked them to write down one of the following on each notecard: the name of their best friend, their most prized possession, their favorite activity, and their life's dream. Then we had them close their eyes. Listeners were guided to visualize their bodies weakening in stages. As their energy began to decline, they were prompted to let go of one card of their choosing; as their strength diminished more markedly, they were asked to let go of a second card of their choosing; when their energy fell to a new low, they were asked to let go of a third card of their choosing; and when they had no energy left, they were prompted to release the fourth card, meaning all the cards were gone and all they had left was themselves. The guided meditation vividly evoked the gradual physical collapse and loss of agency over one's own life brought on by HIV/AIDS. With their eyes still closed, listeners were asked, "Who would you tell that you had AIDS? Who would you not tell? Why? Why not?" This proved to be a powerful experience; people often teared up or even cried.

The traveling outreach teams conveyed the message that every person is of infinite value and worth, gifted with transcendence. Team members were determined to let everyone know that phobias, prejudices, or bigotry should not deter any of us from the path of righteousness—in this case, literally saving lives.

"Prejudice can be insidious, appearing in ways that sometimes even well-meaning and profoundly devout people are not aware of," I remember saying. "Prejudice reduces a human being to a thing—a color, a gender, a sexual orientation, or a disease. It says to the person living with HIV/AIDS, 'You are a disease; you are unclean. I will not take care of you.'"

But I soon saw that I had my own prejudices.

※

At each parish visit, after giving our presentation, we asked those in attendance to break into small groups. Each was led by one of the trio of volunteers.

During one visit, I noticed an older man in the audience, his arms crossed. He struck me as being an old curmudgeon from Greece. *Probably intolerant*, I remember thinking to myself. *I hope I don't get that guy in my group.*

But sure enough, when we broke into three groups, there he was in mine. Another man, forty-something, was also in our group. He dominated the conversation, asking a lot of questions about how AIDS is transmitted and then angrily blaming drug users, sex workers, and homosexuals for transmitting HIV. While he was still speaking, the older man, with a heavy Greek accent and in broken English, interrupted him.

"Leesten," he said, "who care about homseshuals or no homseshuals? Or where disease come from? Our children are dying. What are we going to do about it?"

I looked again at the older man, and now I *saw* him.

I learned a lesson that day (again!), the very lesson we were trying to share with our listeners: do not judge others.

We had accomplished our second goal.

∞

In the summer of 1992, the Democratic and Republican parties held conventions to choose their nominees for the upcoming presidential elections. Anyone watching noticed something strikingly different.

On July 14, 1992, Elizabeth Glaser stood at the podium at the Democratic National Convention in Madison Square Garden in New York and spoke of how years before, she hemorrhaged while giving birth. She recounted that she received seven pints of blood, unknowingly became infected with HIV, and then infected her infant daughter and later her son. Her daughter died at age seven. Glaser, who co-founded the Pediatric AIDS Foundation, looked out at the audience and asked for bold leadership to seek an end to the AIDS pandemic. "I am in a race with the clock. This is not about being a Republican or an Independent or a Democrat. It's about the future—for each and every one of us."[17]

Sixteen days later and 1,400 miles away, Mary Fisher delivered a speech that brought a hush to the crowd gathered at the Republican National Convention in the Houston Astrodome. She asked for an end to the silence around AIDS. She had been infected with HIV by her former husband, and she had two small children. She appealed to her party to take a compassionate public stand. "Tonight, I represent an AIDS community whose members have been reluctantly drafted from every segment of American society. Though I am white, and a mother, I am one with a black infant struggling with tubes in a Philadelphia hospital. Though I am female and contracted this disease in marriage, and enjoy the warm support of my family, I am one with the lonely gay man sheltering a flickering candle from the cold wind of his family's rejection."[18]

Some AIDS activists scoffed at the two political parties for having wealthy white women represent the face of AIDS in America. Others countered that when it comes to saving lives, anything that moves the ball down the field is progress. To me, it seemed a very "sanitized" representation of those living with HIV/AIDS, an implicit acknowledgment that our nation was not yet ready to embrace the majority of those living with HIV/AIDS—gay and bisexual men, illicit drug users, and professional sex workers, people for whom, it seemed, compassion was harder to come by. This saddened me.

Still, because of those two speeches, AIDS was now an issue at the front and center of national politics. For the first time, across both major political parties, the conversation was about "us" rather than "them"—a change worth celebrating. It was a step forward.

∞

Each spring, our diocese held a two-day clergy retreat, a gathering of priests from all fifty-eight parishes in the diocese. It aimed to inspire our clergy and enhance their unity. Shortly after the Task Force was created, we approached Bishop Iakovos and asked if HIV/AIDS could be one of the key topics at the diocese's next clergy retreat in March 1993. We knew it would be our best chance to make a compelling case to our priests, face-to-face. The bishop gave his approval, and we were given a plum spot: the first morning of the retreat would be dedicated to the topic of HIV/AIDS.

It was now July 1992. We had eight months to prepare. The Task Force had highly qualified members, and we tapped two of them to speak at the retreat. I would lead the priests in the guided meditation. We prepared our materials and double-checked every event detail to make sure the retreat would run like clockwork.

∞

March 1993

March 9, 1993, finally arrived, and the clergy gathered from all corners of the diocese—Chicago, Des Moines, St. Paul, Madison, Hammond, St. Louis, and other towns and cities—in a hotel under the leadership of Bishop Iakovos. People milled around that morning, getting coffee and juice outside the conference room and chatting, then filed into the room and took their seats.

Once everyone was seated, I welcomed them to the morning session, introducing myself as chair of the Bishop's Task Force on AIDS. I could see discomfort on the faces of some clergy. Others listened impassively, their arms crossed over their chests. The idea of discussing a pandemic transmitted mostly through sexual activity and the sharing of needles by drug users was understandably met with some hesitation by priests, who had reason to wonder, *Is this really an issue in my parish?* But to my relief, most of my brother priests who were gathered in the room seemed genuinely interested. They wanted to know how to minister to parishioners if any of them were to disclose that they or someone in their family was living with HIV/AIDS. Perhaps some parishioners already had.

Our first speaker that morning was Angelike Mountanis, the director of social services at the Hellenic Foundation. Originally from Greece and educated as a social worker, she was a confident, no-nonsense speaker who compassionately conveyed to her audience the rocky psychological journey traveled by those who were HIV positive: the shock of the diagnosis; the fear of being abandoned by friends and family; the lack of a cure; and the inevitability of HIV progressing to AIDS, then physical decline and death. She reminded her audience that people living with HIV/AIDS are persons who are struggling with a medical condition and worthy of our care.

Angelike related the jarring story of one family, immigrants from Greece who had two sons. The younger son, in his mid-twenties, was living at home when he learned he was HIV positive. He was scared, but he told his family. His frightened parents, afraid that he would infect them and his brother, confined him to his room. They fed him by placing his meal outside his door and then vanishing. When he needed to use the restroom, they all closed themselves into other rooms before he came out. He was not only suffering from the virus, but was also experiencing a type of solitary confinement, living like a leper in his own home, isolated and untouchable. "It was only because his family didn't know much about HIV/AIDS," Angelike said. "They didn't know any better."

When Angelike heard about this troubling situation, she told her audience, she was moved into action by compassion. She reached out to the young man's parents and met with them. She listened to them and told them she understood their fear. She then explained that they did not have to isolate their son because he could not infect any of them. She assured them that he could safely move around the house. They listened, not fully convinced, but they did allow him more freedom in the house. Now he could see them and talk with them. They still wouldn't risk touching him despite Angelike's gentle coaching.

When their son became seriously ill, they followed tradition and spoke with their parish priest, asking him to come to administer Holy Communion to their son. But the priest, like the parents, was afraid. He would not visit. Disheartened, they tried to find a priest who would come, and they finally found one.

"That priest's visit made all the difference," Angelike said. "He visited and administered Holy Communion, and he spoke encouragingly to the young man's parents." The priest knew about HIV/AIDS, she added, so he knew he didn't have to be afraid, and he helped the parents to be less afraid too. Angelike told her listeners that they, too, could make a powerful difference by visiting those living with HIV/AIDS, and they could do so safely, without contracting HIV.

For some priests, her speech may have afforded them their first glimpse into the isolation, fear, and sense of being marginalized that so many who lived with HIV/AIDS experienced at the time; others may have been surprised to learn that it was possible to visit someone living with HIV/AIDS without becoming infected. She galvanized the priests, encouraging them to look past the terrible disease to the person who was suffering. She said that their compassionate calling to visit and pray with the sick was especially needed by this forgotten group, to whom a visit would mean so much.

∞

After a very brief break, our next speaker, Dr. Claudia R. Libertin, took the podium. A faithful Ukrainian Orthodox Christian and a distinguished infectious disease specialist, at forty years of age she already held two patents for HIV protease inhibitors and was a tenured professor of medicine at Loyola University.

Angelike had introduced listeners to the psychological impact of HIV/AIDS, whereas Dr. Libertin was here to educate the clergy about its medical aspects. The Task Force knew that arming our priests with accurate information would simultaneously reduce their fear and make them more effective as shepherds of their parishes.

Much of Dr. Libertin's presentation that morning echoed the information in the HIV/AIDS packets sent to priests, but that was by design. Having a clear understanding of HIV/AIDS and how HIV is transmitted was what our clergy most needed. I listened as Dr. Libertin moved from the basics of HIV/AIDS to a detailed discussion of human sexual behavior, the value of abstinence, and the importance of condom use in preventing HIV transmission.

When she paused for a moment, a prominent priest—evidently finding her frank discussion of sex and sexuality highly inappropriate, and unable to restrain himself against this outrage any longer—leapt up from his chair and interrupted her presentation.

"Do you realize that you are speaking to the Greek Orthodox clergy of the Diocese of Chicago?" he belted out indignantly, fixing her with a hard gaze.

The room fell silent, stunned by this display of brash disrespect.

Standing at the podium, the scientist looked at the priest, unfazed. Pious, resolute, wearing a business suit and a calm expression, Dr. Libertin didn't flinch.

"Yes, Father," she said respectfully, "I'm perfectly aware of whom I am addressing." She stood her ground.

I felt my body tense. The room filled with a deafening silence.

"Father!"

Bishop Iakovos called out sharply to his priest, piercing the silence.

The irate priest, still standing, turned to face his bishop, who sat at the back of the room. Already some of the righteous indignation was draining from the priest's face.

The bishop looked directly at the priest. These men had known each other for years. What passed silently between them in those milliseconds was known only by them.

"The doctor is giving us valuable information to save lives," Bishop Iakovos said to him. "Now sit down and listen." With these words, the bishop took charge of the room. A sense of calm returned. The chastened priest, fuming but obedient, took his seat, and Dr. Libertin resumed her presentation precisely where she had left off.

No one there could have missed the message from the bishop: *This is part of your ministry from now on. Pay attention.*

Breathing a sigh of relief, I leaned back against my chair and relaxed.

There were no further outbursts that morning.

We had accomplished our third goal.

※

At the clergy retreat, Angelike had spoken about a family who kept their son confined in his room. Of course, I knew whom she was talking about.

Angelike had first shared the troubling story with me even before we started working together on the Task Force. I recall being horrified that anyone could treat their child that way. It was only several months later that I realized she was talking about a family that I knew—Bob's family. I was stunned.

Thinking back to my first visit with Bob, I now saw it from a completely different perspective. However unsettled I may have felt when I saw sheets of plastic throughout his home, the truth is, life for Bob was still light-years ahead of what it had once been. Angelike's loving intervention had made a tremendous difference. It was a perfect example of the kind of positive change the Task Force was trying to make throughout the diocese.

※

"How are we going to pay for all of this?"

The Task Force's next challenge was money. We would not receive any funds from the diocese, I explained. It was Bishop Iakovos's standard practice that special ministries and projects, like the Task Force, were always funded by donations. With that understanding in mind, we all agreed: the Task Force would raise the money needed to make the new ministry possible.

Not that much money was needed because speaking to and educating an audience and helping to develop Sunday school protocols are not expensive, but a great deal of time and energy were required. I am grateful to say that people responded to the need and gave graciously of their time, talents, and treasure. Every Task Force project was paid for by donations.

Of course, we worked hard to make this happen. We inserted donor cards into the AIDS ministry packets that we sent to priests to share with their parishioners. We welcomed and received donations whenever our outreach teams spoke at parishes or events. We did mailings and made personal appeals. We received grant funds, a bequest, and donations from people who believed in our mission. The women's charitable group of the diocese, the Philoptochos, partnered with us and annually requested its member chapters at each parish to support the Bishop's Task Force on AIDS. Our own board members, too, supported our work with donations, and printers gave us discounts or donated their printing services.

Remarkably, by the grace of God, we never had a problem funding this meaningful and life-affirming ministry.

※

A few weeks after the clergy retreat, on April 18, 1993, we celebrated Pascha (Easter). After the service, before I left the cathedral, I called Bob to ask if I could stop by to see him on my way to my parents' house. I also asked if it was all right to bring Captain Scott Venable of the US Army, one of my spiritual sons and a catechumen,[19] with me. Bob had said, "Sure, come on over!"

We arrived at his home and received a warm welcome from Bob's father and mother. "*Christos Anesti!* [Christ is risen!]" we said to one another in the traditional Paschal greeting. "I just came by to administer Holy Communion to Bob and to wish him a good Pascha," I told his parents. They welcomed us in, and I introduced Scott. I had brought a couple of red eggs with me from church, and I gave these traditional Pascha gifts to Bob's mother. She went into the kitchen to make some coffee. His father invited us to sit down in the living room, and I noticed that something about the room felt different.

The plastic drop cloths were gone.

Soon Bob joined us, and I introduced Scott to him. I couldn't help but notice the striking contrast between the uniformed man with military bearing and the skeletal man living with HIV/AIDS. Scott was visibly shaken by Bob's appearance. Bob noticed, and with the hint of a smile, he asked Scott, "Have you ever seen a person with AIDS before?" Scott admitted that he hadn't. With that frank admission, the awkwardness diminished. It crossed my mind that Scott, encountering this visibly sick man, might worry about the possibility of contracting HIV.

"Would you like to receive Holy Communion?" I asked Bob.

He was hesitant. "I don't think I should. I haven't fasted," he said.

Hours before, I had read the congregation a famous Pascha homily, written by St. John Chrysostom, which invites everyone—everyone!—to experience the joy of Pascha. It reads in part, *Those who fasted, and those who did not, rejoice today! The table is full, everyone fare sumptuously!*

"The Church gives special dispensation for the sick, especially on Pascha," I said.

Bob received Holy Communion. Then his mother brought out coffee, Pascha bread, cookies, and the traditional red eggs. The five of us sat and chatted comfortably. Exhausted from having been up much of the night celebrating the divine services—and relieved that I had survived the weeklong marathon of services between Palm Sunday and Pascha!—I was euphoric that Pascha, the holiest day of the Christian calendar, had finally come. Bob seemed happy, and his parents seemed relaxed. Even Scott now seemed comfortable.

Over the course of many visits that year, Bob and I had become friends. He and his family knew I would keep our visits and Bob's diagnosis confidential. It felt like we were family.

∞

When it was time to go, I hugged and kissed Bob goodbye in Greek fashion. To my surprise, Scott did too. *"Christos Anesti!"* we called out as we left.

Once the two of us were seated in the car, Scott said, "I've never seen you visiting someone who's sick." He paused. "It was hard to see Bob. It was kind of scary—he's around the same age as us."

"Yes, he is," I said.

"But he really believes," Scott said. "He was more concerned about reverence for the sacrament than about his own body. The moment he received Communion, I knew Christ was there."

We drove on in silence. Once we reached my parents' house, I was about to get out of the car when Scott stopped me.

"You know," he said, "when we were leaving Bob's house, I felt a connection with him. I hugged him because I felt moved to. I didn't expect that."

I smiled. I was proud of these two men: Bob, for generously opening his life up to a stranger, and Scott, for responding to Bob with compassion. For me, it felt like the joy of Pascha.

9

✢

Countdown

March 14, 1999

One of the things I treasure about Chicago is the calm of Sunday mornings. Traffic is light, and the city seems almost at rest. On Sunday, March 14, 1999, I drove through the quiet streets to the Annunciation Cathedral to concelebrate Orthros and the Divine Liturgy. After liturgy, someone gave me an opinion page article from that morning's *Chicago Tribune* written by Locke Bowman, the legal director of the MacArthur Justice Center at the University of Chicago Law School. Only days before, Bowman had penned a letter to Governor Ryan asking him to create a special commission to assess the death penalty in the state and to temporarily suspend executions. Three hundred twenty-one lawyers had signed it.

This morning's op-ed piece zeroed in on Andrew's upcoming execution, only three days away, and placed it squarely at the center of a moral crossroads:

> If the politicians, the lawyers and the civic leaders were serious when they said just last month that our capital punishment system is flawed, error prone, in obvious need of examination before it can be trusted to work fairly, then the time to begin the study and the moratorium is now. Andrew Kokoraleis should be given his hearing. Let us heed the sober lessons of our recent history. Not for Andrew Kokoraleis' sake. For ourselves, and for the integrity of the system of justice on which we all depend.[1]

I couldn't have agreed more. If our political leaders meant what they said, the Illinois death chamber should remain empty, its lights off, at least for now. It should not be used to kill Andrew on Wednesday.

Chapter 9

I assumed that Professor Bowman was making a direct appeal to the governor, and with good reason. After weeks of effort and debate by many people—journalists, judges, attorneys, legislators, and advocates for and against the death penalty—it had come down to this: one man would decide whether Andrew would live or die. Governor Ryan had several options. He could impose a moratorium, as Bowman and so many others urged him to do; he could delay Andrew's execution while reconsidering his case; he could commute his sentence to life in prison without the possibility of parole; or he could sign Andrew's death warrant, step back, and allow the execution to proceed.

The governor was on the hot seat, and everyone knew it. The question before him was, *What to do about Andrew?*

※

I stayed at the cathedral after liturgy to prepare for our press conference that afternoon. Anxious and restless, I was constantly checking my phone messages. I called my assistant from the diocese to confirm that he would join me at the cathedral, and he confirmed that he would be here on time. I reread the statement that I was planning to deliver, which was directed primarily at Governor Ryan.

The governor was by now familiar with my outspoken efforts to press for clemency for Andrew. Far from being a behind-the-scenes lobbyist, for the last two weeks I had loudly and repeatedly used my position as chancellor at the Greek Orthodox Diocese of Chicago to seek mercy for Andrew, arguing that in the Church's view, life—all life—is sacred, a gift from God. I spoke privately to the media; gave speeches before groups of people; worked with other activists seeking to end the death penalty; and spoke with some of those, like Mr. Coutretsis, who might be able to influence the governor.

The press conference today was a group effort. My fellow clergy—devoted pastors, ministers, rabbis, bishops, and priests—were due to arrive at the cathedral in an hour. For the first time, the people of Chicago would become aware that a religious coalition was working together on Andrew's behalf. Over the last few weeks, our letters and those of other clergy had reached the governor's office, urging clemency for Andrew. To our great disappointment, every plea had gone unanswered, as had follow-up calls. "We'll get back to you," callers were assured by the governor's staff, and then—nothing. The governor had ignored us again and again in our attempt to meet with him to plead for Andrew's life.

Perhaps a more public approach would succeed: a press conference.

One goal was to give journalists a clear and compelling story for broadcast news and the newspapers, one that might influence their viewers and readers across the state. We aimed to make a strong case for clemency and a moratorium on executions.

At a deeper level, though, we wanted to make a direct appeal to an audience of one: Governor Ryan. Our press conference would be the high point of our efforts to communicate with him. A determined group of religious leaders, we would stand shoulder to shoulder, unabashedly representing a broad range of faith traditions that opposed the death penalty, and we would urge the governor to have mercy on Andrew and to declare a moratorium on executions. We would challenge the governor to meet with us face-to-face so we could make the case for mercy. We would do this as we stood before a phalanx of reporters with notepads and cameras.

Perhaps the governor would listen to us—would take us seriously—if he saw our message carried in newspapers and on broadcast news to readers, listeners, and viewers throughout the state.

∞

I lit a candle, offered a silent prayer, and stepped into the cool interior of the cathedral's nave, the empty pews facing the altar, chandeliers overhead. The familiar space, quiet, beautiful, and holy, was reassuring. The stained-glass windows were bright with cold afternoon sunlight. I was agitated. I thought of Andrew in his cramped cell, receiving one discouraging update after another from his lawyer. So many disappointments had happened the previous week—Judge Jorgensen denied the request for a new evidentiary hearing, the Illinois Prisoner Review Board hearing had not resulted in clemency, the attorney general's office concluded that Andrew's case needed no further review, and the Illinois Supreme Court dismissed Andrew's appeals. Door after door had closed. Our press conference had unexpectedly taken on greater significance. If the governor did not give him a reprieve, Andrew would be strapped to a gurney and executed in less than sixty hours. I could only imagine how Andrew felt, alone in his "fishbowl," with everyone looking with concern or curiosity at the man scheduled to be killed.

My assistant arrived, and we started setting up. We turned on the lights and moved a podium into place in front of the icon screen and altar. We tested the sound system.

Everything was in place by the time the other clergy began to arrive. Seeing my friends and colleagues in the cathedral, hearing their cheerful greetings, I was convinced of the rightness of our endeavor. It seemed possible that together we might make a difference. When a representative of the Illinois Coalition Against the Death Penalty (ICADP) joined us, our number was complete. More than a dozen of us were there, as was attorney Carol Mavrakis. Fred was there, too, as were many faithful from the cathedral and other advocates from the ICADP, seated in the pews offering their encouragement by their presence.

When the press arrived, we took our places. I was gratified to see so many journalists, from the *Chicago Tribune* to the *Chicago Sun-Times* to several regional television stations.

I opened the press conference with a statement directed at Governor Ryan. "We appeal to the governor's God-given conscience and humanity to commute the sentence from death by lethal injection to life in prison." Speaking for the group, I lamented the fact that despite days of concerted outreach to Governor Ryan, he had refused to meet with or even respond to us. I condemned Andrew's impending execution as a "destructive symmetry of violence mirroring violence" and "a rush toward lethal injection."[2] Then the other clergy, and Carol, took their turns at the podium. As each spoke, the rest of us stood in a semicircle behind the speaker, creating a visual backdrop of support.

We asked the governor to declare a moratorium on executions, recalling the eleven exonerated Illinois death row prisoners and the fact that many of them were freed after new evidence supporting their innocence was introduced. We spoke in fervent opposition to the death penalty. Bishop Vsevolod of Scopelos of the Ukrainian Orthodox Church Western Diocese observed that "those in authority on this earth [have] no right to substitute God's authority by . . . the taking away of the most precious gift of God—life itself—from one of his children."[3]

The press conference was one of the largest and most unified demonstrations of local religious opposition to the death penalty ever seen in Chicago. When it concluded, my colleagues and I were exhilarated. The event had gone well, and the local media had turned out in droves. We were hopeful that our appeal to Governor George Ryan would prompt him to reach out to us or to show mercy to Andrew. I returned home full of hope that the press conference had hit its mark.

That evening, I turned on the news and flipped through the channels. Every station opened with a news story about our press conference.

Other advocates called me to express their delight. We were so happy—it had worked! It was a high-water mark for us. We had grabbed Chicago's attention and made our case. There was no way the governor and his staff could miss it.

My mother called me. "Demetri! What did you *do*?" she asked, her voice a mix of astonishment and pleasure.

"What do you mean?" I asked.

"You're all over the news!" she said. "Pa and I can't believe it!"

I was already in my thirties, but it meant a lot to me that my mother and my pro–death penalty father were proud of me and the success of our anti–death penalty demonstration.

Now came the hard part, waiting to see what the governor would do.

Andrew's life was hanging in the balance. He had only fifty hours left.

∞

Within the governor's inner circle at that time, an intense debate was ongoing as Andrew's execution approached.[4]

Feelings were running high. Pressure on Governor Ryan to declare a moratorium on executions in Illinois before Andrew was executed was building and was intense. Since the death penalty had been reinstated in 1977, eleven people had been executed in Illinois, and eleven other death row inmates had been proven innocent and exonerated—two of them just a month earlier. It was a terrible track record for a system that was purported to be just and fair. Proof that prosecutors were often more interested in winning cases than in justice had undermined claims that only the guilty were convicted in Illinois.[5] The stunning case of Anthony Porter, the innocent man whose life was spared only hours before execution because of the work of journalism students, was still fresh in everyone's memory.

Pressure on the governor to maintain capital punishment in Illinois continued as well, but by that point, even some supporters of the death penalty acknowledged that things had gone wrong and the system needed to be improved. Talk of assessing and "fixing" capital punishment was becoming more common. The only question was, what should be done about Andrew? Should he be executed according to the old, corrupt system, under which he had been convicted? Or should he be spared for now, while the system was being assessed and improved?

Some of Governor Ryan's staff, particularly his close adviser Pete Peters, were urging the governor not to execute Andrew. Peters's own thorough examination of information concerning capital punishment had led him to conclude that the system was unjust.[6] He advised the governor to stay Andrew's execution. He said he would benefit from an abundance of goodwill from religious leaders and the many others in Illinois who were lobbying for a pause in executions to allow a deep analysis of the death penalty system. Pausing Andrew's execution would be a brave decision, Peters argued, and the governor would receive national recognition for his courage. Governor Ryan would be a hero.

Others, including the governor's chief of staff, Robert Newtson, were pushing the governor to proceed with the execution. In the eyes of voters,

Newtson argued, Andrew was the wrong criminal to grant clemency to; his crimes were just too grisly. Demonstrating mercy for Andrew would make the governor's "tough-on-crime" stance ring hollow. Those advisers urged that he introduce a moratorium on capital punishment once Andrew was executed. That way, he could please both those demanding Andrew's life and those seeking a moratorium.

Either way, the governor would be taking a political risk: he would be condemned for being too soft on a convicted murderer, or he would be denounced for allowing Andrew to be executed in light of the recent exonerations of Illinois death row prisoners. Leaving his options open, he asked an aide to prepare a document granting Andrew a gubernatorial ninety-day stay of execution.[7] He already had a death warrant for Andrew on his desk. In the end, he would affix his signature to one document or the other.

∞

"Standing solemnly inside an ornate house of worship, more than a dozen religious leaders on Sunday called on Governor George Ryan to commute the death sentence of Andrew Kokoraleis and for state lawmakers to place a moratorium on all executions." So began the article[8] in the *Chicago Tribune* on Monday, March 15, the day after our press conference. I arrived at work elated and hoped all morning for a call from the governor's office or to hear that one of the other members of the clergy had received a call. I was on pins and needles. I had steeled myself for a meeting with Governor Ryan. My colleagues and I would appeal to his better angels. Perhaps we could persuade him to delay the execution or even to offer Andrew clemency. Even better, perhaps the governor, persuaded to change his mind, was already preparing to release a statement announcing a stay of execution or commutation of Andrew's sentence to life in prison. Every time the phone rang, my heart leapt. Nothing else mattered that day. Whatever other work I had was on hold as we awaited Governor Ryan's response.

Meanwhile, related developments were taking place elsewhere in the state.

Alan Freedman filed motions that morning with the US Supreme Court seeking review of the state court's decision on Friday to dismiss Andrew's appeal.[9] Representative Coy Pugh and others also filed an emergency petition with the Illinois Supreme Court. They petitioned the court to put executions on hold until the Illinois House resolution calling for a moratorium on executions worked its way through the legislature.[10]

A hundred miles south of Chicago, state Representative Dan Rutherford was accompanied by a group of recently elected lawmakers on his annual visit to Pontiac Correctional Center and Dwight Correctional Center, both of which were in his district. While touring the Pontiac facility, he and the other lawmakers overheard journalists from a local newspaper interviewing Andrew about his upcoming execution.[11] During the interview, Andrew sat behind a black metal mesh screen. He told the reporters that he didn't think the last-ditch appeal to the US Supreme Court would prevent his execution, but he understood and appreciated that his lawyers were willing to try. He said that he had made peace with his own death.[12]

∞

Monday afternoon rolled around, and none of my fellow religious leaders had heard from the governor. I hadn't either. No announcements had been issued by the governor's office.

I was puzzled. I had been so sure that our plan would work, but it began to dawn on me that Governor Ryan had never had any intention of contacting us—not even after seeing coverage of our demonstration—and never would. *It hadn't mattered.* He would continue to ignore us just as he had ignored us before, and Andrew would still be executed. This was a devastating realization.

I reached out to Fred, and we commiserated. I had led the charge, believing that a vocal group of religious leaders could press the governor to reconsider and that that would be enough to change his mind. Had I miscalculated? I had. Should we call the governor's office now? No. Was there anything we could do? No—we had pulled out every stop, and it hadn't changed anything. It was crystal clear that the eleventh-hour reprieve I had been hoping for—counting on, I now realized—was not going to happen. Andrew was going to be executed. This was shocking and hard to accept. The truth is that even then, part of me didn't accept it.

Theodora and I spoke by phone. She was very concerned about Andrew and was preparing to go to Tamms the next day. She asked if I wanted to go, too, but I told her no, that I planned to stay in Chicago, knowing that Father Kallinikos would be allowed to visit and pray with him. Meanwhile, I asked that if she spoke with Andrew, would she please let him know that I would welcome a call if he wanted to speak with me. She promised me she would.

I was brokenhearted. I went to the chapel in the diocese and kneeled in front of the icon of Christ, weeping as I prayed for Andrew. I prayed that if it was possible, that somehow, he could be spared. I prayed that if he were to be executed, he would not feel forsaken. Then, spent, I dragged myself back to my office. I kept one eye on the clock, hoping against hope to hear something, anything, that might offer hope.

When five o'clock came without any word from the governor, cold reality hit me like a punch to the gut. None of our efforts had worked: the courts hadn't intervened; the legislature hadn't succeeded; no clemency had been announced; no moratorium had been declared; and the governor had avoided our coalition and hadn't even had the courtesy to say, "I won't meet with you." We had failed, as had everyone else. Nothing anyone had done had stopped or even slowed the steady movement toward state-sanctioned homicide. Andrew was going to be executed in thirty-one hours. I sat in my chair, numb, defeated, mortified, and dazed. As the minutes passed, I felt utterly helpless.

Then I came to terms with reality. I couldn't prevent Andrew from being executed on Wednesday morning, but I needed to do something for him. I thought, *What would I do at the bedside of someone who was dying?* I would pray. Yes, at least we could pray for Andrew. I would invite others to gather at the cathedral tomorrow night just before midnight. Together, we could hold a vigil and pray for Andrew as, 362 miles away in Tamms, a lethal cocktail of three fluids was pumped into his body.

With a heavy heart and heavy steps, I got up from my desk, turned off the light, and made my way home.

∞

I listened to the evening news. Governor Ryan had not yet formally stated that he would allow the execution to go ahead, but all evidence suggested that it was just a matter of time. The governor's aides and staff later reported that he was agonizing over the decision of what to do about Andrew. "He can't make up his mind," one staffer said.[13]

I was skeptical. Based on all I knew about him, I just didn't believe it. Why couldn't he make up his mind? Fear of political fallout? It didn't seem to me that he cared much about Andrew's life or possibly killing an innocent person. It seemed to me that his quandary was political, not moral. Surely, had it been moral, he would have engaged in a discussion with religious people in an effort to find clarity, however hard that discussion and the questions it raised would be. He was talking about allowing the state to take a man's *life*. As it was, he had turned a deaf ear to our pleas.

Later that evening, Governor Ryan's office announced that the governor would release a statement about Andrew sometime on Tuesday.[14] I was feeling hopeless.

However, a glimmer of hope did emerge that evening: Illinois Supreme Court Justice Moses Harrison II issued an extraordinary solo stay of Andrew's execution.[15] It appeared that the execution was off for now.

The justice's unilateral action was wholly unanticipated. I felt like someone had thrown Andrew a lifeline. Elated but guarded, I immediately reached out to Fred, who confirmed that Justice Harrison had made a solo ruling—an unusual move—and it appeared that the execution would not take place on Wednesday. How much more time Andrew might have was not clear, but it seemed he was no longer in immediate danger. His fate was no longer dependent only on the pro–death penalty governor, which was a relief.

The execution was stayed for now, but we learned that that could change if one of two things happened: if the full Illinois Supreme Court overturned Harrison's ruling or if the US Supreme Court ruled quickly on the motions. In Alan Freedman's view, neither seemed likely. Freedman did not believe that the Illinois Supreme Court had the authority to overturn Justice Harrison's ruling. Further, now that Justice Harrison had issued a stay of execution at the state level, the US Supreme Court might not feel an urgency to expedite Andrew's petitions.[16]

I went to bed, hopeful that at least Andrew now had a chance.

∞

The following day, Tuesday, March 16, at 7:00 a.m., Andrew was airlifted by helicopter from Pontiac to the state's new maximum-security prison at Tamms, where he was scheduled to be the first person ever executed there.[17]

This was confusing. Wasn't Justice Harrison's stay enough to stop that? Apparently not. Governor Ryan did not order corrections officials to cancel their preparations for an execution, so they proceeded as planned.[18] I needed more information, so I reached out to Fred and to Carol.

"Will Justice Harrison's stay prevent Andrew from being executed?" I asked. I was told that the full Illinois Supreme Court was taking up the matter of Justice Harrison's stay that day and that they might overturn it. Just as quickly as the hope of the evening before had come, it now turned to ashes.

At Tamms, Andrew fasted all day, drinking only water. He was described by Corrections Department spokesman Nic Howell as being "polite, cooperative and calm."[19] Andrew turned down the opportunity to watch television, listen to radio, or use the Valium offered by prison staff. His younger brother Nick was allowed to visit with him at Tamms all afternoon starting at about one o'clock.[20] I had been hoping to receive a call from Andrew, but so far, I hadn't heard from him.

Meanwhile, in Springfield, the Illinois Supreme Court expressed its displeasure at Justice Harrison's solo ruling of the previous night. In a four-to-three decision, they overturned Andrew's stay of execution, and another door had closed. I wasn't surprised. I felt defeated. Whatever glimmer of hope I once had was gone.

The US Supreme Court acted swiftly. Three hours after the Illinois Supreme Court overturned Justice Harrison's ruling, Justice John Paul Stevens issued a two-sentence order that denied Andrew's first motion, requesting an emergency stay of execution, as well as his second motion, to review the state court's recent dismissal of Andrew's appeal.[21]

Finally, the Illinois Supreme Court wrapped up its work that day without taking up Representative Pugh's petition for an emergency stay of execution, noting that he and the other petitioners might not have standing to bring the motion.

Andrew's defense team was out of options.

※

Late in the afternoon, a call came to the diocese for me from Andrew's lawyer, who was able to put Andrew through on the phone. Without our knowing it, the diocese's phone system had disconnected the many collect calls Andrew had tried to make from the prison that day, even after the system had accepted the charges. Fortunately, his attorney had figured out another way for Andrew to reach me.

Andrew sounded calm. I asked him how he was doing. I told him we had tried, that I was so sorry we had not succeeded in stopping the execution. He said he had never expected that our efforts would change things and that that was all right. He told me that Father Kallinikos would be allowed to pray with him in his cell and that he and Theodora had spoken by phone. She was now in a car in the parking lot at Tamms with Father Kallinikos and his wife. Andrew said he felt even more like he was in a fishbowl than he had before.

"Andrew, you are in our prayers and always will be," I said as we finished; then we said goodbye. I hung up the phone feeling completely defeated, my faith shaken. I had believed that righteousness would prevail. But now I knew the man at the other end of the phone would be executed that night and would never see another sunrise.

Andrew had been right to have low expectations. He understood that he was just a pawn on the Illinois political chessboard. I was glad that he was prepared for what was happening and grateful that his brother had come to be with him.

After I hung up the phone, I faxed an invitation to many people. It read, "Will you join me tonight at the Annunciation Cathedral for a midnight memorial service for Andrew?"

∽

At around 7:30 Tuesday evening, the governor's office issued a three-page public statement announcing that Andrew would be executed.[22] Governor Ryan asked for the prayers of Illinois residents in the belief that he had "acted wisely" by allowing the execution.[23] His statement also read, "I have struggled with the pleas of our clergy and others who ask that I commute or stay the execution of Andrew Kokoraleis."[24]

In my anger and grief, I marveled at the governor's hubris. He had never even met with us. *How could he possibly have struggled with our pleas if he hadn't spoken with or even acknowledged us*, I wondered. Now, when he wanted to justify the killing of Andrew, he was shamelessly using us—referencing "our clergy"—and presenting a distorted narrative that he had engaged in discussion with us. It sickened me. I suspected it was all politics.

Very soon, I was proven right.

∽

I arrived at the cathedral at 11:30 p.m. It was a cold night, and my coat flapped in the wind as I unlocked the front doors and stepped inside the dark cathedral. Only two days ago, we had been here, making a plea for mercy to the governor. It had failed. We had failed. I sighed and turned on the lights, then dimmed them.

Soon I heard the cathedral doors open and turned to see people arriving, for which I was so grateful. We were an unlikely group: Father Kyprianos Bouboutsis, Fred, Carol, a handful of parishioners, me, some members of our religious coalition, and advocates from the ICADP. We carried a shared sadness, knowing that Andrew was going to be killed soon. We had tried to prevent his execution, and there was some solace in that knowledge. Mostly, it was reassuring to be together on that difficult night.

As people took their places in the pews, I walked to the front, put on my priest's stole, and opened the Royal Doors at the center of the icon screen. I stood before the Holy Altar, shaken, and tried to hold it together. I opened my prayer book, and now everything was ready.

At 11:55 p.m., I turned to face the group that had gathered and reminded everyone that Andrew's execution was scheduled for 12:01 a.m. Then I described the main parts of the service I would be offering: the prayer of the separation of soul from body and the trisagion ("thrice-holy")—the traditional funerary memorial prayers—and their deep, centuries-old place in our tradition concerning the dead and the dying. Finally, I spoke about the simple chant that we would sing in Andrew's memory. Then we stood in silence in the dimly lit church, waiting.

At midnight, the church bells began to toll. They resounded in the mostly empty church and sent a sad, haunting sound down windy city streets lit by streetlights and the headlights of passing cars. People who were awake at that hour probably wondered why the night was pierced with the pealing of bells. Inside the cathedral, we listened with heavy hearts, as the vibrations of the cathedral bells reverberated through each of us.

When the bells were quiet, I began the service. My eyes filled with tears for Andrew, whose execution, we all knew, was scheduled to begin. We were helpless to change what was happening in Tamms, but at least, we were together, somehow joined with Andrew in his last moments on earth, supporting him with prayer. It was staggering to believe that hundreds of miles south of us, near the rich, agricultural fields of the small town of Tamms, the killing of a human being with the "blessings" of the governor was being carried out in the name of the people of Illinois.

⁂

Unbeknownst to us, a mirror image of our vigil, but a far more public one, was being held in southern Illinois.[25] At 11:00 p.m., Father Carl Scherrer; Father Tom Miller; forty other death penalty opponents, mostly Roman Catholics from the downstate cities of Carbondale, Harrisburg, Anna, and Marion; and four members of the Southern Illinois Death Penalty Moratorium Committee gathered to hold a candlelight vigil for Andrew near the prison grounds of the Tamms facility. They, too, were praying and singing, standing together in the cold darkness and carrying signs protesting the death penalty.

About the time their demonstration began, any visitors still in Andrew's cell—a cell reserved for the condemned prisoner—were asked to leave. Andrew passed an hour in solitude. At midnight, prison staff at Tamms directed Andrew to lie down on his back on a gurney. They used leather straps to tie down his chest, legs, and wrists and then wheeled him into the execution chamber. Andrew told them he understood why Governor Ryan had decided to go ahead with the execution, and he said he forgave the governor.[26]

The execution chamber featured two-way mirrors, behind which were hidden five rooms.[27] When Andrew was wheeled in, curtains covered the windows. Someone wiped the crook of Andrew's left elbow with an alcohol swab—giving the impression that what was about to happen was a medical procedure—then inserted an IV. They covered Andrew with a sheet so that only his face was visible.

The curtains of the execution chamber windows were then opened, allowing the media and witnesses—among them, the director of corrections and Lorraine Borowski's family—to view the execution. The prison warden, George Welborn, and at least one member of the correctional staff were inside the chamber with Andrew. An executioner and assistant were ready, as was a physician (to pronounce Andrew dead).

As required, the order of execution was then read aloud.

Andrew was given an opportunity to say any last words. He made a final statement in which he said, in part, "To the Borowski family, I'm truly sorry for your loss. I mean this sincerely." His last words were recorded.

After completing his statement, he appeared to be praying under his breath. Then, at the warden's signal, the anonymous executioner injected three drugs in succession into Andrew's veins—sodium thiopental, pancuronium bromide, and potassium chloride—as the onlookers watched.[28] Those who witnessed the execution observed that Andrew quickly lost consciousness and seemed to be hyperventilating. The color drained from his face. Andrew Kokoraleis, thirty-five years old, was dead four minutes after the fatal combination of drugs was injected into his arm. Prison officials closed the curtains.[29]

Hundreds of miles away in the Chicago cathedral, we raised our voices to sing the centuries-old chant, "May his memory be eternal."

10

✣

"Be Careful the AIDS!"

July 1993

I received the call at the diocese on July 8, 1993, a sweltering summer day. It was early afternoon.

"Father Demetri? It's George." It was Bob's brother calling to tell me, "Bob is in the hospital. He's dying. Can you come see him?"

"I'm on my way," I said.

I hung up the phone, picked up my priest's case, and headed up the stairs. "I'm not sure when I'll be back," I said to the diocese receptionist. I stepped into the warm afternoon sunshine and hailed a cab.

This would probably be the last time I would see Bob alive, I realized, as I stepped into the cab and pulled the door closed. "Illinois Masonic Hospital," I said to the cabbie.

∞

It was because of Bob that we started the Bishop's Task Force on AIDS, and by God's grace, our work was bearing fruit. Throughout the diocese, as Greek Orthodox priests and laypeople exhibited newfound empathy, many people living with HIV/AIDS experienced a passage from isolation to loving acceptance by their Church, and the Task Force received handwritten notes of appreciation from grateful parishioners. Face-to-face and over the phone, priests related moving accounts of their own HIV/AIDS ministry, which I shared with Bishop Iakovos. He was touched and pleased that God's work was being done one person at a time.

For thirteen years, the bishop had been my mentor. He had influenced my spiritual journey and my maturity as a person. Once I was a priest, he mentored me in a more hands-off way, giving me enough leeway to do what I thought was needed but always stopping me if he thought I was headed down the wrong path.

This was also true of the Task Force. He asked me questions about our progress, suggested improvements, gave his blessing to new aspects of the ministry, and talked with me about developments he saw in the news concerning HIV/AIDS. He even attended one or two Task Force meetings, but, mostly, he left responsibility for the Task Force on my shoulders.

When Bishop Iakovos gave me, a newly ordained priest, his blessing to chair the Task Force, he demonstrated his belief that I could be trusted with this ministry, which meant a great deal to me. From that day forward, I was determined to prove that his faith in me was not misplaced.

∞

The elevator doors opened, and I stepped onto the AIDS floor. Beyond the nurses' station, I entered Bob's room. A cool fluorescent light mounted on the wall behind him illuminated his skeletal face and the oxygen mask that covered his nose and mouth. He wore a faded blue hospital gown, and his body under the covers looked frail. An IV was in one arm. Unconscious and breathing heavily, he appeared to be sleeping. His mother, father, brother, and AIDS buddy[1] were on either side of his bed.

The nurse came in and checked on him. She let us know it would not be long. Then the nurse left the room, quietly closing the door behind her.

I prayed for Bob and anointed him. His teary-eyed mother was holding and stroking his hand, and she kept saying that he felt cold. She attempted to cover him to make him more comfortable. His father sat quietly, his face drawn. Bob's brother, who was four years older than Bob, tried to be strong for his parents and, at the same time, tried to soothe his little brother. They were at Bob's side supporting, consoling, and reassuring him that it was okay to leave. It was beautiful to see how much they loved him and heart-wrenching to see their pain.

Turning to Bob's parents, I gently suggested, "It might be time to say goodbye to Bob now while he is still alive and can hear you."

They agreed, gathered their things, then came to stand by their son's bedside. They held his hand and told him they loved him, tears streaming unabashedly down their faces. Mother and father tenderly kissed their dying boy on the forehead. Bob's mother stroked his cheek. Then they left, sobbing as they closed the door.

On one side of the bed, George sat holding Bob's hand. His AIDS buddy sat opposite, holding the other. When Bob's breathing became more labored, the three of us looked at each other in shared understanding; it would not be long. I got up and stood at the foot of the bed, donned my stole, and prayed the prayer of the separation of the body from the soul, asking God to ease Bob's transition from this life to the next. Part of it reads, "Receive in peace the soul of this Your servant, Bob, and give it rest in the everlasting mansions, with Your saints."

When Bob took his final breath, the three of us were beside him. I looked at Bob and realized he had become my friend. Tears ran down my cheeks as I prayed the memorial prayers over his body. "May his memory be eternal," I said to George, and we hugged. Bob's AIDS buddy was sad and silent; her eyes were full of tears, but she managed to smile at me.

It was then, standing beside Bob's lifeless body, that I understood how deeply his life had touched mine. I was a brand-new priest when he first called me—working at the diocese offices, managing paperwork, projects, and meetings. It was work that had to be done, and in its way, it glorified God. But Bob needed a priest to look into his eyes and reassure him that God loved him. This man had pulled me out from behind my paper-filled desk into his flesh-and-blood life.

For sixteen months, Bob had allowed me to walk beside him on the most difficult part of his life's journey—a profound gift. He had made the priesthood real for me, and he had become my friend. Now he was gone, and my heart was broken in two.

⚯

I emerged from Bob's room into the hallway and encountered an older gentleman in a hospital gown and robe, walking with a rolling IV beside him. He stopped.

"How is Bob doing?" the man asked me. "I know he had a couple of rough nights recently."

"He just died," I said.

"I'm so sorry," the man said.

"Thank you," I said, grateful for his kindness. The priest's bag in my hand felt unbearably heavy and so did my shoulders. I rode the elevator downstairs and made my way through the noisy hospital corridors, past medical staff and patients. Now, I just wanted to be outside, free of the building, noise, and other people. I felt raw. I reached the outer door and pushed it open. A warm afternoon breeze touched my face, somehow comforting me.

I went to find a cab, all the while viewing the world around me with detachment; my mind was still back on the AIDS floor, in the hospital room where Bob lay dead.

The sky was blue, the sun was bright, and traffic was moving. People walked past me, some of them laughing. I felt a flash of anger that the world seemed to go on as before, as if Bob's death was inconsequential. I hailed a cab, and from the back seat, I looked out at the people in passing cars. They were caught up in their own worlds. To them, Bob's death didn't matter. I was filled with anger at the world's callous nonchalance.

Then I was pierced by reality: Bob was dead, and despite my love for him, most of Chicago didn't care. I slumped back against the seat, emotionally and spiritually spent. When we arrived at the diocese, I paid the driver, packed up my things, and headed home.

A few days later, I presided over Bob's funeral at his home parish. In the last months of his life, Bob and his family had started telling people he was HIV positive, and Bob told me that many people had said to him, "You should have told me sooner! I could've been there for you!" As a result of his candor, he was surrounded by people in the final days and weeks of his life. I believe that he no longer felt like an outcast. On the day of his funeral, the church was full of family and friends who gathered to say a final goodbye to him. I was heartened to see Bob's parish priest there, too, although he chose not to concelebrate the service, instead keeping a safe distance from the casket by joining the chanter off at the side to chant the funeral hymns. But he was there.

Bob's family and I followed the hearse to Elmwood Park Cemetery, where a freshly dug grave in his parish's section of the cemetery waited to receive Bob's casket. We said a prayer standing beside the grave, and then Bob was laid to rest, surrounded by many who loved him. Some years later, his parents joined him there.

∞

The year Bob died was the year many Americans, sitting in theaters, saw a compassionate portrayal of a person living with HIV/AIDS on the big screen for the first time. Tom Hanks played attorney Andrew Beckett in the movie *Philadelphia*. Based on a true story, it was the first major Hollywood film about HIV/AIDS. In it, Beckett hires a personal injury attorney to take on his law firm, which fired him after discovering he had AIDS. That same year, playwright Tony Kushner won the Tony Award for Best Play and the Pulitzer Prize for Drama for his play about AIDS, *Angels in America*.

It was also a year marked by another turn in national policy. On June 25, 1993, President Bill Clinton established a new White House Office of

National AIDS Policy.[2] That same month, Congress enacted the National Institutes of Health (NIH) Revitalization Act. It changed the NIH's structure to better coordinate AIDS research, giving the Office of AIDS Research primary oversight of all AIDS research by the NIH and requiring that AIDS research be expanded to include women and minorities.[3]

For those of us involved in AIDS advocacy, these developments, however limited, were welcome news. Discussion of AIDS was finally becoming mainstream, which was both sensible and timely. In 1992, AIDS had been the number one cause of death in the United States for men ages twenty-five to forty-four. Coordinating and funding efforts to end the pandemic were proving to be a matter of national self-interest.

∞

The work of the Task Force focused on ministry to Greek Orthodox people, but the suffering we saw around us was profound. In Chicago, as in New York and San Francisco, enormous numbers of people were dying from complications due to AIDS: some of them in hospice care or hospital rooms; some of them home alone; and some of them on gurneys in the hallways of hospitals, where the number of people needing treatment overwhelmed medical resources. AIDS was seen by much of mainstream society as a pandemic that affected gay people and illicit drug users, not "people like me and my friends." Those living with HIV/AIDS were routinely dismissed or marginalized. They were feared. ("He touched that doorknob; if I touch it, I might 'catch' AIDS." "She is HIV positive; if I ride the elevator with her, I might become infected.") They were considered untouchable. Throughout Chicago, people living with HIV/AIDS were abandoned by family, shunned by friends, sometimes evicted from their apartments, or even blocked from renting an apartment in the first place. The stigma clung to them even after they died because some funeral directors refused the bodies of people who were HIV positive. Others were willing to accept them but demanded a surcharge for their services.

Witnessing the outcast status of these modern-day lepers, Roman Catholic seminarian Stephen Martz[4] and Reverend Jim Corrigan had been moved by compassion to form the AIDS Pastoral Care Network (APCN) in Chicago in April 1985. This organization brought together faith leaders from disparate faith communities and spiritual traditions to combine their energies to care for those living with HIV/AIDS. When the Task Force started, APCN played an important role in helping us develop our unique ministry to serve our Greek Orthodox parishes. But as the Task Force came face-to-face with the widespread distress in our city, we felt called to do more. This inspired us to work with people of other faith traditions to help those living with HIV/AIDS in Chicago. The Task Force jumped in with both feet.

One early example of shared ministry through APCN began in September 1992. The Task Force partnered with other faith-based AIDS ministries to launch a series of free bimonthly seminars called "Interfaith Response to AIDS," which were open to the public. The distinctive character of Chicago—one of the most religiously diverse cities in the world—means that it is home to many faith communities. The seminars were designed to equip HIV/AIDS pastoral care workers to see beyond their own cultural assumptions and minister more effectively to people from a wide spectrum of religious backgrounds.

Each seminar focused on one faith tradition and opened with a reflection from that tradition. For instance, when Bahá'í physician Dr. Ahmad Bastani was the speaker, he read from the words of Bahá'u'lláh, founder of the Bahá'í faith. Then he informed the audience of the unique cultural sensitivities they would encounter in ministering to Bahá'í adherents living with HIV/AIDS. Audience members were encouraged to ask him questions, and this back-and-forth interaction about theology, medicine, and personal experience created an interfaith understanding that went well beyond HIV/AIDS. Each seminar helped us emerge from our respective cultural and religious "ghettos" and to see the other person as a *person*. They helped us understand one another better, even as they helped us become more effective in AIDS ministry.

The Task Force had the honor of hosting these seminars at the Annunciation Cathedral, a location that made it convenient for people who worked downtown to attend. These sessions were so successful that the series continued for three years.

Another early, meaningful step was taken by the Task Force in fall 1992. Each year, on the second Sunday of October, the Episcopalian, Lutheran, and Roman Catholic dioceses of Greater Chicago jointly declared and celebrated an annual Day of Prayer for People Living with HIV/AIDS. Beginning in 1992, we, too, participated in this annual ecumenical observation. With the approval of Bishop Iakovos, this day of prayer was declared and recognized in every Greek Orthodox parish throughout the diocese.

∞

The term "faith-based AIDS ministries" may evoke an image of pious people with folded hands moving silently in cassocks, or kippot, or saffron robes among those who are ill, whispering prayers under their breath. While that likely reflected a slice of reality, the truth was wonderfully more complex and beautiful. Each of us was unique.

One member of the APCN board of directors who made a particularly deep impression on me was Rae Lewis-Thornton, MDiv. She learned she was HIV positive in 1987.[5] A national political organizer who worked on electoral campaigns and issues, such as health care reform, she spoke locally about AIDS. *Essence* magazine featured her as their cover story in December 1994, the first cover story of an African American woman living with AIDS. This groundbreaking story changed the face of AIDS for Black women, and Rae was propelled into the national arena as an AIDS spokesperson. As a contributing editor in television, she won an Emmy Award in 1995 for her series *Living with AIDS*.

Rae Lewis-Thornton's cover story, *Essence* magazine, December 1994. © Reverend Rae Lewis-Thornton

She was passionate about educating people—especially teens—to protect themselves from contracting HIV.[6] She did this dynamic outreach while very ill, with a T-cell count in the range of 75 to 80 (the normal range is 750–1,500).

Rae told the other APCN board members about her AIDS awareness outreach to youth. She had speaking engagements around the nation at high schools and colleges. She was strikingly beautiful and would dress in an intentionally provocative manner. Putting on a sexy persona, she would strut in front of students and say things like, "If you saw me in a club, would you want to get with me?" or "Do you think I'm fine?"

After all the nods and whistles, she would pause and say, "I have AIDS."

The room would go silent in disbelief and shock. Once she had the students' attention, then the real education began. She'd tell the students about her journey with HIV/AIDS. Rae said that if they believed they weren't vulnerable to AIDS because they were well dressed, well educated, Christian, and heterosexual and never used drugs and didn't sleep around, she was proof that they were wrong: these things were true of her, and she still contracted HIV. She warned them to protect themselves by always using a condom, every time.[7]

The impact of these presentations by a *woman* was powerful. She was a straight woman, not a gay man.

Like Rae, each of us brought our passion, skills, and faith tradition to this important work. We were bold enough to spearhead outreach in a way that would reach people. Our shared vision of AIDS ministry led to fruitful working relationships among diverse religious communities that had previously had little reason to collaborate. Yet our strong desire to work together didn't magically erase our religious and cultural differences. These were sometimes thorny.

For instance, the transmission of HIV was primarily a result of men having sex with men. This raised a question about definitions: was a man who had sex with other men considered gay? In some cultures, the answer was yes and, in others, no.

The use of condoms, a key recommendation for safer sex, could be a complicated topic. The Roman Catholic position on birth control meant that the Roman Catholic Church taught married heterosexual couples not to use condoms. That teaching sometimes made the discussion of condom use difficult even for gay Catholics or for heterosexual Catholic couples in which one person was HIV positive.

In the Episcopal Church and in some Protestant denominations, gay men and women could be ordained. That was not true of all faith traditions.

Theological or cultural clashes sometimes came to the fore as people of goodwill but from different backgrounds solved problems together to serve those living with HIV/AIDS. Had we chosen to, we could have allowed those differences to become stumbling blocks. Instead, we focused on our points of agreement and let the rest go. In tackling the HIV/AIDS epidemic, we always discovered a willingness, even a resolute desire, to cross organizational and sectarian boundaries to save lives—a willingness that none of us had ever encountered before.

As a result, interfaith HIV/AIDS ministry in Chicago was marked by a profound cooperation. *Our work together strengthened our belief in the possibility of Christian unity.* In the words of the Gospel according to Mark, "And these signs will follow those who believe: In My name they will cast out demons; they will speak with new tongues . . . they will lay hands on the sick, and they will recover" (Mark 16: 17, 18, NKJV). Together, we were casting out the demons of our age; together we were speaking about our interfaith efforts and activities in a new language, not wrestling with our differences in doctrinal theory as much as coordinating pastoral practice. In ministry to persons living with HIV/AIDS, we were laying our hands on the sick together. Working together allowed us all to recognize powerfully that those who are not against us are for us.

This was unexpected. Those of us who experienced this unity in ministry realized that the divisions we thought existed, in theology or doctrine, were not as wide or unbridgeable as we once believed. In our shared work together, we often discovered that these distinctions were less divisive than many of us had previously thought. Our work together helped us see that we weren't so different after all. For the diocese, it dramatically enhanced our understanding of and dialogue with fellow religious leaders.

❧

My Yiayia Maria (my maternal grandmother) was an educated woman, one of the first teachers ever hired to teach at Greek-language afternoon schools and Saturday day schools in Chicago. She had heard about HIV/AIDS but did not fully know how it was transmitted. She did know that if it was contracted, it could be fatal.

When my siblings or I went out for the evening and she happened to be at our parents' home, she would sharply caution us, "Be careful the AIDS!"

"We will, Yiayia!" we promised. "We will!"

❧

The Task Force was not immune to conflicts. At one meeting, I proposed the idea of a pediatric AIDS quilt-a-thon in partnership with the Philoptochos of our diocese. I had heard about this ministry from another parish[8] where I had recently been invited to speak. Volunteers would gather at one parish, bringing hundreds of yards of donated festive material and batting, pairs of scissors, a bank of sewing machines, and yarn for tying, and set up a "factory" to produce dozens of quilts in a single day. The quilts would be given to children living with HIV/AIDS in area hospitals. Around the Task Force conference table, board members agreed it would be a caring way to help children.

"Those children are innocent, after all," said one Task Force member, who happened to be a member of the Philoptochos.

I bristled with anger.

"Okay," I said, taking a deep breath and looking at her. "What I'm going to say, I'm going say as calmly as possible. We are not and will not divide people into categories of 'innocent' and 'guilty.' We are talking about combating a disease. HIV positive adults are not 'guilty.' No one deserves this. They are infected with a virus."

There was a pause.

She sighed, nodding in agreement, and the meeting continued.

Women from several parishes gather at Saints Constantine and Helen Greek Orthodox Church, Palos Hills, Illinois, for a Philoptochos Pediatric AIDS Quilt-a-thon, 2007. Private collection of Bishop Demetrios C. Kantzavelos

Years into our work together as a Task Force, each of us still wrestled with the complex issues raised by AIDS. It was, as I had discovered myself, so easy to judge.

❧

Just as each person involved in AIDS ministry was different and unique, so was each person living with HIV/AIDS. I remember visiting forty-two-year-old AIDS patient Jimmy Stamatakos in the hospital a few times. Jimmy was a gay man with an outlandish sense of humor, a natural entertainer. Thin and drawn, his body was riddled with purple Kaposi's sarcoma lesions.

During our second visit, he said, "I've noticed that I have some more Kaposi's sarcoma lesions."

"I'm sorry to hear that," I said.

"That's okay," he said with a sudden smile. "I've learned I can play connect the dots with them!" His irresistible laughter filled the room, and I couldn't help but join in.

Later that same visit, he told me he had watched Jacqueline Kennedy Onassis's funeral service. "I was so excited and moved when I heard Leontyne Price sing 'Amazing Grace' that I have decided that I want that sung at my funeral, just like at Jackie's. I want to bring the house down! Can you arrange that?"

"I really don't think I can get Leontyne Price," I protested, laughing.

"Oh, I understand that, but promise me you will find a fabulous Black woman to sing it! Her voice will fill the church!"

"I promise you, I will!" I said, even as part of my mind doubted whether Jimmy's parish priest would agree to this unorthodox request. Well, I would somehow deal with it when the time came.

When I went to see Jimmy at the hospital the third time, on October 7, 1994, it was because his family called. Would I come pray the memorial prayers over his body? I arrived to find Jimmy's mother, Bessie; his two sisters, Pamela and Diana; and Diana's husband, Jim Lukis, there, all of their eyelashes still wet with tears—but, as I soon discovered, still with a sense of humor.

After the prayers, Bessie leaned right over her son's body and pointed an insistent finger at me. "You made him a promise!" she reminded me dramatically, wagging her finger at me with faux ferocity. Her daughters looked on, smiling at their mother's audacity despite their sorrow.

"What was that?" I asked. I leaned in, eyebrows lifted, playing along.

"*You* know," she said, eyebrows knit sternly. "That 'Amazing Grace' would be sung at his funeral"—a final gesture of love for her son.

I pondered this, and getting momentarily serious, told her that anything outside the traditional Orthodox Christian service was not really allowed during the funeral. "How about at the graveside?" I offered.

"Okay. At the *graveside*," she conceded, rolling her eyes at me in mock irritation.

Several days later, I was driving to Jimmy's funeral service at Saints Constantine and Helen Greek Orthodox Church in Palos Hills. Seated beside me was a talented African American singer who was recommended to me by a friend, J. Michael Thompson, at the time, the director of music ministry at St. Peter's in the Loop, a famous downtown Roman Catholic parish. The singer sat respectfully in the church during the service; then we drove together to the cemetery. At the graveside, I celebrated the brief service of committal, removed my stole, and offered a few words, informing the mourners that "Prior to his death, I made Jimmy a promise." That promise, I told them, was a bit outside our ordinary tradition; however, I added, Jimmy was anything but ordinary. People smiled. I took a step or two backward, allowing the singer to take center stage.

It was a perfect blue-sky October day. The young singer's voice filled the autumn air with the redemptive tones of "Amazing Grace." Her performance was stirring, a beautifully fitting tribute to Jimmy. When she finished, everyone was silent for a moment.

Breaking that sacred silence with perfect comedic timing, Jimmy's mother turned to me and said, "How absolutely beautiful. Do I pay her now?"

∞

Word of the Bishop's Task Force on AIDS traveled beyond the Chicago diocese and throughout the country, often by word of mouth. I received an increasing number of calls from gay Greek Orthodox Christians and from Greek Orthodox Christians living with HIV/AIDS. Some requested medical information, but more often, callers were seeking spiritual guidance. As the saying goes, there are no atheists in foxholes. Receiving a diagnosis of "HIV positive" or hearing "You have AIDS" pulled the rug out from under people's confidence. I could hear the anger, fear, or surprise, or a combination of all three, in their voices.

"Why is God punishing me?" and "Why me?" were among the most common questions that I heard. To the latter question, I would usually respond, "When you ask that question, you should probably ask the opposite question as well, 'Why *not* me?'" I would listen to their shock and despair and help them begin to come to terms with their circumstances, whatever they might be, offering care and comfort. I would encourage them to remember that God was not punishing them and did not "give"

HIV/AIDS to them (or their spouse or their child) but that the Lord had promised to help bear them up through the difficult journey. I encouraged them to reach out to their parish priest for further support but added that if they did not feel comfortable doing so, they could call us back. Many requested anonymity and discretion because their (or family member's) sexual orientation or health condition was not public knowledge.

Among the most poignant were calls from closeted gay clergy. These men were often relieved to have someone to talk to, someone to listen to them without judgment who understood the demands of their calling. These faithful men, as broken and as human as the people they served, often struggled to reconcile their priesthood (and, for some of them, their marriage) with being gay. For them, it was a relief to hear someone say, "I understand," "Yes, we have information about that," or "Here's the name of a doctor who can help you." Sometimes, all that was needed was the "sacrament of presence," in other words, being present for them, just listening to them or being with them.

One day, the diocese's receptionist buzzed me. "A woman on the line would like to speak with you about the Task Force," she said, sounding a note of caution.

"Thanks," I said. I prepared myself to hear an earful of complaints, and I picked up the call.

"Hello, Father Demetri," said Demetra Patukas, a cheerful Greek Orthodox woman from Coatesville, Pennsylvania. "I just read about the Bishop's Task Force on AIDS in the *Orthodox Observer*. I'm so glad to hear that the Church has an AIDS ministry." I listened with relief. "My son, George, was diagnosed with AIDS in 1980–81, before the term 'AIDS' was even used," Mrs. Patukas continued. "He died on January 4, 1992."

I asked her to tell me about George.

He had always been a wonderful son, loving and delightful, she said. He had taken charge of his own medical care, although little was known about AIDS in the early days. The years passed and he began to grow progressively weaker. She, her husband, Tom, and their other son, Kostantinos, had stayed by George's side and supported him. They often felt helpless. George had tried to stay brave and upbeat. It had been hard for his family to see him die.

Then Mrs. Patukas asked me to tell her about the Task Force. I shared the story of why we had started and some of our earliest steps. She was interested in our work, so I told her about our current ministries in Chicago and throughout the diocese. She asked a lot of thoughtful questions. I noticed that Mrs. Patukas was impassioned and articulate about AIDS. As we spoke, an idea suggested itself to me, so I asked her if she would consider working with the Task Force. My question surprised her, but after a few minutes, she said she would like to help. I promised to be in touch.

※

In 1994, AIDS was the leading cause of death for *all* Americans ages twenty-five to forty-four. Things were getting worse. This terrible loss of our youth motivated the Task Force to keep expanding our work of AIDS ministry and education. We looked for every opportunity available.

The Hellenic Foundation applied for and secured a grant from the City of Chicago's Department of Human Services to create a bilingual AIDS awareness campaign in 1995. That's when Executive Director Cynthia Yiannias and Angelike Mountanis of the Hellenic Foundation reached out to the Task Force. Together, we developed a sleek media campaign targeted at the Greeks and Greek Americans of Chicago.

We designed a poster featuring the famous carved bust of Hermes, the messenger god. Perfectly balanced, harmonious in its shape, the beautiful sculpture on the poster was marred by a jagged line that ran from the upper right corner and diagonally down to the left across the image of Hermes. The poster read, "Who can get AIDS? Even we Greeks can get AIDS." One version was in Greek, and the other was in English. We distributed the posters to all our parishes in the diocese and to any public space that Greeks and Greek Americans frequented, such as the Hellenic Foundation; Greek grocery stores in Chicago's Greek-town; and AIDS-related social service agencies, such as the APCN and Test Positive Aware (TPA). We also produced engaging Greek/English bilingual infomercials for television and public service announcements for both English- and Greek-language radio stations in Chicago. The campaign was well received.

※

One day, Mrs. Patukas called and informed me that she had been invited to speak at the Mothers March Against AIDS in Washington, DC. The march was held on Sunday, May 7, 1995, a week before Mother's Day. Mrs. Patukas and her husband joined more than 1,100 mothers and fathers marching to the White House. At the podium, she spoke movingly about her son and the need to urge government to find a cure for AIDS. Many of the marchers carried placards featuring photos of their children. The march was the first of its kind. It included mothers living with HIV/AIDS; mothers worried about their HIV-positive children; and mothers, like Mrs. Patukas, who had lost a child from complications due to AIDS.[9]

A significant medical breakthrough in HIV treatment occurred in June 1995, the month after the Mothers March Against AIDS, when the Food and Drug Administration (FDA) approved the first protease inhibitor. (Protease inhibitors treat viral infections. They work by preventing a virus from making more copies of itself.[10]) Protease inhibitors were quickly followed by another group of medications, non-nucleoside reverse transcriptase inhibitors, nicknamed "non-nukes" or NNRTIs. (NNRTIs likewise interfere with the ability of a virus to multiply or reproduce but in a different way than protease inhibitors.[11])

The introduction of these drugs was a breakthrough, ushering in a new era of highly active antiretroviral therapy (HAART): Doctors now had medications that acted on HIV at different times as the virus attempted to make copies of itself. Together, the medications shut down the virus, allowing the person to regain health. This was extraordinary news, potentially affecting millions of lives around the globe. In fact, in 1996, the number of new AIDS cases diagnosed in the United States declined for the first time since the pandemic began,[12] but at the same time, the number of new HIV infections in the United States continued to climb.

Like other AIDS advocates, the Task Force looked forward to a day when HIV and even AIDS would be treatable and manageable, like diabetes. We didn't think there was a cure in sight, but if a person who was HIV positive could live a normal lifespan, even if it meant taking medication all their life, that would be a remarkable outcome, a quantum leap of hope.

The Task Force had its own good news, albeit more modest, that same year. The documentary *Mothers March* was released. Based on the march held in Washington the previous year, it profiled four women who had lost children to AIDS and were mobilized in the fight against the disease. Mrs. Patukas was one of the four.

Mrs. Patukas truly became a spokesperson for the Task Force when she partnered with us in 1997 to produce a video titled *A Family Like Ours*, featuring actor John Stamos as the host. The video related the Patukas family's journey with AIDS and included some clips from the *Mothers March* documentary. Our target audience was Greek Orthodox parishes. We were confident that the Patukases' story would help others to view people living with HIV/AIDS with greater compassion.

When we screened *A Family Like Ours* for the Diocese Philoptochos Board, which had donated funds for its production, there was not a dry eye in the place. We knew we had a winner. The Task Force screened the video at parishes throughout Chicago and sent copies of it to all fifty-eight of our parishes. Eventually, the Task Force sent the video to all Greek Orthodox parishes in the United States, encouraging their priests, Philoptochos chapters, and youth groups to show it. Mrs. Patukas and I went

Front row, from left: Father Demetri Kantzavelos; John Stamos; Nicholas J. Furris, director, producer. Back row: Tom Denove, director of photography. Private collection of Bishop Demetrios C. Kantzavelos

on a speaking tour to parishes and Philoptochos chapters—anywhere we were invited. In this way, we made people aware of HIV/AIDS and of the Bishop's Task Force on AIDS, a resource for any priest or parish.

That year was also notable for several consequential developments in the effort to end the AIDS pandemic. As a result, 1997 was an astonishing year for AIDS advocates and the AIDS community.

- HAART became the new standard for HIV care.
- For the first time since the start of the epidemic, the CDC reported a significant decline in AIDS deaths in the United States, mostly due to the use of HAART. *AIDS-related deaths in 1997 declined by 47 percent compared to 1996 in the United States.*
- The FDA approved a combination of two antiretroviral drugs in one tablet called Combivir. This greatly improved the ability of people living with HIV to keep track of and take their medications.
- Congress enacted the FDA Modernization Act of 1997. The act codified an accelerated drug-approval process[13] and allowed dissemination of information about off-label uses of existing drugs.

All these developments were greeted with enthusiasm by the Task Force and the other faith-based ministries with which we worked. We were beginning to witness a change of attitude toward those living with HIV/AIDS. By that time, the virus was so widespread in all circles of American society that prejudices were diminishing, as were stereotypes about who is or is not HIV positive. We were able to imagine a day that our ministries would not be needed.

One major concern that emerged around this time was drug resistance, and this concern became increasingly worse. As ever larger numbers of people used protease inhibitors, resistance to the drugs became more common. This became an enormous concern within the AIDS community. The development of resistance to these medications spurred research to find new categories of drugs that worked in slightly different ways to treat HIV.

※

In January 1998, we received a letter telling us that the Greek Orthodox Diocese of San Francisco was planning to establish an AIDS ministry. They asked me to join them at a pivotal planning meeting, and I was honored to do so.

The Task Force had been doing its work for more than six years. Over that time, we had educated our clergy about HIV/AIDS and provided them with useful tools to minister to those living with HIV/AIDS and their families. We had successfully disseminated accurate medical information about HIV/AIDS to Greeks, Greek Americans, and others throughout the diocese. Our speakers' bureau was so successful that in its first two years, we had visited every parish that invited us, as well as every major organization in the diocese: Philoptochos, Sunday school teachers, Greek Orthodox Youth of America (GOYA), Young Adult League (YAL), and Clergy/Laity Assemblies, to name a few. Our work with other faith-based AIDS ministries created new opportunities for interfaith and ecumenical understanding. We worked arm in arm with other people of faith on the streets of Chicago and in homeless shelters, hospitals, and hospices—wherever there was a need we could help address.

By the end of 1998, the despair of the early days, when no treatment was available, had been eclipsed by new hope. The beginning of the end was finally in sight as new therapies emerged and new policies promoted HIV/AIDS education and treatment. But even within our own Greek Orthodox community, the need for HIV/AIDS ministry and support continued. Our work was far from done.

11

✢

Lows and Highs

March 17, 1999

The morning Andrew was executed, I awoke sad, angry, and disillusioned. I was a wreck. I reached out to Fred, Theodora, confidantes, advisers, and friends. That afternoon, I left work early and went to a bar, where I sat alone, grieving.

Up until the very end, I had believed that something would prevent Andrew's execution. As I attempted to numb my feelings of grief and failure with a few glasses of scotch, I realized, finally, what I had always been up against but had not understood until now—a purely political state apparatus that benefited some in power and readily executed the less powerful. I had naively believed that an appeal to morality and conscience could change things and now grasped that that's not how it works in Illinois politics. I finished my drink and headed home.

Before I went upstairs, I stopped to check my mail. Among the bills and assorted mailers, a typewritten envelope with a return address from Pontiac postmarked March 15, 1999, stood out. I hurried upstairs, left the rest of the mail on a table, and sat down.

The letter in my hands seemed almost sacred. I carefully opened the envelope and pulled out the enclosed greeting card on which was written a note from Andrew:

March 1999

Rev. Demetri,
    I know we haven't known each other very long, but like you, you have impressed me a great deal with your honesty and straightforwardness. From where I sit, I don't meet very many people with those kinds of qualities.

Handwritten note from Andrew. Private collection of Bishop Demetrios C. Kantzavelos

    I wanted to thank you again for everything you've tried to do for me. Perhaps, as I mentioned during our first visit, God might use my execution to finally end all executions in this State.
    I will not say "goodbye". I'll see you in heaven, my brother!

In Christ's love,
Andrew Kokoraleis

    I caught my breath and tears filled my eyes. I savored the words of a man who had become my friend. As I read and reread the card, I saw, too, that his message was full of hope. It suggested that Andrew had felt ready for what was coming and that in his last hours on earth, he knew he was loved.

Before I met Andrew, I hadn't thought much about the death penalty. Once we met, the sheer horror of the idea that he would be killed by the state spurred me to action. Everything I had done to advocate against the death penalty had been done for Andrew's sake.

But in that brief span of a few weeks, I had looked behind the curtain of the death penalty system and discovered that corruption could and often did occur at every level: during police interrogations, in court when prosecutors overlooked or even misrepresented the truth or defense attorneys offered an incompetent defense (or even fell asleep during a trial), or when a judge knowingly acquitted the guilty for the sake of a bribe. Even geography influenced who was put on death row, with those prosecuted in rural Illinois being sentenced to death at a much higher rate than those in urban areas. The whole system of capital punishment was demonstrably capricious, making anything like the idea of objective "justice" frankly impossible.

Holding Andrew's greeting card in my hand, I called Fred. My voice faltered as I read the note aloud, and it broke Fred's heart too. As we said goodbye, we shared the traditional Greek Orthodox Christian phrase, *Zoe se sas*—"Life to you" and "Life to yours." One sentence in Andrew's note stood out to me as I read it again. "Perhaps, as I mentioned during our first visit, God might use my execution to finally end all executions in this State." It felt almost like a personal call from beyond the grave.

∞

I fired off a letter to the *Chicago Tribune* opinion page, which they published ten days after Andrew's execution. In it, I questioned Governor Ryan's reported "agonizing" over whether to execute Andrew and pilloried the governor for putting political expediency ahead of human life.

> All religious people of good conscience can agree that using the death of any individual, criminal or innocent, for individual political gain is indicative of a cold indifference to the life that was lost. It is immoral. We regret the governor of Illinois has chosen personal political gain rather than leading the people of this state based on morality and a proper civil ethic.[1]

It was my first salvo, and I was not going to hold back. The governor had chosen to permit Andrew's execution despite a lack of evidence, claims that Andrew's confession was coerced by police, and a growing public outcry for a moratorium on executions. The death penalty system that had sentenced Andrew to death had been shown to be unjust and unfair, and yet the governor allowed the execution to proceed. As Bishop Iakovos said to me when he returned to Chicago and learned that Andrew had been executed, "They shouldn't have killed him." The idea of working to end executions in Illinois now became a priority for me.

∞

I was new to the Illinois Coalition Against the Death Penalty (ICADP) board, and in board meetings, I was passionate. I suggested new approaches and stronger alliances with other anti–death penalty groups and recruited new members from the Chicago interfaith community.

In our meetings, we had lively conversations about our next steps. Our aim was the abolition of the death penalty and nothing less, but we could read the political tea leaves. For the short term, we concluded, it made sense to support the newly energized campaign for a moratorium on executions and the creation of a commission to assess the death penalty. It was a first step toward abolition. Anything that would educate the public and elected leaders about the flaws of capital punishment would be progress toward our long-term goal: abolition.

I became familiar with several critiques of capital punishment:

Conviction. Rather than righting the wrong of murder by convicting the guilty, the death penalty system often convicts the innocent and sends them to death row.

Sentencing. Rather than sentencing only "the worst of the worst" to death, the death penalty is instead imposed upon the poorest people, people of color, and those with the worst legal representation in court. Only rarely are women, those linked to organized crime, the educated, or the wealthy executed.

Cost. Rather than saving the state the expense of life imprisonment, the death penalty costs taxpayers significantly more. This is largely but not exclusively because of the higher court costs related to the number of judicial appeals defendants are allowed (in an effort to prevent convicting and executing the innocent).[2]

Deterrence. Rather than the death penalty acting as a deterrent, states with the death penalty generally have higher rates of homicide and overall crime.[3]

Safety. Sentences of life without parole and supermax prisons ensure that people who are dangerous will not be a threat to anyone, in prison or out.

Closure. Rather than giving families of victims closure, the death penalty forces them to obsess on vengeance and to continually reopen old wounds.

Cycle of violence. Rather than addressing the complex social problems that provoke violent crime in the first place, the death penalty contributes to the worsening climate of violence.

I also became acquainted with the advocacy efforts undertaken by allied organizations working to end the death penalty. The Death Penalty Moratorium Campaign, started in Illinois by Bill Ryan, had, as far back as March 1997, proposed a moratorium on executions and a commission to study the death penalty. The following year, in 1998, the Illinois Campaign to End the Death Penalty broadcast "Live from Death Row" events at Pontiac Correctional Center to allow listeners to hear the stories of ten men on Illinois's death row who claimed to be innocent. In 1999, Lawrence Marshall and Rob Warden would establish the new Center on Wrongful Convictions and the Death Penalty at Northwestern University School of Law.

※

To my surprise, the appetite for assessing Illinois's capital punishment system increased in the days and weeks after Andrew's execution. It was as if the question of how to fix a death penalty system that almost everyone now seemed to agree was broken was top of mind. A plethora of task forces and committees were announced that spring, all with the purpose of critiquing and improving the death penalty system: Attorney General Jim Ryan said he was creating a twenty-six-member group to study the death penalty; Illinois Senate Minority Leader Emil Jones announced the formation of a seventeen-member task force to reform the criminal justice system; the Illinois House was establishing a new task force on the death penalty;[4] Representative Coy Pugh reissued his call for a six-month moratorium on executions to allow the death penalty to be assessed; and Illinois Supreme Court Chief Justice Charles Freeman announced the formation of a seventeen-member committee of trial court judges to study the death penalty.[5] All of this was very good news.

Two weeks after Andrew's execution, on April 2, 1999—Good Friday,[6] the day commemorating Jesus's crucifixion at the hands of the state— the Roman Catholic bishops in the United States launched a campaign to abolish the death penalty domestically, consistent with the message delivered by Pope John Paul II on his visit to the United States earlier that year.[7] It meant a great deal to me personally because April 2 is my birthday.

On May 17, another Illinois death row inmate, Ronald Jones, was exonerated. Convicted of rape and murder in 1989, Jones claimed that his confession had been the result of an eighteen-hour-long interrogation and beating that left him with a raised bump on his head after which he signed a confession that he immediately recanted. Once DNA testing became a standard legal tool, his attorney had asked that Jones's DNA be compared to the DNA on the victim's vaginal swab. The judge denied that request, but the Illinois Supreme Court allowed it. Two years later, in 1997, Jones was excluded as the source of the semen. Two more years passed before prosecutors finally dismissed the charges. Shortly after Jones's exoneration, Illinois House Speaker Mike Madigan announced a task force to study legislation requiring the videotaping of confessions.[8]

Of course, not everyone was on board. The Illinois State's Attorneys Association voiced their opposition to a moratorium on executions.[9] In August, a proposed bill arrived on Governor Ryan's desk. It created and provided money for a new Capital Litigation Trust Fund, making funds available for both defense attorneys and prosecutors in capital cases. Its intent was to *increase* the use of the death penalty across the state. The bill was passed unanimously by the Illinois House and Senate, and the governor signed it.[10]

※

Summer passed, the autumn leaves began to fall, and on Sunday, November 14, 1999, the *Chicago Tribune* published the first part of another blockbuster front-page investigative series, "The failure of the death penalty in Illinois." Journalists Ken Armstrong and Steve Mills concluded that "the findings reveal a system so plagued by unprofessionalism, imprecision and bias that they have rendered the state's ultimate form of punishment its least credible."[11] Errors were made by trial judges, suspects were represented in court by incompetent and inexperienced attorneys, police tortured suspects to extract false confessions, prosecutors made unscientific use of evidence (such as misidentifying dog hair as human hair), and some prosecutors intentionally sought to select all-white juries when trying African American or Latino defendants.

The journalists also presented proof of the faulty system's ineffectiveness in convicting the guilty. Of the 285 cases of defendants sentenced to death in Illinois, 259 had gone through at least one round of judicial appeals. The result? Of the 259 defendants, the court hearing their appeal reversed either their conviction or their sentence in 127 of the cases—nearly half of them. In total, 127 death row inmates were deemed as deserving either a new trial (57 cases) or a new hearing about the fairness of their sentence (73 cases).

That same week, the *Chicago Tribune*'s opinion page published a letter I wrote on the heels of Governor Ryan's recent five-day trip to Cuba seeking trade opportunities for the state.[12] He had publicly expressed concern about Cuba's human rights record. I commended the governor for his concern for the people of Cuba but noted:

[The governor's] "humanitarian" record here at home needs attention....

Back in March, religious leaders ... called on the governor to reconsider the policy of capital punishment as exercised in Illinois. In light of the numerous people on death row exonerated prior to execution, and the numerous allegations of judicial and prosecutorial misconduct in Illinois, we assume *either the governor is ignorant of these facts and allegations, in which case his ability to govern is in serious question, or he chooses to act in an inhumane manner by refusing to acknowledge that which he knows to be true* [emphasis added]. In either case, his criticism of Cuba's government and record of human rights, not to mention his acknowledgment of a need for humanitarian efforts in Cuba, is simply political hypocrisy....

If the governor wishes to be a humanitarian, he needs to begin at home.[13]

I was determined to keep pressing the governor for change concerning the death penalty.

Shortly before Thanksgiving, the Illinois Supreme Court's seventeen-person committee issued recommendations to improve the fairness of the death penalty system. Among them was a requirement that prosecutors and defense attorneys in capital cases must have a minimum amount of training and experience and that police interrogations (not just confessions) be videotaped,[14] two recommendations that would make a tremendous difference for defendants.

At the end of November, Representative Coy Pugh introduced a new bill into the House calling for an eighteen-month moratorium on the death penalty and the creation of a commission to take a hard look at the death penalty. Pugh observed that aside from the recommendations just issued by the Illinois Supreme Court, there had as yet been no real change in the death penalty system in Illinois.[15] Sadly, he was right. Andrew had been executed in March, and although early on, Illinois leaders had demonstrated a great deal of sound and fury—"signifying nothing," as Shakespeare might have observed—about improving the system of capital punishment, little of substance had changed by the end of 1999.

The new year came, ushering in a new millennium, and Steve Manning, a former police officer sentenced to death in Illinois, was exonerated. On January 27, 2000, another death row inmate, Murray Blue, had his murder conviction and death sentence reversed as well.[16]

It was around this time that Governor Ryan received a call from Attorney General Jim Ryan. The attorney general said it was time for the governor to schedule the next batch of executions.[17] Ten months earlier, in a visit to Murphysboro High School, Governor Ryan had told death penalty opponents that after Andrew's execution, there would be a de facto moratorium since no other executions were scheduled. Now, that window was closing.

∞

"Governor to halt executions," read the front-page headline in the *Chicago Tribune* on Sunday, January 30, 2000. In the exclusive interview with the *Chicago Tribune*, Governor Ryan's spokesman, Dennis Culloton, announced the governor's intention to declare a moratorium on executions in Illinois. Culloton said that the governor decided to do so owing to "the state's troubling track record of exonerating more Death Row inmates than it has executed and in response to a recent *Tribune* investigation that exposed the death-penalty system's flaws."[18] The governor planned to hold a press conference the following day. The unanticipated announcement was a dream come true for opponents of the death penalty.

I must admit, I read the article with skepticism. Still, a flicker of hope ignited in me. Maybe—just maybe—the firestorm of controversy and advocacy before, during, and after Andrew's execution had helped set political change in motion in Illinois.

∞

The next day, Governor Ryan told a room of reporters, "I cannot support a system which . . . has proven so fraught with error and has come so close to the ultimate nightmare, the state's taking of innocent life." He announced that he was declaring a moratorium. He pledged, "Until I can be sure that everyone sentenced to death in Illinois is truly guilty, until I can be sure with moral certainty that no innocent man or woman is facing a lethal injection, no one will meet that fate."[19] Further, the governor said he intended to create a blue-ribbon commission to study the death penalty.

Governor Ryan's announcement was groundbreaking. It made Illinois the first of the thirty-eight states with the death penalty to declare a moratorium and formally suspend executions. It significantly helped the cause of abolition in the state and in the nation. The ICADP was elated, as were many other advocates. The governor was hailed by many in Illinois, around the nation, and even internationally as a hero. He rightly basked in public acclaim from those opposing the death penalty. He also had to bear criticism from supporters of capital punishment.

I was ecstatic that Governor Ryan had declared a moratorium, but I viewed him as anything but a hero. A hero would have declared a moratorium before Andrew was executed.

I believed the governor had a different reason for his political about-face. An investigation had recently come to light, one that threatened to take down any chance of Governor Ryan successfully running for a second term: allegations of corruption and bribery in his previous role as Illinois's secretary of state.

The corruption investigation began with a terrible tragedy. In 1994, part of a taillight assembly dropped from a semitrailer onto the highway. It bounced beneath a minivan, rupturing its gas tank and causing the minivan to explode in flames. Six children were killed, and their parents, Reverend Duane and Janet Willis, suffered severe burns. An investigation revealed that the trucker may have bribed someone in Ryan's office for a commercial license. Ryan fired the internal investigators and ended their probe. All these years later, federal authorities were investigating and had already indicted some of the employees who worked in the office once headed by Ryan.[20]

These developments prompted me to write a letter to the editorial page of the *Chicago Tribune* that was published only five days after the governor announced a moratorium on executions. I thanked the governor for granting reprieves to those on death row. However, I suggested that considering the corruption investigation, his declaring a moratorium was an act, not of valor, but of political cowardice:

> At the time of the execution of Andrew Kokoraleis, religious leaders of our city and state implored the governor to objectively evaluate a penal system in which more people sentenced to death have been vindicated than executed.... He did not, choosing [instead] what was politically expedient at the time.
>
> Now, under political fire for the bribery scandals during his tenure as secretary of state, it seems too convenient for the governor to reverse himself on this issue. This is a political act, likely intended to defray attention from embarrassing investigations.[21]

That said, this was the first time in US history that a governor had declared a moratorium on executions. Even if I suspected the governor's motives, I had to admit that the declaration of a moratorium was the biggest win ever for death penalty opponents in Illinois. I think Mary Alice Rankin (who established the Illinois Coalition Against the Death Penalty) and Andrew would both have been happy to hear the news. I know I was.

Despite the declaration of a moratorium in Illinois, prosecutors could still request the death penalty, and judges and juries could still sentence people to death. But the final step needed for execution—a signature on a death warrant by the governor—was now on hold. Abolition advocates knew that the distance between a moratorium and an abolition was significant. We also knew that any unilateral action by a governor could easily be reversed by a subsequent governor. We were aiming for a new law to abolish the death penalty. Still, it was a time of real hope.

Five weeks later, on March 9, 2000, Governor Ryan held another press conference, this time to announce the creation of the promised Death Penalty Moratorium Commission and to introduce its fifteen members. Frank McGarr, former chief US district judge in Chicago, was chair. Two vice chairs were former US Senator Paul Simon and Thomas Sullivan, former US Attorney in Chicago and former criminal defense attorney. Also on the commission were former federal judge and FBI and CIA director William Webster and attorney and author Scott Turow. Three of the panel were women; four were people of color. The governor gave the commission three tasks:

- Review the administration of the capital punishment process and determine why it had failed in the past, resulting in innocent people being given death sentences.
- Examine ways to provide safeguards and improvements, from law enforcement to the criminal justice system, from investigation through trial, judicial appeal, and executive review.
- Make recommendations on how to improve the system so that no innocent person will be executed.

Ever the skeptic when it came to Governor Ryan, I had my doubts about the composition of the handpicked commission and questioned whether the governor would allow it true autonomy, including the possibility of suggesting abolition of the death penalty. Would Governor Ryan accept the commission's conclusions, whatever they might be? Or was this just an empty political gesture that would shield him from criticism by allowing others to green-light his future use of the death penalty?

∞

On May 12, 2000, I was in Springfield with six other members of the Illinois Conference of Churches—Bishop Joseph Imesch of the Catholic Diocese of Joliet; Reverend David Anders, executive director of the Illinois Conference of Churches; Reverend Jane Fischer Hoffman, conference minister, Illinois Conference of the United Church of Christ; and Bishop

Peter Beckwith of the Episcopal Diocese of Springfield, and two other people. We were sitting outside Governor Ryan's office.[22] When we were invited into his conference room, the governor shook our hands.

It was my first time meeting the governor face-to-face. As he shook my hand, he growled at me, "I want you to know that you are lucky to be here. I did not want you here, but you are here. I was told that I had to include you. You need to know that you are just lucky to be here."

Taken aback but determined to remain coolheaded, I responded, "It's nice to meet you, too, Mr. Governor." I took a seat with my colleagues at the conference table. Matthew R. Bettenhausen, deputy governor for Criminal Justice and Public Safety, who was helping coordinate the work of the Death Penalty Moratorium Commission, was also at the meeting. We proceeded to discuss a number of issues. Then I raised my hand and said that I had a concern and a question. The governor called on me.

"My concern is that while we are grateful for the declaration of the moratorium, some of us are haunted by the fact that you called the moratorium *after* the execution of Andrew Kokoraleis."

The governor went red in the face. "That animal got everything he deserved!" he said with vehemence. "He butchered a woman. Let me tell you something. I have always been in favor of the death penalty, and I always will be. I reviewed everything, and I have absolutely no remorse for what I did. I have no regrets. I read everything about his case." The tension in the room was palpable. "And let me tell you something else; I read all of your nasty letters. I told you when you walked in you were lucky to be here, and I meant it," he said.

Standing my ground, I continued. "My question, Mr. Governor, is with regard to the commission you have appointed. It seems that the majority of the members are from the legal profession. Do you have any intention of broadening the commission to include representatives from the religious community, anti–death penalty advocates, the medical community, ethicists, and social service professionals, not to mention representatives from diverse minority groups?"

"Absolutely not," the governor responded abruptly. Looking around the table, he asked, "Are there any more questions?" At this point, Bishop Imesch turned to me and whispered, "You are a very patient man." To which I whispered, "Not really."

Bishop Imesch spoke up. "Governor, you were quoted in the media yesterday as saying that if the commission came back to you with the suggestion of abolition that you would support it," he said.

"Your Excellency," Governor Ryan responded, visibly unhappy, "don't believe everything you read in the papers and, more importantly, don't believe everything you believe you have read."[23]

The meeting concluded, and we took a group photograph with the governor. He was probably as relieved as I was when we left his office.

∾

That fall was marked by a few significant developments.

At a death penalty conference in Virginia, Lawrence Marshall and Rob Warden met up with Chicago colleague Chick Hoffman, well known for representing indigent defendants in capital cases in Illinois[24] The Illinois moratorium had been in place for several months, but there had been little movement toward changing existing death penalty law. The three men discussed ways to advance the cause of abolition and came up with an idea: Perhaps Governor Ryan could commute the death sentence of everyone on Illinois's death row to life in prison.[25]

Governor Ryan, meanwhile, was gaining a reputation as a speaker who questioned the death penalty and who, by declaring a moratorium in Illinois, had shown moxie by putting his words into action. That fall, he was participating in various anti–death penalty conferences.

On October 11, former First Lady Rosalynn Carter spoke at a luncheon at the Carter Center before lawyers, judges, and policymakers gathered for the American Bar Association conference "Call to Action: A Moratorium on Executions." She expressed her view: "I am morally and spiritually opposed to the death penalty."[26] Following Mrs. Carter, Governor Ryan spoke to the audience.

On November 18, Governor Ryan attended the "Committing to Conscience: Building a Unified Strategy to End the Death Penalty" conference in San Francisco, where he received an outstanding public service award. He met Sister Helen Prejean, who had written the personal account *Dead Man Walking*; Mike Farrell of the television show *M.A.S.H.*, who was the president of Death Penalty Focus in California; and US Senator Russell Feingold of Wisconsin. He told them all that he was awaiting the recommendations from his blue-ribbon commission before doing anything further.

That month, two more death sentences were reversed by the Illinois Supreme Court.

In December, nine months after it began its work, the governor's Death Penalty Moratorium Commission met for the third and final time. During that meeting, Chair Frank McGarr said the commission might even recommend eliminating the death penalty.[27]

∾

January 31, 2001, was the first anniversary of the moratorium declaration by the governor. On that day, the Illinois Supreme Court enacted the new standards their committee had previously proposed for capital cases.

In February, Illinois legislators introduced a bill to abolish the death penalty, but it went nowhere. On March 29, the Illinois House approved a raft of meaningful reforms to reduce prosecutorial misconduct and prevent wrongful convictions, but they all died in the Senate.

Meanwhile, Governor Ryan continued to be on the road as a guest speaker—at Harvard Law School, UCLA, and Pepperdine University. He regularly mentioned Anthony Porter and Andrew Kokoraleis in his speeches. The governor always noted that, in addition to declaring a moratorium, he had established a blue-ribbon commission to study the death penalty and was looking forward to receiving its recommendations.

∞

The next year, in March 2002, Governor Ryan was at a death penalty conference in Oregon, where he was asked if he would consider blanket clemency. "That's not something that's out of the question. I'll consider that," he said. Knowing that his answer would likely anger police, prosecutors, and victims' families back home in Illinois, he added, "I'd rather have somebody angry than an innocent person killed."[28]

Chick Hoffman, Lawrence Marshall, and Rob Warden noticed what the governor had said. They dusted off the idea they had developed eighteen months earlier: blanket clemency to all of the approximately 150 people on death row. They hoped they could persuade the governor to do it.

But there was a catch. An Illinois law on the books stated that unless a death row inmate requested clemency, the governor could not grant it.[29] The trio of lawyers determined to prepare clemency appeals for all of the death row inmates, hoping they could recruit other attorneys to help. Soon, a dedicated team of attorneys got to work filing the clemency petitions. Getting wind of it, prosecutors countered: they requested a formal hearing for each case.[30]

It was eventually determined that the Illinois Prisoner Review Board would be given the responsibility to hold a hearing for each appeal in order to allow prosecutors, the families of victims, and defense attorneys to speak. All petitions for clemency had to be submitted by August 29, 2002.

∞

Meanwhile, on April 15, 2002, Governor Ryan and Frank McGarr, chair of the Death Penalty Moratorium Commission, unveiled the commission's long-awaited report at a press conference. The 207-page report concluded that the capital punishment system in Illinois was broken. The commission made eighty-five recommendations to improve it, but acknowledged that even if all recommendations were put in place, there was still no way to guarantee that innocent people would not be killed. The governor urged Illinois lawmakers to take up the recommendations and translate them into law.

Commission member Tom Sullivan succinctly summarized the commission's findings: "Repair or repeal."

"The commission's report opened the door to considerable hope," Reverend Paul Rutgers, executive director of the Council of Religious Leaders of Metropolitan Chicago (CRLMC), later recalled.[31]

For months, the governor had been touting the significance of the anticipated report. Despite high expectations, however, no sweeping reforms came on the heels of its release. A legislative package that included the commission's recommendations was developed and received some welcome in the Illinois House, but it didn't gain a foothold in the Senate; it was an election year, and few wanted to consider supporting a controversial bill in the monthslong run-up to November. The governor, with accusations of corruption hanging over his head, had decided not to run for a second term, and he had little political capital to bring about change in the last nine months of his governorship. There did not seem to be enough political will in the state to keep moving forward on reforming the capital punishment system.

Lawrence Marshall, Rob Ward, Chick Hoffman, and their colleagues successfully filed petitions for clemency for Illinois's death row inmates, having met the August 29 deadline. By September 30, Illinois prosecutors filed responses to each of the petitions.[32] The Illinois Prisoner Review Board now faced the Herculean task of holding appeal hearings for each of the death row inmates. The hearings were scheduled for mid-October.

Meanwhile, in September 2002, Chief Justice Moses Harrison II retired. He was asked whether he thought that Governor Ryan should commute all death sentences to life without the possibility of parole. "He has the power to do it, and he should do it," he recommended.[33]

∞

On October 15, 2002, the Illinois Prisoner Review Board held its first day of hearings. Prosecutors and the families of victims painfully recounted the murders of which each inmate had been convicted. Defense attorneys made the case for clemency for their clients.

Day after day of relentless, back-to-back murder hearings were deeply upsetting to everyone, including the Prisoner Review Board members.

Over two weeks, some of the worst crimes ever committed in Illinois were recounted, often in devastating detail, resurrecting disturbing, violent memories and causing victims' families deep distress. Daily media coverage of the hearings carried harrowing details of the murders.

Everyone knew that the hearings were being held because Governor Ryan was considering commuting everyone's death sentence to life in prison. This further upset some of the victims' families, who had long expected the convicted murderers to be executed eventually. Brokenhearted family members tearfully pleaded to see someone held accountable for the murders of their loved ones. Many requested that death row inmates be executed.

Eventually, the wisdom of holding the hearings began to be questioned in the media.

> From the start, Gov. George Ryan and his top aides knew they would take a hit when the families of murder victims recounted their gruesome, heartbreaking stories at the 142 clemency hearings for Death Row inmates.
>
> But neither the governor's office nor the state's leading critics of the death penalty fully expected just how potent that testimony would be.
>
> The debate over reforming the capital punishment system was quickly overpowered by the emotion of it all, leading Ryan to retreat and say he was having "second thoughts" about granting a blanket commutation for the state's condemned prisoners. . . .
>
> Rob Warden, of the Center on Wrongful Convictions at Northwestern University and a coordinator of the clemency requests, was more blunt.
>
> "I would have to admit that we probably underestimated it. It's pretty much overpowering," he said.[34]

In the wake of the emotional hearings, the pressure to abandon the idea of blanket clemency was immense.

Governor Ryan, in a speech in Washington, acknowledged the pain of victims' families in the hearings being held in Illinois. However, he also made a point of reminding his audience that he had broad clemency powers as governor.

After returning to Illinois, the governor learned that families of victims hoped to appeal to the governor in person to ask him not to grant blanket clemency. Governor Ryan agreed to and did meet with them at a town hall–style meeting, with no media present.[35]

In November, the Prisoner Review Board sent its confidential, nonbinding recommendations to the governor.

∞

At this time, the leadership of the Center on Wrongful Convictions, the ICADP, and Murder Victims' Families for Reconciliation were having joint discussions. The governor would leave office in mid-January, and it was important to keep encouraging him to move forward on the idea of blanket clemency so that he could accomplish it while still in office. Everyone agreed that a major publicity campaign was needed in the next several weeks. Advocates worked together to create three highly visible events that would take place over the course of two days, Sunday, December 15, and Monday, December 16. Each was carefully planned for maximum impact and media coverage.

On December 15, 2002, the Center on Wrongful Convictions at Northwestern University School of Law held a "National Gathering of Death Penalty Exonerated," a moving event that featured forty-four exonerated people and attracted advocates seeking an end to the death penalty. At the well-attended event, Reverend Jesse Jackson made an appeal to Governor Ryan, who was not there, "You can make a choice that will change the course of a nation."[36]

The next morning, at 4:30, exoneree Gary Gauger and his wife stood in the dark on a stretch of Illinois Highway 53 near Joliet. Across the highway was the Statesville Correctional Center, where Gauger had been wrongfully imprisoned for years. The couple was joined by Lawrence Marshall. Together, the three set off on the first one-mile leg of a thirty-seven-mile relay walk, known as "Dead Men Walking," that started near the prison and ended at the governor's office in downtown Chicago. Gauger and other exonerees hoped to convince Governor George Ryan to grant clemency to condemned prisoners on death row. In Gauger's hand was a scroll. It read:

> We are the exonerated. We have each walked in the valley of the shadow of death. The courts and the public were certain that we were guilty and that we had forfeited our right to live. Only through miracles did the truth emerge. The truth proved we were victims of wrongful convictions.[37]

For thirty-seven miles, people handed off the scroll like a baton, exoneree to exoneree. For the last ten miles, exonerees who had already handed off the scroll kept walking, and soon a large group of people were marching together. The last leg of the relay was led by Anthony Porter and Professor David Protess. I and many other people joined them. Porter delivered the scroll, followed by a crowd, to a member of the governor's staff in downtown Chicago.

That evening, a one-night performance of the off-Broadway show *The Exonerated* was held at the Chicago Center for the Performing Arts. Starring Jill Clayburgh, Richard Dreyfuss, Mike Farrell, and Danny Glover, the play dramatized the stories of six death row exonerees; five of them were in the audience that night to watch it. Also in the audience were

Governor Ryan; his wife, Lura Lynn; his top staff; and some members of the General Assembly. At the end of the performance, the actors gathered on stage and thanked Governor Ryan for having declared a moratorium in Illinois. The audience burst into applause and gave the governor a standing ovation.[38]

Afterward, the sister of a death row inmate approached Governor Ryan and asked if the governor would be willing to meet with the families of those on death row, just as he had met with the families of victims. He agreed. Soon after he met with death row inmates' families at Old St. Mary's Church in Chicago.

∞

Anti–death penalty advocates continued to appeal to the governor to offer blanket commutation. Nelson Mandela called him, as did Archbishop Tutu, encouraging him to be merciful. Other leaders from around the world—Mexico, Poland, the Vatican, and the European Union—also supported commutation. Closer to home, Lawrence Marshall asked the governor to dinner and suggested that Governor Ryan might consider the possibility that it was for this very moment that he had been brought to power. The governor also received a letter supporting blanket commutation signed by 428 law professors from around the United States. When asked, spokespeople from the governor's office consistently stated that blanket commutation was "on the back burner."

Reverend Jesse Jackson visited inmates on death row at Pontiac Correctional Center on December 31, 2002, and afterward, he too appealed to the governor for blanket commutation. Around that time, Professor Francis Boyle of the University of Illinois Law School in Champaign, Illinois, announced that he was going to nominate the governor for the Nobel Peace Prize owing to his work against the death penalty system in Illinois.[39]

∞

On January 10, 2003, Governor Ryan delivered a speech at the DePaul University School of Law, where Andrea Lyon, known as the "angel of death row," was a professor. During that speech, which was televised, the governor announced that he was pardoning four men on death row, for which he received several standing ovations.

The next day, January 11, 2003, the governor entered a packed hall at Northwestern University Law School. On live television, Governor George Ryan stood before students, professors, exonerees, death row inmates' families, and the media. He gave his last speech as governor. As part of it, he said:

> Our systemic case-by-case review has found more cases of innocent men wrongfully sentenced to death row. Because our three-year study has found only more questions about the fairness of the sentencing; because of the spectacular failure to reform the system; because we have seen justice delayed for countless death row inmates with potentially meritorious claims; because the Illinois death penalty system is arbitrary and capricious—and therefore immoral—I no longer shall tinker with the machinery of death.... The legislature couldn't reform it. Lawmakers won't repeal it. But I will not stand for it. I must act. Our capital system is haunted by the demon of error: error in determining guilt, and error in determining who among the guilty deserves to die.
>
> Because of all these reasons, today I am commuting the sentences of all death row inmates. This is a blanket commutation.[40]

Governor Ryan concluded his speech by saying, "Lincoln once said: 'I have always found that mercy bears richer fruits than strict justice.' I can only hope that will be so. God bless you. And God bless the people of Illinois."

The applause was resounding, and the governor received a standing ovation. That night, he had commuted three death row inmates' sentences to forty years in prison and commuted the death sentences of the remaining 164 people on death row to life in prison without the possibility of parole. He had emptied out Illinois's death row. Two days later, he stepped down as governor.

❦

I listened to Governor Ryan's historic speech and was reminded of a meaningful scripture, Isaiah 61:1–2: "He has sent me to bring good news to the oppressed, to bind up the broken-hearted, to proclaim liberty to the captives, and to release the prisoners; to proclaim the year of the Lord's favor." It was a memorable moment in Illinois history.

Journalist Cathleen Falsani of the *Chicago Sun-Times* reached out to me and some of the members of the CRLMC to hear our thoughts about the announcement. My colleagues expressed a range of opinions. Reverend Paul Rutgers, executive director of the CRLMC, said, "I believe that the religious leadership around the Council table has been consistently in support of the suspension of the death penalty and, under those circumstances, of commutations."

When asked how I felt, I said, "It's bittersweet. I wish that announcement came three-and-a-half years ago."[41] However, this step encouraged me and other advocates to double down on our efforts to seek abolition.

12

✣

Fulfillment amid Heartbreak

December 2002

The Bishop's Task Force on AIDS was at its height in December 2002 when I first met Peter in the reception room of the Diocese of Chicago, a room bright with Christmas decorations. Peter's mother, whom I had known for years, brought him to meet with me.

"So, Father, tell us about the Task Force and this AIDS stuff," she said.

"She's asking because I'm HIV positive," Peter explained.

Peter's mother said, "He's just returned to Chicago from Florida, and we're wondering what we should do." She looked at her son, her face full of worry.

He was a bright guy. While still in college, Peter had worked with the Chicago Board of Trade as an independent trader with the MidAmerica Commodity Exchange. He had never been interested in drugs or even cigarettes, but he took up smoking in 1990 while working on the high-pressure trading floor. He left Chicago in 1991 after graduating from DePaul University with a degree in economics and finance and took a job at Chemical Bank in New York. There, he was introduced to the city's club scene, where he discovered he loved the music and was drawn to the idea of being a DJ, and like most of the people on the dance floor, he started using drugs. Peter worked in banking by day but honed his DJ skills after hours. Eventually, clients in New York and elsewhere began hiring him to DJ their events, especially tea dances, which are afternoon dance events. In 1994, he left banking and became a full-time DJ in New York.

Five years later, Peter moved to South Beach, Florida, as a "geographic cure" in an effort to stop doing drugs. He applied himself full-time to DJ work. He was quite successful, and the work was as lucrative as banking had been. Soon, he was being sought after to DJ parties all over the country. He was particularly famous for his tea dances, playing upbeat music with a positive vibe. Those events were often fundraisers for HIV/AIDS organizations. His father and mother were supportive of his transition from the financial world into the world of music, but they didn't know that he was using drugs or that he was HIV positive.

Then, in what appeared to be a setup, he was arrested for conspiracy to sell and distribute illegal drugs, which is a federal offense. When he called his parents from jail, he told them everything: his HIV status, drug use, and arrest and conviction. Hundreds of miles away in Chicago, his parents just wanted to do whatever they could to help him, so they mortgaged their home to cover his bail and urged him to come home to Chicago. He was now out on bail, awaiting a sentencing hearing in Florida. It was Christmastime.

Peter had never heard of the Bishop's Task Force on AIDS, so I told him a little about its history. I suggested that he make an appointment to see Catherine Creticos, a physician and infectious disease specialist on the Task Force board of directors who worked at Howard Brown Health Center and Illinois Masonic Hospital. Dr. Creticos, a Greek Orthodox Christian, was a person of action. During the height of the HIV/AIDS pandemic, she made a point of standing at the end of the line to receive Holy Communion each Sunday to demonstrate to others that no matter how many people had already received from the Communion spoon, she (and they) would not become infected with HIV or anything else.

Peter did go to see Dr. Creticos. As he sat on the exam table, he told her that in the past he had used methamphetamine and had somehow convinced himself that meth was so powerful that it would "kill" the HIV in his body. She quickly corrected that falsehood.

"Meth did the opposite; it sped up the virus," she said. She checked Peter's T-cell count, which was very low, at about 200. After a thorough assessment, she started Peter on a cocktail of four different drugs, including HIV protease inhibitors.

Peter followed Dr. Creticos's instructions, and his body began to respond to the treatment. His T-cell count recovered, and the HIV viral load kept dropping until it became undetectable.

∞

Soon it was time for Peter to return to Florida for his sentencing hearing. He knew he could try to cut a deal by turning state's evidence and identifying other people involved in the drug trade but concluded that it would be dangerous to testify against them. He also knew he could be facing ten to twenty-five years in prison.

Peter's mother asked me to appear at the hearing as a character witness for her son, which I agreed to. On the appointed day, Peter arrived in Florida accompanied by an entourage: his father, mother, one of his brothers, and me. Peter's father was weak and very ill from battling cancer, diabetes, and heart disease, but he wanted to be there for his son. We understood that the hearing would be brief, so we planned to fly back the same day.

We arrived at the courthouse, and when we entered, Peter's attorneys were waiting for him. They whisked him off into a small room nearby, and moments later, one of the attorneys came out and asked me to join them. When I walked in, I saw that Peter was crying; I looked at the attorney for an explanation.

"You're not going to be a character witness for Peter, Father," the attorney said to me bluntly. He then turned to Peter and said, "Tell Father Demetri what happened."

"I got caught selling Viagra [a prescription drug] online," Peter admitted, his face wet with tears, a violation of his bail. All hope of the judge's showing mercy in Peter's sentencing had evaporated. Under those circumstances, having a character witness wouldn't make any difference. One of his attorneys shook his head.

"You've got to tell your parents," I said, and the attorneys agreed.

"No, I can't." No matter what we said, he insisted he couldn't tell them. Yet he was the only one who could because attorney/client privilege and clergy/penitent confidentiality meant that we were prevented from disclosing this to anyone. At that point, it was almost time for the hearing. After some back-and-forth, the four of us came out to where Peter's family was seated on a bench in the hallway.

They looked at Peter's tearstained face, unsure about what was happening, and then looked at me pleadingly as if to ask, *What's wrong?* Just then, Peter's name was called, summoning him to court for the hearing. With tears streaming down his face, he blurted out to his parents and brother what he had done; then he and his attorneys turned to enter the courtroom, and the doors closed behind them.

Peter's family, dumbfounded and in shock, stayed where they were. We had all intended to go into the hearing with him, but instead, we stayed outside. I explained in greater detail what Peter had done, what his attorneys had said, and why having me testify now would not do Peter any good.

"What's going to happen next?" we asked a nearby court official, explaining briefly what had just happened.

"He'll be processed and sent to prison," the official answered.

"Can we see him after he is processed?" we asked.

"Yes, but that will take several hours."

I looked at Peter's father, whose tired shoulders sagged under the weight of the news. I asked Peter's family, "What do you think? Do you want to wait?" They looked despondent, weary, exhausted.

"No," Peter's father decided, "let's just go." He appeared deflated; no one had expected this. Deeply discouraged, worried for Peter, and suddenly unable to help, we headed to the airport and caught a flight back to Chicago. In the end, Peter's attorneys asked that his prison time be reduced to five to ten years, and he was sentenced to six and a half years in prison.

Peter's father died a few months later while Peter was in prison.

∞

In January 2003, the Greek Orthodox Archdiocese of America experienced a reorganization. Each of the eight dioceses was elevated to metropolis, and each bishop who headed a diocese was elected to the status of metropolitan. Thus, Bishop Iakovos of the Greek Orthodox Diocese of Chicago was elected Metropolitan Iakovos of the Greek Orthodox Metropolis of Chicago.

Most of the work accomplished by the Bishop's Task Force on AIDS had been done, geographically speaking, within the borders of the Diocese (later, Metropolis) of Chicago. In 2004, however, the Task Force received national recognition. The Greek Orthodox Archdiocese of America invited the Bishop's Task Force on AIDS to give a presentation about HIV/AIDS at the archdiocese's biennial conference, the national Clergy/Laity Assembly. Mrs. Demetra Patukas spoke and shared the story of her son, George, and I spoke about Bob and the history and impact of the Task Force. Our joint presentation was warmly received. To our delight, the archdiocese was utilizing the Task Force as a resource for AIDS-related pastoral outreach, and Greek Orthodox faithful from around the nation with concerns or questions about HIV/AIDS were often referred directly to us. This embrace by the national leadership of the Greek Orthodox Church was deeply affirming.

The Task Force was also a resource for other Orthodox Christian communities in the United States, such as those from the Antiochian Orthodox, Romanian Orthodox, and Serbian Orthodox traditions.

Perhaps the greatest honor, however, was an international opportunity given to us by His All Holiness, Ecumenical Patriarch Bartholomew of Constantinople (the modern city of Istanbul, Turkey). The Ecumenical Patriarch is the archbishop of Constantinople and is also the most senior figure in the Orthodox Christian world—the "first among equals."

Ecumenical Patriarch Bartholomew had, as a young man, studied theology at the Ecumenical Institute in Switzerland. While there, he became friends with Koshy Chacko from India, who had been raised in the Indian Orthodox Church.[1] (The Indian Orthodox Church traces its origins to St. Thomas the Apostle, who traveled to the Malabar coast of India in 52 CE.)

Decades later, HIV/AIDS was rapidly spreading through India. Reverend Chacko saw an urgent need to expand the facilities and services of an existing HIV/AIDS clinic in the rural town of Vazhuvady, in the state of Kerala. He explained the need and his vision to his old friend, the Ecumenical Patriarch.

Ecumenical Patriarch Bartholomew knew about the work of the Bishop's Task Force on AIDS through his communicatons with Metropolitan Iakovos of Chicago as well as from Greek media and others who reported on our ministry.

Thus, in 2004—the year India overtook South Africa as the nation with the greatest number of people living with HIV/AIDS[2]—Ecumenical Patriarch Bartholomew directed the Metropolis of Chicago to sponsor an international AIDS project in India.

We took on this challenge and launched a campaign to significantly fund the expansion of the HIV/AIDS clinic in Vazhuvady.[3] First, we shared the vision with Greek Orthodox believers and Indian businesspeople in Chicagoland and appealed for their financial support. Next, we partnered with my spiritual son and dear friend, Gregory Pappas, the founder and president of the Greek America Foundation, and organized a fundraising concert featuring the internationally acclaimed Greek vocalist Glykeria. With the generosity of many, we raised the necessary funds for the project. The clinic expansion was completed and the clinic named in honor of Ecumenical Patriarch Bartholomew, whose intervention had helped make it possible.

Funding the expansion of an AIDS clinic in India was a welcome opportunity to support AIDS ministry beyond our own borders. This outreach also opened a door to develop a relationship with the Indian community of Chicago and the Midwest.

It was a relief to see that AIDS was increasingly seen as a medical problem. The Church was tending the sick, and the work of the Task Force, once seen as groundbreaking and even risky by some, was being embraced as mainstream.

It was a time of success and satisfaction in my work on HIV/AIDS, but it proved to be a difficult season for my family.

When my father was a young man, the idea of smoking still had cachet, and he made an early habit of it. By the time he was in his sixties, his body was feeling the effects of it, even though by then he had long since stopped smoking. He was plagued with health problems related to smoking, primarily kidney decline and then failure. For a few years, he underwent dialysis to compensate, but even that began to take a toll on him.

In 2005, my father ended up in the hospital. He called us all together in his hospital room and said that he had decided that he was going to stop dialysis, that he just couldn't take it anymore and wanted to die at home. The day he made his announcement, we had a hospital bed delivered to my parents' home and put it in the middle of the family room, and we had him transported home, where he would receive hospice care.

My siblings and I visited him and my mother daily. About a week later, all of us—George and his wife, Kelly; Maria; Mike; and me—came to see him one morning. He would have none of it and shooed us away, demanding that everyone go to work.

"You all owe your bosses a full day's work," he insisted. His strong work ethic was one of his defining features, and he instilled that value in all of us. My siblings and I obediently left for work.

Later that day, I was leading an event planning meeting at the metropolis when I received a call from my mother.

"He's taken a turn for the worse," she said. "Come home soon."

I was still in the meeting twenty minutes later and hoping to finish when a second call came.

"Your father just died," my mother said. "Can you pick up your sister from work?" I hung up the phone and, thunderstruck, turned to look at everyone.

"I think I need to go home," I said, evidently so dazed by this news that I didn't explain myself or show any emotion. I was still trying to take in what my mother had just said.

"You can't go home; you're running the meeting," someone said.

"My father just died; I really think that I need to go home," I clarified. Everyone now got up, expressed their condolences, hugged me, and urged me to leave.

I went to retrieve my jacket and saw Metropolitan Iakovos.

"I need to go home," I said.

"Why?" he asked.

"My father died."

"So quickly—?" he said. "Go!"

I drove to my sister's workplace and picked her up.

"Pa *died*?" she said with a doubtful tone.

"Yeah."

"It doesn't seem real," she said, mirroring my shock.

"No, it doesn't."

We reached my parents' house, and I put on my stole and read prayers over my father's body. As I said the words, my eyes filled with tears, and I realized that he was really gone. My mother was weeping, and everyone was sad but not inconsolable. My father had been ill for so long, and he had said he was ready to go.

I called the funeral director, and two people from the funeral home arrived to transport my father's body. My sister asked them, "Is he really dead?"

They assured her he was.

My larger-than-life father, Christ J. Kantzavelos, died on October 7, 2005, at 10:40 a.m. at the age of seventy.

Later, my mother told us about my father's death.

"He was conscious until the end," she said. "Sometime after you all left, I asked the hospice physician if he would care for a cup of coffee, and he said yes. I stood beside your father and told him that we were going into the kitchen for a cup of coffee.

"Pa said, 'I love you,'" my mother said. "I gently kissed him on the cheek and told him, 'I love you too.' The physician then followed me into the kitchen."

Once they were out of the room, my father died.

My mother, my siblings, and I arranged for the visitation to be at the funeral home and the funeral service to be held at the Assumption Church, the church where my father had been baptized and married. Among the guests at the visitation was Francis Cardinal George. I was so grateful to see him.

"How did you know?" I asked him.

"Metropolitan Iakovos called and told me."

The day of the funeral, Metropolitan Iakovos officiated. Approximately twenty-eight priests were in attendance. I was preparing to sit beside my mother in the front pew, but she said emphatically, "No. You are a priest. That's your father, and you are going to serve." So I did.

Keeping with old-school tradition, on the way from the church to the cemetery, my mother had the funeral procession stop for a few moments in front of our house where they had lived and where we grew up.

A year later almost to the day my father died, on Monday, October 30, 2006, I was elected to be an auxiliary bishop with the title of Bishop Demetrios of Mokissos.[4] The ordination ceremony was held at my home parish, the Assumption Church, two months later, on December 9, 2006. I was forty-four years old, the youngest Greek Orthodox bishop in the United States.[5]

The church was packed. I was the first member of the parish to become a bishop, and it was the first time that a bishop's elevation ceremony had ever been held at the Assumption Church. The ceremony for ordaining a bishop is ancient, one of the oldest in Christian history. Archbishop Demetrios came from the archdiocese in New York to officiate, and all the metropolitans and bishops in the United States who were able to attended. Ten priests served that day, and more than a hundred priests and a few deacons were sitting in the congregation. There was also a meaningful contingent of ecumenical and interfaith guests, people with whom I worked over the years who became very close friends. Perhaps most visible among them were four Roman Catholic auxiliary bishops, all dressed in their magenta robes.

I recall the ordination vividly, and one moment in particular. I was kneeling on both knees in front of the altar with both my hands—right over left—resting on the altar and my forehead resting on top of my hands. One of the bishops opened the gospel book and placed it, text-side down, across my shoulders and the nape of my neck, and I felt the weight of it. Then the archbishop and the twelve metropolitans and bishops who were present each placed a hand on me—and if they couldn't reach me, then on the right shoulder of the bishop ahead of him, who had his hand on me—and the archbishop began to pray.

As Archbishop Demetrios prayed the prayer of ordination, I felt a burning sensation inside my whole being, an intense heat, strange and unfamiliar but somehow welcome, almost as if God were purifying me by the power of the Holy Spirit. *Was this how the Apostles felt on Pentecost?* I wondered, marveling. This amazing feeling was paired with a sudden surge of energy welling up inside me. I was still on my knees with my head bowed, but I felt like standing up and throwing off one reality and emerging into another—like casting off an old garment that I didn't need any more or shedding a cocoon like a butterfly. I felt *new*. Something had changed. Then the archbishop, metropolitans, and bishops removed their hands and the gospel book, and I stood up and was led out in front of the icon screen by the archbishop, who proclaimed, "Axios!"

At that moment, I knew that I was not the same. My sense of self, who and what I was, had changed. My understanding of myself as a priest had undergone a metamorphosis, and I felt complete in a way I never had before. This confirmed what a bishop friend of mine in Greece told me, that once I was ordained a bishop, I would feel different, changed even.

Newly ordained Bishop Demetrios of Mokissos bows to Metropolitan Iakovos of Chicago, December 9, 2006. © Gus Psichogios, photographer

The ceremony was followed by a wonderful party celebrating the event. Gardenias on every table filled the room with their fragrance, and my family was there celebrating with me. It was the dream of a lifetime. But I missed my father.

∞

After Peter completed his prison sentence, some years after he and I first met, he returned to Chicago, and we reconnected. He told me he had taken steps to clean up. Looking back, Peter recalled: "Every day when I awoke, I thanked God that I was alive. I prayed and prayed each day that God would help carry me on this new path of sobriety." He learned to take life one day at a time, and he worked hard to stay clean by regularly attending Alcoholics Anonymous and Narcotics Anonymous meetings. When he found himself wanting a pipe or cigarette, he picked up a Twizzler[6] instead. His family was proud of him, as was I.

Peter discovered that he did not have to leave behind the music and DJ work in order to live drug free. Still drawn by the beauty and power of music and the joy of mixing sounds that he developed as a DJ, he began to use those skills to explore music and sound in a different way—as therapy—to heal himself and others. Utilizing everything from Tibetan

Michael Kantzavelos, Maria-Magdalene Kantzavelos, Merope Kantzavelos, Bishop Demetrios of Mokissos, and Kelly and George Kantzavelos, December 9, 2006. © Gus Psichogios, photographer

singing bowls to Gregorian chants, to gongs, recorded music, and more, he creates immersive soundscapes to promote physical and psychological healing. He has his own personal sound healing studio where others can come to heal and be helped to release tension, and he works with people who have addictions.

I think about Peter, whom I met in 2002, and Bob, whom I met in 1992, and I am aware of the profound difference that ten years made in the Task Force's response to each of them. When Bob reached out to me in 1992, we were able to support him and his family by showing up, sharing medical information, and letting Bob know that God loved him and we did too. We let him know that he was not an outcast. Medically, however, we didn't have much to offer. In 2002, when Peter reached out to the Task Force, our toolbox had expanded significantly and included information about medical providers and highly effective pharmaceuticals.

Recently, I was in earshot of someone asking Peter where he would have been today if the Task Force had not existed. Without hesitation he answered, "I would be dead."

∞

The Task Force started its work modestly but boldly in 1992. By 1994, the speakers' bureau we had set up for parish visits was no longer needed because information on HIV/AIDS was more widely available. In 1995, we wrapped up our interfaith seminar series and, instead, worked arm in arm with other faith leaders on the streets of Chicago, in homeless shelters, and in hospitals and hospices.

Our understanding of our clergy kept improving too. For instance, I learned that the priest who was so disruptive at the clergy retreat had, in fact, already been visiting AIDS patients in the hospital even before the retreat. What had upset him at the retreat was the candid discussion of sex. Younger priests, by and large, were more comfortable with the topic.

The more priests we spoke with, the more we came to understand that, early on, many of them had agreed there was a need to minister to people living with HIV/AIDS; they just didn't know how. Our efforts to arm them with information and a tool kit, to help coach them and to serve as a resource, had encouraged them to step out with confidence. To their credit, they had done so admirably.

With each change in government policy concerning HIV/AIDS and each medical breakthrough, we in the Task Force kept nimbly doing our best to carry out our mission to minister effectively to those living with HIV/AIDS and their families. Under pressure from AIDS activists, new treatments emerged. New legislation allowed HIV treatment drugs to be fast-tracked, and combinations of drugs were proving effective against the virus. The need for the Bishop's Task Force on AIDS was diminishing. HIV was gradually becoming what AIDS activists once hoped it would, a chronic, manageable virus.[7]

It was obvious that the Bishop's Task Force on AIDS had completed its work. In our own parishes throughout the metropolis and working side by side with people of many faith traditions in Chicagoland, we had done the work we had set out to do.

It had been an exhilarating endeavor, and it all began with a phone call from Bob.

13

✟

To Sign or Not to Sign

March 8, 2011

It was March 8, 2011, a cool, bright Chicago morning, when the call came on my cell phone in the car.

"Hello," I answered, "this is Bishop Demetrios." I was a little groggy. I had just had a minor medical procedure, and the lingering effects of anesthesia prevented me from taking the wheel. My assistant, Dean Kartsimas, was driving me home.

"Hello, Your Grace," said the voice at the other end of the line. "I'm calling on behalf of Governor Quinn, who would like to see you tomorrow in Springfield."

Even in my somewhat compromised state, I registered the significance of the message. I pushed the remaining fog from my mind and sat up a little straighter in the passenger seat.

"Can you be here at the capital at 10:00 a.m.?" she asked.

"If the governor wants to see me, I'll be there at 6:00 a.m.!" I said, my mind now clear. I felt a thrill of happiness in my chest. I had the presence of mind to ask, "Why does the governor want to see me?"

"I think you know why," she said cryptically and added, "We'll see you at his office at the Illinois State Capitol tomorrow morning at ten o'clock."

I was looking out the windshield at the street scenes going by, but my thoughts flashed back twelve years to my first meeting with Andrew, then to the day of his execution, and finally to the call I had just received. There in the midst of Chicago traffic, tears welled up in my eyes.

"Pull over," I exclaimed.

"What is it? What's wrong?" Dean asked, alarmed, eyes still on the traffic.
"Pull over," I said.

He did, then looked at me with concern.

I let out a deep breath, then looked at him and said that the governor wanted to see me in Springfield the next morning. When he asked me why, I told him I wasn't sure, but then it dawned on him.

"Holy crap!" he exclaimed.

If we were right, I needed to make some calls.

∞

Eight Years Earlier, January 2003

In January 2003, Rod Blagojevich was sworn in as governor. When still a gubernatorial candidate in 2002, he had expressed his views about the death penalty after the Death Penalty Moratorium Commission released its report. He was a supporter of capital punishment, he had said, but he saw many of the commission's recommendations as having merit.[1] Once he came into office, he said he would not consider lifting the moratorium Governor Ryan put in place until death penalty reforms were passed by the legislature.[2]

The new governor also saw the mixed response to blanket commutation. For instance, various leaders in Illinois had praised Governor Ryan. Jane Ramsey, executive director of the Jewish Council of Urban Affairs in Chicago said that the commutations "deserve to be applauded as an important steppingstone toward making the changes necessary to create a moral justice system in Illinois and to abolish the death penalty." I concurred, "I think we're on the threshold of a new moral awakening in this country, and the final step is abolition. . . . People are thinking differently now, and they're seeing a different side of the debate."[3] Others did not agree. The office of the Illinois Attorney General sought to prove that the blanket clemency was unconstitutional, taking the matter to the Illinois Supreme Court. However, the court confirmed the legitimacy of the former governor's action in January 2004.

In 2003, the Illinois Coalition Against the Death Penalty (ICADP) was thrilled that death row had been emptied but meanwhile kept pressing for the true prize: abolition of the death penalty. Some people, we discovered, had the misconception that former Governor George Ryan's declaring a moratorium on executions in 2000 and granting commutations in 2003 meant that the death penalty had already been abolished. Instead, soon after the commutation, prosecutors had begun to repopulate death row. The difference now was that death row inmates in Illinois were not being executed.

Representatives of the ICADP gave public presentations throughout the state letting people know that "executions could begin tomorrow" if Governor Rod Blagojevich decided they should. We urged people to demand abolition of the death penalty.[4]

In 2003, the Illinois General Assembly passed legislation reflecting some of the recommendations of the Death Penalty Moratorium Commission. This bipartisan legislation reforming capital punishment—a package of six bills developed by state lawmakers—was championed by State Senator Barack Obama of Chicago. It also created an independent Capital Punishment Reform Study Committee to study the effectiveness of the new reforms and make an annual report to the legislature. Governor Rod Blagojevich signed it.[5]

The year 2003, which had started with Governor George Ryan's issuing a historic blanket commutation for those on death row, ended with the former governor being named in a federal indictment. The charges included racketeering, bribery, extortion, money laundering, tax fraud, and more.[6]

∞

Governor Blagojevich left the moratorium in place during his first term in office, which lasted from 2003 through reelection in 2006. In 2007, when he began his second term, he continued this policy. In March of that year, the *Chicago Tribune* abandoned its long-standing pro–death penalty position, one it had promoted in its pages in 1869, 1952, and 1976. It now urged abolition of capital punishment in Illinois.[7]

In 2008, the ICADP brought in a dynamic new executive director, Jeremy Schroeder, who took a fresh approach. He secured grant funds that allowed him to commission an independent statewide poll and to hire a public relations firm.[8] The poll revealed that a majority of registered voters (more than 60 percent) preferred sentences of life without parole over the death sentence. The PR firm helped coordinate a campaign seeking editorial support from newspapers. Both efforts moved the cause of abolishing the death penalty forward. That year, for the first time ever, the Illinois State Bar Association's governing body voted eighty-two to thirty-eight in support of abolition.[9]

∞

In the years after Andrew was executed, I was interviewed on a Chicago radio talk show about the Greek Orthodox Metropolis of Chicago's advocacy to end capital punishment in the state. The host asked me, "What business does the Church have involving itself in issues like the death penalty?"

"We are simply reclaiming our historic role," I answered. I told him that for hundreds of years, the early Christian Church boldly identified with those who suffer. Jesus didn't spend his time with powerful people, and he didn't seek their approval. He was usually found among those who suffered physically or socially: he touched and healed lepers, who were outcasts; he defended a prostitute who was about to be stoned; he talked to a Samaritan woman—something that observant Jewish men did not do; he healed the child of a Roman centurion, even though the centurion represented the empire that occupied the land of Israel; he ate with tax collectors, considered traitors because they were Jews who collaborated with the Romans; he cared for a widow and a blind beggar, both of whom had terribly low social status; and he delighted in being with children, who have no power.

Jesus taught his followers to feed the hungry, clothe the naked, visit the sick and imprisoned, and welcome the stranger. After his death and resurrection, his followers obeyed his teachings, often in unconventional ways.

"As a result," I said, "many early Christians did what we refer to today as social justice. In their view, of course, it was just carrying out the message of the gospel."

"Are you saying that social justice was part of the early church?" my host asked, surprised.

"Yes," I said. When my host requested examples, I obliged.

"Hospitals and soup kitchens," I said. I told him the first hospitals on record were established by Christians. Among these was a famous one created by St. Basil, Bishop of Cappadocia, circa 370 CE. During a famine, he also created what appears to have been the first soup kitchen in history and fed the hungry of his city. I told the radio host that from the start, the early Christian Church has cared for those who suffer as part of its ministry.

"Fighting to end the death penalty today," I said, "is simply reclaiming our historic role."

∞

In 2009, Governor Rod Blagojevich was impeached, convicted, and removed from office.[10] Blagojevich's lieutenant governor, Pat Quinn, assumed the governorship that year. Governor Quinn, too, continued the moratorium on executions.

In 2010, two sisters, Jeanne Bishop and Jennifer Bishop Jenkins, added their voices to the abolition effort in Illinois. They recalled their journey of grief after the 1990 murders of their pregnant sister and her husband,

Nancy and Richard Langert, in their home in suburban Chicago. Their late sister's final message—a heart, followed by a *U*, written in Nancy's own blood at the scene of the murder—was one of love. The sisters, inspired by Nancy's example, also chose to focus on love by advocating for abolition of the death penalty.

"Nancy would never want the memorial to her life to be the death of another human being," said Jennifer Bishop Jenkins.[11]

That year, 2010, was an election year. Governor Quinn decided to run for governor.

In the Illinois General Assembly, the Capital Punishment Reform Study Committee, established by a bill passed in 2003, issued its final report that year. Among its conclusions was that the cost to the state (i.e., taxpayers) of maintaining a system of capital punishment was enormous.

Death penalty opponents had been making gradual inroads over the seven years since George Ryan left office, but we always knew that abolishing the death penalty in Illinois was never going to be a slam dunk. Since 2010 was an election year, we did not expect the passage of a bill to abolish the death penalty because no politician wanted to risk introducing a bill as controversial as that just before an election.

After the election, however, in the lame-duck session, Illinois State Representative Karen Yarbrough, who had again won her seat in the recent election, saw a window of opportunity. She aimed to get the proposal to abolish capital punishment before the Illinois House for a vote. Given that it was a lame-duck session, she could not introduce a new bill. Her only option was to attach an amendment to a bill that was already moving through the General Assembly. So she found one, a bill related to the qualifications of probation officers, and added the amendment.[12]

The amended bill was scheduled for a vote in the Illinois House on January 6, 2011. In the chamber of 118 members, Yarbrough needed sixty votes for the amended bill to pass, and in speaking with colleagues, she found them. At the eleventh hour, however, two of the representatives who had promised Representative Yarbrough that they would support it withdrew their support, and the measure failed. Yarbrough sought a reconsideration, and a second vote was held. On the second round of voting, one of the defectors relented, and two other representatives changed their votes to yes, which was enough for the measure to pass the Illinois House, sixty to fifty-four.[13]

Five days later, on January 11, the bill was voted on in the Senate, sponsored by State Senator Kwame Raoul. It passed by a vote of thirty-five to twenty-two. Senator Raoul credited a dedicated team of people for bringing abolition "ninety-nine yards downfield," allowing him to carry it the final yard. He singled out the ICADP, the Center on Wrongful Convictions, the Illinois State Bar Association, murder victims' survivors, exoneree Randy Steidl, and Representative Karen Yarbrough.[14] The abolition amendment, so significant in its consequences, was only two sentences in length:

> Beginning on the effective date of this amendatory Act of this 96th General Assembly, notwithstanding any other law to the contrary, the death penalty is abolished and a sentence to death may not be imposed.
>
> All unobligated and unexpended moneys remaining in the Capital Litigation Trust Fund on the effective date of this amendatory Act of the 96th General Assembly shall be transferred into the Death Penalty Abolition Fund, a special fund in the State treasury, to be expended by the Illinois Criminal Justice Information Authority, for services for families of victims of homicide or murder and for training of law enforcement personnel.[15]

On January 16, 2011, the bill with the abolition amendment was sent to Governor Quinn. He had sixty days to sign or veto it. If he did nothing, it would automatically go into effect on March 18, 2011.

As a result of the spotlight put on this issue for more than twelve years, public opinion—and, therefore, the opinion of many politicians—had shifted. Supporting the moratorium and abolition of capital punishment was less of a political risk now than in the past.

But for Governor Pat Quinn, it was anything but an easy decision. The governor was getting political pressure from all sides. Many of his constituents supported the idea of abolishing the death penalty, and many did not. Significantly, his attorney general, Lisa Madigan, disagreed with the idea of abolition, and so did the police.

Governor Quinn and I had met on several occasions. I had spoken to him personally in the past regarding the abolition of the death penalty, and we had developed a positive relationship. Now, some of my colleagues suggested that I go see him. I called the governor's office and made an appointment to meet with him in his Chicago office to discuss the bill.

I arrived a few minutes early at his office and was asked to wait. As the minutes passed, every ten to fifteen minutes a young staffer came out to check on me and repeatedly apologized for the long wait. I was eventually told the reason for the delay: Governor Quinn was on the phone with Archbishop Desmond Tutu, who was urging him to sign the abolition bill. Finally, about an hour after I had arrived, I was ushered into the governor's office, where an attorney joined us as a legal adviser.

The governor, referring to the death penalty legislation on his desk, said candidly, "Tell me why I should sign this." He then went over the arguments for the death penalty, raising the concerns he had heard from constituents and others. I countered each argument, drawing on the reasoning that had been developed over decades by death penalty abolition advocates and highlighting the new scientific tools that were overwhelmingly proving the injustice of the current system of execution. As we talked, the governor took notes. By the end of an intense discussion, I was tired. I got in a cab, went to the office to pick up my car, and headed home, hoping I had made a difference. The governor had until March 18 to make a decision.

※

March 9, 2011

On the morning of March 9—the day after I received the call from the governor's office—my assistant, Dean, and I drove the two hundred miles from Chicago to Springfield.

The previous day, I had spoken with Metropolitan Iakovos, Fred, Theodora, and my friends and colleagues in the world of abolition advocacy about my invitation to Springfield. They, too, were excited, and some of them had similarly been invited. Together, we were holding our collective breath.

When the silvery façade of the capitol dome came into view, the enormity of the occasion hit me full force. I all but floated up the steps of the state capitol and into the reception room of Governor Pat Quinn's office, where several other invited guests were already gathered. I exchanged greetings, smiles, and hugs with many of them, people with whom I had collaborated for years and others whom I recognized who were leaders in the cause. It was a lively and dedicated group. We had all come to the same conclusion, and a celebratory energy filled the room.

Governor Quinn was in his office, we were told.

Soon, we were ushered into a large room, where members of the media stood ready with cameras and notepads. "The governor will begin the press conference now," one of the governor's staff announced.

The governor entered the room and stood at the podium. The anticipation was intense as he looked around the room.

Governor Quinn announced that he had just signed the legislation abolishing the death penalty in Illinois. My heart leapt, and I couldn't contain a smile. Like the rest of the abolition advocates in the room, I kept quiet, even though all of us were elated. The governor explained the reasons for his decision. Then he added that he was commuting the sentences of the fifteen men on death row to life in prison without the possibility of parole.

The press asked the governor pointed questions about his decision and how he would respond to the concerns of those who supported the death penalty, including the families of victims. Many of the answers he gave were those we had discussed in our private meeting. After the press conference, people in the room joyfully celebrated, and I thanked Governor Quinn and hugged him. Representatives from various news outlets requested interviews with activists, and I was among them. I went with a group of others to a room where we were interviewed, and I took my turn at the podium.

Astonishingly, the day had finally come. That day, Illinois became the sixteenth state to abolish the death penalty.

I was honored to have been invited to attend the press conference. As the only clergy present, I stood in for a large and dedicated group of faith leaders from across several religious traditions who had worked together for years for this very outcome. Today, it had happened. I was presented with one of the pens the governor had used to sign the bill—a sacred treasure.

The movement to end the death penalty in Illinois had formally started in 1976 when the visionary Mary Alice Rankin established the Illinois Coalition Against the Death Penalty. Thirty-five years later, her goal had been achieved, and the organization she had established had played a major role. Andrew's hope, which proved to be prophetic—that God might use his execution to finally end all executions in this state—had also been fulfilled. So many people had made this day possible, and so many had cared for Andrew and his fate—Metropolitan Iakovos, Theodora, Fred, Tina, Carol, and many others. I was grateful to have been part of that history.

14

✢

An End, and a Beginning

June 2, 2017

On Friday, June 2, 2017, I was in a conference room in Plymouth, Michigan, attending a meeting of the Joint Committee of Orthodox and Roman Catholic Bishops, when I received an urgent call from Metropolitan Iakovos's nephew. I discreetly stepped out of the room and took the call.

I was told that Metropolitan Iakovos had been taken to the hospital two nights ago, on Wednesday, May 31. This was a surprise; that was the day I had left for Michigan, and he was fine when I had said goodbye to him that morning. I told the metropolitan's nephew, as well as a few of the meeting organizers, that I would be returning to Chicago immediately.

When I landed in Chicago, my assistant, William Kallas, picked me up from the airport, and we sped through the streets of Chicago. We arrived at the hospital to find the metropolitan unconscious and his breathing labored. I was surprised to see him in this weakened condition. Even in his eighties, he was fit. In his room were Fred Chapekis, his personal lawyer; Fred's wife, Tina; Deacon Chris Avramopoulos, his deacon; and his nephew. They told me that Metropolitan Iakovos had had emergency abdominal surgery, and his prognosis was not good. We were all stunned at the metropolitan's rapid decline.

My head was spinning. I had known Metropolitan Iakovos for thirty-seven years, and now, unexpectedly, his life was ebbing. I wasn't ready for him to go. My heart was breaking. Yet, as chancellor, I realized that it was my responsibility to help guide the metropolis through this crisis.

I called my confidante, close friend, and special assistant to the metropolitan, Father David Bissias, and asked him to meet me at the metropolis as fast as humanly possible so that we could coordinate urgent practical matters. Then, from an adjacent room at the hospital, with Fred and the metropolitan's nephew by my side, I called the archdiocese to speak with Archbishop Demetrios. The director of his office told me that the archbishop was unavailable because he was meeting with another bishop. I insisted that the matter could not wait, that I needed to speak with the archbishop urgently. When he finally came to the phone, I told him that Metropolitan Iakovos was in the hospital, dying. He was sympathetic and asked me to keep him informed. I promised I would.

I returned to the metropolitan's room, and we all gathered at his bedside. His breathing had become shallow. We had a decision to make. Do we put Metropolitan Iakovos on life support to keep him alive and hope for a miracle, or not? Fortunately, Fred produced a document signed by Metropolitan Iakovos years earlier stating that the metropolitan did not want to be kept alive artificially if there was no medically recognized chance of recovery. With that, it was out of our hands. We knew it would not be long.

I asked everyone to leave the room so that I could have a few private moments with His Eminence. He was not conscious, but I had learned that people in that condition are often able to hear. I leaned close to his ear and whispered words of gratitude, respect, and love. Through my tears, I was confident that Metropolitan Iakovos heard me.

It was already after 5:00 p.m. when I arrived at the metropolis office to meet with Father David to prepare for the inevitable. We prepared press releases, notifications to the metropolis clergy, and other necessary documents. In the midst of our work that evening, I received a call from Fred telling me the metropolitan had just died. I heard Fred's words, but it didn't seem real. I immediately returned to the hospital.

His Eminence, Metropolitan Iakovos of Chicago, died on June 2, 2017, at 9:27 p.m. at the age of eighty-nine. His deacon, Chris, and Fred and his wife, Tina, were there by his side when he stopped breathing. I arrived at the hospital just after he had passed and broke down crying. We all cried together. I offered the prayer for the separation of the soul from the body and the memorial prayers. Metropolitan Iakovos had led the metropolis for so many years. It seemed impossible that in a matter of two days, everything had changed, and he was gone.

I was crushed, trying to come to terms with his death, but I knew I had obligations to fulfill. I went to the adjacent room once again and called Archbishop Demetrios. Even though it was late, I was able to reach him on his direct office number. Through sometimes uncontrollable sobbing, I conveyed to him that the metropolitan had died. The archbishop began by offering formal words of condolence, but soon he was instructing me about the plans he and the other metropolitans had made for Metropolitan Nicholas of Detroit to temporarily oversee the Metropolis of Chicago until a new metropolitan was elected. I knew they needed to move on and make plans for succession, but in the rawness of my grief, just thirty minutes after my hierarch and mentor died, I wasn't ready. To me, it felt unloving and coldly practical, as if the metropolitan's passing were simply an administrative problem to be solved.

The succeeding days were a blur. Grief was mixed with the demands of letting people around the world—particularly his family in Greece—know of Metropolitan Iakovos's death and making funeral plans befitting the metropolitan's stature. In his thirty-eight years as bishop and then metropolitan, he had done so much good and was well loved by many people. The telephone at the metropolis rang continually, and my mailbox and email box were filled with expressions of sympathy. The pressure of responding to so many people and planning the details of the funeral demanded that I focus on the tasks before me. When I was alone, however, my sadness sometimes overwhelmed me.

The visitation and funeral services were held at the Annunciation Greek Orthodox Cathedral in downtown Chicago on Thursday, June 8, and Friday, June 9. With Archbishop Demetrios's blessings and permission, I celebrated Orthros and the Divine Liturgy, as is our custom, before the funeral service. Thus, I was able to offer my personal reflections in the form of a sermon. This gentleman, in every sense of the word, had been my mentor and spiritual father for more than half of my life.

Archbishop Demetrios, the metropolitans and bishops of the archdiocese, and other Orthodox hierarchs concelebrated the funeral service for Metropolitan Iakovos, honoring one of their own. The interment was at the Saint John Chrysostom Monastery in Pleasant Prairie, Wisconsin.

∞

For the next eight months, I worked under the temporary authority of Metropolitan Nicholas of Detroit in an administrative capacity, keeping the metropolis functioning and carrying out the day-to-day work.

On February 7, 2018, a new metropolitan of Chicago was elected.

That day, I received a call from Archbishop Demetrios informing me that after my having served at the Diocese and, later, Metropolis of Chicago for more than thirty years, my assignment had changed. I would no longer be at the Metropolis of Chicago.

His words cut me off at the knees. With the archbishop still on the line, I sat stunned at my desk, the telephone in my hand. We proceeded to have a long and difficult conversation. This wasn't planned, and my life was now in turmoil. It wasn't what I wanted nor what I and many others had anticipated. Yet I realized it was something I would have to accept. I knew that my duty was to be obedient to the archbishop. That obedience had been instilled in me by my spiritual father and mentor, Metropolitan Iakovos of blessed memory. It is at the core of what it means to be a deacon, priest, or bishop in the Church.

Archbishop Demetrios suggested that I take a sabbatical. I requested a year, and he granted it. I thanked him, hung up the phone, and tried to process what was happening.

One of my spiritual sons, John Balourdos, heard the news and soon after arrived at the metropolis. He helped me pack up my belongings from my office and put them in the car. I said goodbye to and tearfully hugged everyone at the metropolis. Then John drove me home.

∞

"Here is the key to the shrine," said the woman I had met only a day or two before. Polexeni (Polly) Maouris Hillier handed me a key on a keyring. We were sitting on a bench in the courtyard of the St. Photios Greek Orthodox National Shrine. The sky above us was clear with various sunset hues of orange and red. It was 4:15 p.m., and the day was finally cooling down.

"Thank you," I said, pocketing the key. It was October 2019.

Polly was the executive director of the St. Photios Shrine. I had been given a new assignment in St. Augustine, Florida, by our new archbishop, Archbishop Elpidophoros of America. Part of my assignment was to serve as a resource to accelerate the growth and recognition of the shrine, which was supported by Greek Orthodox faithful. It included a chapel, a museum highlighting local Greek history, and a gift shop, and it was all located within Avero House, a well-maintained historic building.

I had two other roles in St. Augustine. I was to serve as the liaison—a "bishop–ambassador"—between the Assembly of Canonical Orthodox Bishops of the United States of America and one of its agencies, the Orthodox Christian Mission Center (OCMC), which was also based in St. Augustine. The OCMC was involved with Orthodox missions around the world, and part of my work was to serve on its board. I was also tasked with initiating a new Spanish-language outreach of the Greek Orthodox Archdiocese of America, although my Spanish-language skills were limited at best.

During our meeting and tour that day, Polly told me that the Avero House, in which the shrine is located, is historically significant, one of only thirty remaining houses in the historic district that predate 1821. The

An End, and a Beginning 189

Avero House faces St. George Street, a welcoming pedestrian walkway in the St. Augustine Historic District, the most charming part of the city.

The first documented Greek immigrants to North America, Polly said, had landed in Florida on June 26, 1768, full of dreams for the future. They and hundreds of Corsicans, Italians, and Minorcans left their homelands on a convoy of eight ships seeking a new life. The Greeks, many coming from the Mani region and other regions that were brutally subjugated by the Ottoman Empire, saw the opportunity to leave for North America as a door of escape from an empire that kept the majority of its Christian subjects under its heel. They pledged years of indentured service on a British colony in North America in return for passage there and a tract of land.

Only 1,255 of the 1,403 original group members survived the ocean voyage. Once they arrived, they were assigned to the New Smyrna Colony. Conditions there were so unbearable that in 1777, approximately six hundred colonists walked and swam seventy-five miles north to St. Augustine. The Greeks established a community there, and under the British (and later, the Spaniards), who ruled St. Augustine, they were allowed to hold liturgical services and socialize in Avero House. Some of the Greeks still lived in St. Augustine in 1822 when Florida became part of the United States. In 1965, the Greek Orthodox Archdiocese purchased the Avero House and later converted it into the St. Photios Shrine. It seemed a fitting way to commemorate the Greeks who were part of St. Augustine, itself the oldest continuously inhabited city in the United States.

"How many Greek Americans live in St. Augustine these days?" I asked Polly.

"Not a lot, but the Orthodox Christian community here is growing," she said and explained that over the previous two hundred years, much of the Greek population had moved on, seeking opportunities elsewhere. The first Greek Orthodox parish opened in St. Augustine in 1976. In 2007, a new church, Holy Trinity, was built.

In my new role in St. Augustine, I had almost no liturgical responsibilities. As a result, I felt starved because I missed serving the liturgy. I worked hard at the shrine, but it didn't feel like the type of work that made the best use of my abilities, interests, talents, and skills. The truth is, I felt sad and irrelevant, like a fish out of water. I missed Chicago: the culture—the opera, the theater, the restaurants, the Greek Orthodox community, the vibrant mix of various ethnic communities, and the interfaith and ecumenical engagements and friendships—and above all, the people I loved. I missed liturgical life and work in the field of social justice, the rough-and-tumble of Chicago, and my family and friends.

St. Augustine, Florida, had a population of fifteen thousand. It enjoyed a tropical climate, was beautifully situated right on the Atlantic Ocean, and was a popular vacation getaway. Yet, for me, it felt like exile.

That said, my duty was to obey our new Archbishop Elpidophoros, who had assigned me here. This was my job, so I poured myself into it.

I am grateful to say that the work was fruitful. I worked hard to increase the shrine's social media presence, and this also increased foot traffic to the shrine. We created a video in partnership with a Jacksonville-based marketing and production company, Spectrum Films, that told the story of the first Greek immigrants who arrived on the Florida shores. It won three national film awards. One year, we enhanced the annual celebration of "Greek Landing Day," even being interviewed about it on a New York radio station. We expanded our outreach to the local media and the local clergy—including the Roman Catholic bishop of St. Augustine. We increasingly made the shrine a place vibrant with Greek Orthodox faith. We wanted those who lived in St. Augustine to rediscover us and wanted an even greater number of those who visited St. Augustine from around the world to discover Greek history and Greek Orthodoxy's deep roots in the United States.

However, when I sat on my porch after work and looked out at the ocean, I often found myself wondering, with some sadness, *Aside from helping promote and grow a Greek Orthodox shrine, what is my priestly ministry here? What am I doing here?*

Chicago felt very far away.

☙

Beginning in 2021, with the blessing of Archbishop Elpidophoros, I was allowed, for one week each year, to carry a blissful burden of liturgical responsibility on my shoulders: I was assigned to celebrate Holy Week and Pascha (Easter) services in New York City and the surrounding area—the district that the archbishop himself oversees. This meant that for eight days I would move from city to city, celebrating Lazarus Saturday, Palm Sunday, then each of the beautiful and agony-filled daily services that lead up to Pascha and finally, Pascha itself.

Just before Holy Week in 2022, I boarded a plane in Jacksonville, Florida. Of course, I knew I wouldn't see my family at Pascha, and I wouldn't see my home city. I had once felt fruitful in a divine orchard, doing the work of the Church—working toward social change—at the Metropolis of Chicago. Now I was an outsider, "useful" to the Church but an afterthought. As I received my bag of peanuts and first beverage from the flight attendant, I found myself thinking back to Bob and Andrew. Meeting them had changed my life: Bob, whom I met when I was still a wet-behind-the-ears priest, and Andrew, whom I visited when I was a more seasoned priest, responding to a request from Theodora, a woman of faith.

When as an altar boy all those years ago I had first approached Bishop Iakovos, I had so wanted to serve God. It was at the altar that I felt at home, in the splendor of the liturgy, surrounded by ancient Byzantine chants and meaningful gospel readings. It was a world of deep mystery, one that drew me in a powerful way, and it was also safe and insular. Despite my parents' misgivings (and with their financial support), I had gone to seminary.

During seven years of study, my original vision of ministry—to be a parish priest—had changed drastically. While employed at the diocese during summers and holidays since I was nineteen, I discovered a new aspect of my calling: I had a gift for administration. Out of this experience emerged the idea of serving as an administrative priest. I still served God at the altar on Sundays—which I treasured—but I mostly served Him in the offices of the diocese during the workweek. I must admit, that work didn't seem very spiritual, though it was rewarding in its own right.

Then Bob called. I had had no idea when I woke up that morning that encountering him face-to-face would fill me with compassion for him and pull me out of the office and into the world. Yet that single meeting with a man living with HIV/AIDS propelled the creation of a new ministry. The Bishop's Task Force on AIDS served Bob and other people, so many of whom were suffering.

When Theodora had called years later and asked me to visit Andrew, I encountered a bald, shackled, friendly man in the Pontiac Correctional Center, and my heart was moved when I saw his suffering. Compassion for Andrew prompted me to do all I could to save his life and, later, to seek the end of the death penalty in Illinois.

In both instances, I came to understand my ministry in a new and unexpected way. To paraphrase Immanuel Kant, I was "awakened from my dogmatic slumber."[1] That's how it felt for me. My ministry, I discovered, was not only to celebrate the divine services and to be an administrator, but also to serve the suffering and marginalized out in the world and to bring about social change. That was my ministry for twenty-six years.

Until it wasn't.

I once had such high expectations, but now, I was a bishop in exile. I looked out the airplane window and wondered, *What is my ministry now?*

Overhead, I heard the pilot's voice telling us we were beginning our descent. Our plane would soon touch down, so I readied myself to disembark.

It was Holy Monday, 2022. I had already been at two different parishes in Queens, New York, in the two previous days, and now I was on my way to a third. The man who had volunteered to drive me each day, a talkative man named Basil, pulled the car up to the church and helped me carry my liturgical bags inside.

The first days of Holy Week had rejuvenated me. The priests and parishioners welcomed me warmly. I knew that for them, it was both an honor and a challenge to host a bishop. A bishop's presence modified the service and the role of the priest, and it made most priests, chanters, and altar boys a little anxious. So I did my best to alleviate their anxiety by intentionally being affable. After all, I was just as nervous as they were since I'd never met these people before. I was a stranger among strangers.

During each service, I reveled in the magnificence and joy of serving at the altar and being among parishioners. Holy Week features its own special music, and hearing and chanting it in this holy season lifted my heart. At each service, I offered a brief homily. Afterward, I was treated as a special guest and was often invited into the parish social hall to share a light Lenten meal with the priest and members of the parish council. This was deeply touching. Each parish had its own character. Some were large, and others were more modest in size. Some priests were young, with small children, and others were older and more established. What was consistent was the warmth and piety that I encountered.

After Holy Monday services and before we had sat down for the meal, Basil whispered in my ear and asked if I would briefly speak with someone who wanted to see me.

"Of course I will," I said.

∞

A man who attended church that evening had been wanting to go to confession for some time. He'd considered the possibility of confessing to a couple of different priests, but somehow, he hadn't felt comfortable. When he heard me give a homily that night, something about how I spoke and what I said appealed to him. As he sat in the pew listening, he reflected on how hard the last year had been. He knew he needed to sort out his life and his relationship with God. After the service he had gone outside to his car and called a friend. He mentioned that he had just heard a bishop speak and had felt like he should speak to him.

"Then you should go speak with him," his friend had encouraged him. "He's there now; go talk to him." Ten minutes after walking out of the church, he was walking back in.

Basil, my volunteer driver, gestured to a middle-aged gentleman. The man approached me, and we went to one side of the social hall to speak. He kissed my hand in traditional fashion.

"I have to talk to you, Your Grace," he said. "Everyone says yes to God, but they don't do His will—and I am the biggest hypocrite of all. I really need to come to confession. Would you hear my confession?"

"But I'm located in St. Augustine, Florida. You would have to come there. Can you?" I asked.

"Yes, of course, Your Grace," he said. I gave him my business card, and he kissed my hand again and promised to be in touch.

The rest of the week was a mix of ecstasy and pain as we recalled Christ's obedient journey to the cross and a joyful celebration of His triumph over death. Basil was my kind companion each day, arriving to pick me up and bring me back. I had the great pleasure of staying in the home of a dear friend and mentor, Father Eugene Pappas, and when Pascha came, I was graciously included in his family's celebration. It was nice to be in the orbit of a large East Coast city and to encounter the sometimes-brash elements of city life. It reminded me of Chicago. When I returned to St. Augustine, I felt the joy of the resurrection. It had been a good week.

I answered the phone a couple of weeks after Holy Week, and it was the man from Queens. We arranged for him to come see me on the morning of the feast day of St. Augustine, June 15,[2] one of the rare days I could celebrate Divine Liturgy in the chapel. Since many people were visiting the shrine and the chapel that day, Polly let us use her office for his confession. I put on my bishop's stole, and we stood before an icon of Christ.

"Are you ready?" I asked.

"Yes," he said.

I offered the opening prayers, then turned to him and said the traditional words, "My brother, do not be ashamed to relate to God, before me, all that you came to tell; because you are not telling these things to me but to God, before whom you stand."

He began to tell his story, and as he did, his eyes filled with tears. I listened. For the better part of an hour, he poured out his heart and expressed the pain, guilt, and sorrow that he had kept pent up for so many years. He had come home one day to find that his mother, who lived with him, had died. Years before, he and his wife had divorced. He expressed deep pain over the loss of his marriage. He was sad that it had ended as it had and that he had hurt his wife and their children. He felt responsible—not for all of it, but for his part in it. He hadn't ever gone to spiritual court (where he would explain what happened in their marriage to a group of priests who would grant him an ecclesiastical, or spiritual, divorce). It just seemed too hard, even embarrassing, to do. But as a result, he couldn't receive Holy Communion and he didn't go to confession. Especially after the death of his mother, these things weighed on his heart.

Anyone looking at him would conclude that he was successful and had his act together. The truth was, he said, he felt very far from God, disconnected from Him. He wanted to put things right again in his life.

When he was done, we talked. I asked him questions about himself, and he answered. He asked me questions about faith and life and God, and I answered. Then I put the end of my stole on his head and prayed the prayer of absolution, asking that God would forgive him. When I lifted my stole from his head, I saw tears and relief on his face. He had experienced the life-changing power of divine mercy and forgiveness. As an act of pastoral compassion, I directed him to receive Holy Communion that day in the chapel and to obtain an ecclesiastical divorce. I told him I was glad he had come, embraced him, and kissed him on both cheeks in the traditional Greek manner. He kissed my hand.

"Thank you, Your Grace," he said, smiling and wiping the tears from his face. I took off my stole, and we walked out of the office and down to the chapel, where people were already beginning to assemble.

I celebrated the Divine Liturgy that morning. The casual observer could be forgiven for not recognizing a miracle: a man standing in line and receiving Holy Communion. After years of separation, longing, and brokenness, his relationship with God had been restored. For him, it was the beginning of what has proven to be a renewed, faith-filled walk with Christ.

For me, it was yet another epiphany. There in the tiny chapel of the St. Photios Shrine, with the morning sun streaming through the windows, I understood. *This, too, is why I became a priest.*

Epilogue

The official announcement of my retirement from active ministry was publicized on March 15, 2023. Soon after, I flew to Greece for a holiday. I looked out my window and saw white clouds below. My thoughts drifted to the English mountaineer, George Mallory, who made the first modern attempts to ascend Mount Everest. To the question, "Why do you want to climb Mount Everest?" he famously responded, "Because it is there."[1] Mallory's dedication to his purpose kept him going and inspired, even when his circumstances were unbelievably grim and deeply discouraging. One day he wrote in his diary, "I look back on tremendous effort and exhaustion and dismal looking out of a tent door into a world of snow and vanishing hopes—and yet, and yet, and yet there have been a good many things to set on the other side."[2]

In my experience, the struggle for social justice and the affirmation of human life often feels like an attempt to ascend a high, seemingly unscalable mountain. The challenge doesn't stop us, though, just as it didn't stop Mallory. We must keep trying.

Life is a precious gift. My religious tradition, Orthodox Christianity, teaches that we have a sacred responsibility to affirm life, all life. It is a responsibility to work toward a life-affirming, just society in the here and now. What does that look like?

One of the things I have learned is that love is not a mere humanitarian concern for abstract justice and the anonymous poor but, rather, concrete and personal care for each person whom God allows us to encounter in our daily lives. The things that Jesus emphasizes—giving a hungry person a meal or a thirsty person a drink, welcoming a stranger, cheering the sick, and visiting the prisoner—are things that anyone can do. It is helping for no reason but for the sake of helping the person in front of us. It is putting love into action.

George Mallory died on his third expedition to Mount Everest, and the debate continues as to whether he ever reached the summit.[3] Like his expeditions, the ascent to a better world often entails a tremendous effort, exhaustion, and a dismal view of vanishing hope by those seeking to right the wrongs of the world. In my life's journey, I started in a small, safe, comfortable place, worshipping with others of my faith tradition and managing administrative responsibilities (all of which was good and necessary). Gradually, I moved into a larger space that was riskier and less comfortable. I worked with and learned from those from different faith traditions and began to identify with the marginalized and the suffering and to advocate for them. Not only did I seek justice for them, but I also strived for something deeper—mercy and compassion.

Through struggles, triumphs, and sacrifices, and by putting love into action, we can find the more excellent way.[4] Thus, all may become true agents of change. It is daunting and yet . . .

Every new beginning comes from some other beginning's end.
  —Attributed to Lucius Annaeus Seneca (ca. 4 BC–65 AD)

Notes

CHAPTER 1

1. One of Fred's law partners, Tina, and other members of his firm also served pro bono as legal counsel to the diocese.

2. Denise Crosby, "Thomas Kokoraleis, Ripper Crew killer released from prison: 'I want to go on with my life and be left alone,'" *Chicago Tribune*, April 4, 2019.

3. In the administrative structure of the Greek Orthodox Church, the chancellor is second in command to the ruling hierarch.

4. "The Orthodox Church rejects capital punishment and does so out of faithfulness to the Gospel and to the example of the Apostolic Church. It upholds the laws of forgiveness and reconciliation as the chief imperatives of Christian culture, while ever pointing to the potential and promise of transformation in Christ. The Church insists upon the responsibility of all governments to limit violence in every way that they can. Inasmuch as capital punishment returns evil for evil, it cannot be considered a virtuous or even tolerable practice. While some might seek to justify the death penalty as an expression of proportional justice, Christians may not adopt such a logic. In the Gospels, Christ repeatedly rejects the very principle of proportionality. He requires of his followers a rule of forgiveness that not only exceeds the demands of 'natural' justice, but that even sets the wrath of the law aside in favor of its own much deeper logic of mercy (as in the case of the woman taken in adultery)." From "For the Life of the World: Toward a Social Ethos of the Orthodox Church," Chapter 48, Greek Orthodox Archdiocese of America, accessed December 12, 2023, https://www.goarch.org/social-ethos.

5. On June 15, 1779, a man, identified only as Manuel, was tied to a stake, and someone lit the woodpile at his feet. He went up in flames, punished for the crime of witchcraft. Death Penalty Information Center, accessed May 1, 2023,

https://www.deathpenaltyinfo.org/executions/executions-overview/; https://www.deathpenaltyinfo.org/executions/executions-overview/executions-by-state-and-year/.

6. Of the fifty-eight parishes of the Greek Orthodox Metropolis (formerly Diocese) of Chicago, seven are in Chicago proper and eighteen in the suburbs. There are about 250,000 faithful in Chicagoland.

7. Later, it was discovered that Carole Pappas had driven into a lake and drowned.

8. Her name has been changed.

9. "Timeline: Sadistic exploits, innocent victims of the Ripper Crew," *Chicago Tribune*, November 7, 1982, accessed December 13, 2023, https://www.chicagotribune.com/2019/03/29/timeline-sadistic-exploits-innocent-victims-of-the-ripper-crew/.

CHAPTER 2

1. Pronounced PAH-skuh. There is no equivalent word for "Easter" in Greek (Πάσχα) since the word "Easter" is the Anglo-Saxon name for a pagan festival held in honor of the Teutonic goddess Eastra or Ostara. The word "Pascha" is derived from the Jewish word "Pesach," which means "Passover."

2. An icon is a mural, mosaic, or painting on wood representing a sacred event or sacred individual—a "window on heaven"—that is venerated by Orthodox Christians.

3. Eggs that have been dyed red are blessed at the end of the Easter (Pascha) service. The red color symbolizes the blood and sacrifice of Christ on the cross, whose resurrection is celebrated on Pascha. The hard shell represents the sealed tomb of Jesus—the cracking of which symbolizes His resurrection from the dead and exit from the tomb.

CHAPTER 3

1. Andrew told me that his coerced confession was beaten out of him by the same police officers who had beaten out a confession from Rolando Cruz, an innocent man who was also convicted of murder and imprisoned on death row.

In Cruz's case, detectives falsely claimed that Cruz revealed details of the crime that only someone who took part in it would know. A high-ranking police officer later admitted that he had testified falsely and acknowledged that Cruz had never made the inculpatory statement that detectives had formerly attributed to him. Innocent of the charges, Cruz was finally set free in 1995. From Rob Warden, "How and Why Illinois Abolished the Death Penalty," *Law & Inequality: A Journal of Theory and Practice* 30 (2012): 249.

2. *People v. Kokoraleis*, 132 Ill. 2d 235, 547 N.E.2d 202 (Ill. 1989), 251–54.

3. "A 21-year-old man, suspected in the mutilation slayings of . . ." UPI Archives, February 12, 1985, accessed December 13, 2023, https://www.upi.com/

Archives/1985/02/12/A-21-year-old-man-suspected-in-the-mutilation-slayings-of/3621477032400/.

4. Dee Longfellow, "Villa Park man who murdered Elmhurst woman likely to be released," *Bensenville Independent*, November 2, 2017, front page, https://issuu.com/southernlakesnewspapersllc/docs/bi_11.2.17.

5. "Gecht has never confessed to a killing, and prosecutors have been unable to charge him with murder because his alleged accomplices have refused to testify against him." From Eric Zorn, "Sentence of death may aid 2d case," *Chicago Tribune*, March 21, 1986.

CHAPTER 4

1. Now Bishop Andonios of Phasiane.
2. As of this writing, Father Manuel Burdusi of Lanham, Maryland.
3. "The 'Mass,' a term taken from the final words of the Catholic liturgy in Latin, *ite, missa est* (literally, 'go, you are sent'), is used only by Catholics. Eastern Christians use the term Divine Liturgy." From Father David Endres, "The Divine Liturgy and the Mass. What's the difference?" *Catholic Digest*, accessed October 21, 2024, https://www.catholicdigest.com/from-the-magazine/outside-perspectives/the-divine-liturgy-and-the-mass/#:~:text=For%20one%20example%2C%20the%20terminology,use%20the%20term%20Divine%20Liturgy/.
4. The *exorasson* is also worn by laypeople when functioning in a liturgical role, such as reading or chanting.
5. This is known as the Schism of 1054 (alternately, the Great Schism).
6. The Greek Orthodox Archdiocese of America (formerly known as the Greek Orthodox Archdiocese of North and South America, 1922–1996) is composed of an Archdiocesan District (New York) and eight metropolises: Boston, Atlanta, Detroit, Pittsburgh, San Francisco, New Jersey, Chicago, and Denver. It is governed by the Eparchial Synod of Bishops (the council comprising the archbishop and the eight metropolitans, which is headed by the archbishop).

There are 540 parishes, 800 priests, and approximately 1.5 million faithful in the Greek Orthodox Archdiocese of America. Its headquarters is located in New York City.

The Greek Orthodox Archdiocese of America is a province under the spiritual authority of the Ecumenical Patriarchate of Constantinople (Istanbul, Turkey). Source: Greek Orthodox Archdiocese of America, https://www.goarch.org/about.

7. As of this writing, Metropolitan Isaiah of Denver.
8. Philoptochos means "friends of the poor."

CHAPTER 5

1. Sharman Stein, "Police union to fight ruling in brutality case," *Chicago Tribune*, February 13, 1993, p. 5.
2. Matt O'Connor, "Judge Maloney found guilty in corruption case," *Chicago Tribune*, April 17, 1993, pp. 1, 6.

3. Glen Elsasser and Judy Peres, "Death Row inmate wins appeal over judge's bribe," *Chicago Tribune*, June 10, 1997, pp. 1, 20.

4. The one exception is that the American Bar Association's policy has long stated that offenders who are persons with intellectual disabilities or were under age eighteen when they committed their crime should not be executed.

5. Associated Press, "Lawyers' group takes on death penalty; current system called 'unfair,'" *El Paso Times*, February 3, 1997, p. 1.

6. Henry Weinstein, "Bar Association Calls for a Halt to Executions," *Los Angeles Times*, February 4, 1997, pp. 1, 11.

7. "Innocence and the Death Penalty: The Increasing Danger of Executing the Innocent," Death Penalty Information Center, published July 1, 1997, accessed April 2, 2024, https://deathpenaltyinfo.org/facts-and-research/dpic-reports/in-depth/innocence-and-the-death-penalty-the-increasing-danger-of-executing-the-innocent/.

8. Norman Alexandroff, "'Thank God for Mike Falconer': A Prosecutor Testifies for the Defense—and Saves Two Innocent Men from Death Row," *Chicago Lawyer*, February 1987, p. 1. Cobb and Tillis were among those sentenced to death by disgraced judge Thomas Maloney.

9. George H. Ryan Sr., with Maurice Possley, *Until I Could Be Sure* (New York: Rowman & Littlefield, 2020), 8–9.

10. Peter Rooney, "Chance at Trial: 'New Lease on Life' for Burrows, *Champaign News-Gazette*, May 15, 1994, p. A1.

11. "Innocence and the Death Penalty."

12. Rob Warden, "How and Why Illinois Abolished the Death Penalty," *Minnesota Journal of Law & Inequality: A Journal of Theory and Practice* 30 (2012): 249.

13. Don Terry, "DNA Tests and a Confession Set Three on the Path to Freedom in 1978 Murders," *New York Times*, June 15, 1996, p. A6, accessed April 23, 2024, https://dpic-cdn.org/production/legacy/DNA1978.pdf.

14. Dave Daley, "Biker is convicted of '93 killings of Richmond couple," *Chicago Tribune*, June 16, 2000, p. 199, accessed April 22, 2024, https://www.newspapers.com/image/169534185/?match=1&terms=%22Biker%22/.

15. Warden, "How and Why Illinois Abolished the Death Penalty," 251–52.

16. Don Terry, "Survivors Make the Case Against Death Row," *New York Times*, November 16, 1998, accessed May 18, 2024, https://www.nytimes.com/1998/11/16/us/survivors-make-the-case-against-death-row.html/.

17. Warden, "How and Why Illinois Abolished the Death Penalty," 253.

18. Terry, "Survivors Make the Case Against Death Row."

19. In 1997, according to a Gallup Poll, Americans approved of capital punishment by a margin of more than two to one. "Are You in Favor of the Death Penalty for a Person Convicted of Murder?" Gallup Poll, 1997, accessed January 23, 2024, http://www.gallup.com/poll/1606/death-penalty.asps/.

20. Ryan, *Until I Could Be Sure*, 17.

21. Ken Armstrong and Maurice Possley, "Part 1, The verdict: Dishonor," *Chicago Tribune*, published January 10, 1999, modified May 13, 2019, https://www.chicagotribune.com/1999/01/11/part-1-the-verdict-dishonor/.

22. Warden, "How and Why Illinois Abolished the Death Penalty," 256.

23. Christi Parson, "Court stalls execution, asks if killer is smart enough to die," *Chicago Tribune*, September 22, 1998, pp. 1, 64.

24. Warden, "How and Why Illinois Abolished the Death Penalty," 256–57.

25. Rick Pearson and Cornelia Grumman, "A Change of Heart on Execution Cases," *Chicago Tribune*, February 11, 1999, p. 1.

26. Ryan, *Until I Could Be Sure*, 22.

27. Editorial, "Fatal Flaws of Capital Punishment," *Chicago Tribune*, February 12, 1999, p. 26.

28. Lorin Granger, "Cases in Brief: Furman v. Georgia with Carol Steiker," Harvard Law Today, published August 15, 2022, accessed April 15, 2024, https://hls.harvard.edu/today/cases-in-brief-furman-v-georgia-with-carol-steiker/#:~:text=Georgia%2C%20a%201972%20landmark%20Supreme,for%20a%20four%2Dyear%20period/.

29. "Death penalty opponent Mary Alice Rankin, 73," obituary in *Chicago Tribune*, September 11, 1990.

30. Eric Zorn, "Deserving death doesn't justify death penalty," *Chicago Tribune*, March 1, 1999, p. 101, accessed February 25, 2024, https://www.newspapers.com/image/168859833/?terms=Andrew%20Kokoraleis&match=1/.

31. *People v. Kokoraleis*, 149 Ill. App. 3d 1000, 501 N.E.2d 207 (Ill. App. Ct. 1986), 1013.

32. Jaye Slade Fletcher, *Deadly Thrills* (New York: Onyx, Penguin Books, 1995), 55.

33. Bonita Brodt, "Police investigate tips of 'Manson'-like mastermind in 'Ripper' murders," *Chicago Tribune*, November 21, 1982, Section 1, p. 8.

34. Eric Zorn, "Sentence of death may aid 2d case," *Chicago Tribune*, March 21, 1986.

35. "A man described as 'Robin the Ripper,' suspected along . . . ," UPI, November 11, 1982.

36. Brodt, "Police investigate tips of 'Manson'-like mastermind in 'Ripper' murders."

37. *People v. Kokoraleis*, 132 Ill. 2d 235, 547 N.E.2d 202 (Ill. 1989), 251.

38. Brodt, "Police investigate tips of 'Manson'-like mastermind in 'Ripper' murders."

39. Edward Baumann and John O'Brien, "Trail's End," *Chicago Tribune*, October 12, 1987.

40. Brodt, "Police investigate tips of 'Manson'-like mastermind in 'Ripper' murders."

41. *People v. Kokoraleis*, 132 Ill. 2d 235, 547 N.E.2d 202 (Ill. 1989), 251–53.

42. A psychological assessment of Andrew by Dr. Robert Miller, psychiatrist, introduced by Andrew's attorneys, Alan M. Freedman, Bruce H. Bornstein, and Jane Raley, concluded that the death of Andrew's mother, coupled with the rigid and detached personality of his father, rendered the defendant "psychologically adrift," leaving him vulnerable to the influence of Robin Gecht. *People v. Kokoraleis*, 159 Ill. 2d 325, 637 N.E.2d 1015 (Ill. 1994), 1017–18.

43. Fletcher, *Deadly Thrills*, 63–64.

44. Brodt, "Police investigate tips of 'Manson'-like mastermind in 'Ripper' murders"; Fletcher, *Deadly Thrills*, 143–45.

45. "A man described as 'Robin the Ripper,' suspected along . . . ," November 11, 1982, UPI Archives, accessed March 4, 2024, https://www.upi.com/amp/Archives/1982/11/11/A-man-described-as-Robin-the-Ripper-suspected along/9665405838800/; Marianne Taylor, "Gecht guilty of cutting, rape of teen," *Chicago Tribune*, September 30, 1983, p. 27; Fletcher, *Deadly Thrills*, 215.

46. Brodt, "Police investigate tips of 'Manson'-like mastermind in 'Ripper' murders."

47. Gustav Niebuhr, "Governor Grants Pope's Plea For Life of a Missouri Inmate," *New York Times*, January 29, 1999, Section A, p. 1, accessed March 22, 2024, https://www.nytimes.com/1999/01/29/us/governor-grants-pope-s-plea-for-life-of-a-missouri-inmate.html#after-story-ad-2.

48. "Jesus left that place and went away to the district of Tyre and Sidon. Just then a Canaanite woman from that region came out and started shouting, 'Have mercy on me, Lord, Son of David; my daughter is tormented by a demon.' But he did not answer her at all. And his disciples came and urged him, saying, 'Send her away, for she keeps shouting after us.' He answered, 'I was sent only to the lost sheep of the house of Israel.' But she came and knelt before him, saying, 'Lord, help me.' He answered, 'It is not fair to take the children's food and throw it to the dogs.' She said, 'Yes, Lord, yet even the dogs eat the crumbs that fall from their masters' table.' Then Jesus answered her, 'Woman, great is your faith! Let it be done for you as you wish.' And her daughter was healed instantly." (Matthew 15:21–28, NRSV).

CHAPTER 6

1. "Bob" is the diminutive of his baptismal name, Haralambos.

2. Michael S. Gottlieb et al., "*Pneumocystis* Pneumonia – Los Angeles," *Morbidity and Mortality Weekly Report* 30, no. 21 (1981, June 5): 1–3.

3. A. Friedman-Kien et al., "Kaposi's Sarcoma and *Pneumocystis* Pneumonia Among Homosexual Men—New York City and California," *Morbidity and Mortality Weekly Report* 30, no. 25 (1981, July 3): 305–308.

4. Lawrence Altman, "Rare Cancer Seen in 41 Homosexuals," *New York Times*, July 3, 1981.

5. S. Fannin et al., "A Cluster of Kaposi's Sarcoma and *Pneumocystis carinii* Pneumonia among Homosexual Male Residents of Los Angeles and Orange Counties, California," *Morbidity and Mortality Weekly Report* 31, no. 23 (1982, June 18): 305–307.

6. "HIV/AIDS Timeline: 1981," New York City AIDS Memorial, accessed February 13, 2023, https://www.nycaidsmemorial.org/timeline.

7. Maia Szalavitz, "*How to Survive a Plague*: Q&A with Act-Up's Peter Staley on Effective Activism," *Time*, September 27, 2012, accessed February 19, 2023, https://healthland.time.com/2012/09/27/how-to-survive-a-plague-qa-with-act-ups-peter-staley-on-effective-activism/.

8. *Understanding AIDS: A Message From The Surgeon General*, 1988, 2–3, https://stacks.cdc.gov/view/cdc/6927.

Notes 205

CHAPTER 7

1. Richard Goldstein, "Ryan meets death penalty protesters at Murphysboro," *Southern Illinoisan*, March 6, 1999, p. 2, accessed February 15, 2024, https://newspapers.com/image/85492148/.
2. "Postpone execution," *Chicago Tribune*, March 6, 1999, p. 19, accessed February 25, 2024, written by Ed McManus, Chairman, Committee on the Death Penalty, Chicago Council of Lawyers and the Appleseed Fund for Justice, http://www.newspapers.com/image/168861270/?terms=Andrew%20Kokoraleis&match=1.
3. "Bar association recommends case-by-case review of Illinois executions," *Taylorville Daily Breeze Courier*, March 10, 1999, p. 10.
4. Thomas Beaumont, "Judge won't allow new evidence in murder," *Southern Illinoisan*, March 10, 1999, p. 4A.
5. Jaye Slade Fletcher, *Deadly Thrills* (New York: Onyx, Penguin Books, 1995).
6. Beaumont, "Judge won't allow new evidence in murder."
7. "Bar association recommends case-by-case review of Illinois executions."
8. George H. Ryan Sr., with Maurice Possley, *Until I Could Be Sure* (Lanham, MD: Rowman & Littlefield, 2020), 36.
9. "Lawyers press Ryan for a new study on death penalty—and a moratorium," *Chicago Tribune*, March 11, 1999, p. 209.
10. "Attorneys say Kokoraleis is innocent of murder for which he's condemned," *The Taylorville Daily Breeze Courier*, March 12, 1999, p. 16.
11. "Attorneys say Kokoraleis innocent of murder for which he is condemned," *Journal Gazette*, March 12, 1999, p. 7.
12. John O'Connor, "State Supreme Court denies final appeal by Kokoraleis," *Journal Gazette*, March 13, 1999, p. 8.
13. *People v. Kokoraleis*, 65229, 72862, and 87168, 707 N.E.2d 978 (Ill. 1999).
14. Steve Kloehn, "New Episcopal bishop decries death penalty: Cleric joins in protest of execution," *Chicago Tribune*, March 13, 1999, p. 42.

CHAPTER 8

1. "Current Trends Mortality Attributable to HIV Infection/AIDS—United States, 1981–1990," *Morbidity and Mortality Weekly Report* 40, no. 3 (1991, January 25): 41–44, accessed November 20, 2023, https://www.cdc.gov/mmwr/preview/mmwrhtml/00001880.html/.
2. "HIV and AIDS—United States, 1981–2000," *Morbidity and Mortality Weekly Report* 50, no. 21 (2001, June 1): 430–34, accessed November 20, 2023, https://www.cdc.gov/mmwr/preview/mmwrhtml/mm5021a2.html/.
3. "1990 Talk Show with ACT UP: Larry Kramer, Mark Harrington, Peter Staley, Ann Northrop, Robert Garcia," video 46:00, accessed January 4, 2024, https://www.google.com/search?q=Phil+Donahue+Show%2C+1990%2C+featuring+Larry+Kramer+of+ACT+UP&rlz=1C5CHFA_enUS883US883&oq=Phil+Donahue+Show%2C+1990%2C+featuring+Larry+Kramer+of+ACT+UP&gs_lcrp=EgZjaHJvbWUyBggAEEUYOTIHCAEQIRirAjIHCAIQIRirAtIBCTE

2OTMxajFqN6gCALACAA&sourceid=chrome&ie=UTF-8#fpstate=ive&vld=cid:1d505185,vid:JDA0NShQL8s,st:0/.

4. "AIDS Activists Stage Protest," *The Dispatch* (Lexington, NC), April 26, 1989, accessed January 5, 2024, https://news.google.com/newspapers?nid=1734&dat=19890426&id=K1McAAAAIBAJ&pg=6752,6087718/.

5. "ACT UP Demonstrations on Wall Street," NYC LGBT Historic Sites Project, accessed June 28, 2024, https://www.nyclgbtsites.org/site/act-up-demonstration-at-the-new-york-stock-exchange/; "AIDS Activists Take Aim At Gilead To Lower Price Of HIV Drug PrEP," Shots: Health News from NPR, May 30, 2019, accessed January 17, 2024, https://www.npr.org/sections/health-shots/2019/05/30/727731380/old-fight-new-front-aids-activists-want-lower-drug-prices-now#:~:text=And%20we%20threw%20out%20fake,after%20that%2C%22%20Staley%20says; "ACT UP Capsule History 1989," ACT UP Historical Archive, accessed January 16, 2024, https://actupny.org/documents/cron-89.html/.

6. Philip J. Hilts, "AIDS Drug's Maker Cuts Price By 20%," *New York Times*, September 19, 1989, accessed June 28, 2024, https://www.nytimes.com/1989/09/19/us/aids-drug-s-maker-cuts-price-by-20.html/; Jennifer Kabat, "Never Enough: AIDS activism now and then – 25 years of ACT UP and Gran Fury," *Frieze* 149 (September 1, 2012), accessed October 22, 2024, https://www.frieze.com/article/never-enough/.

7. "111 Held in St. Patrick's AIDS Protest," *New York Times*, December 11, 1989, accessed January 5, 2024, https://www.nytimes.com/1989/12/11/nyregion/111-held-in-st-patrick-s-,-protest.html/.

8. Veronica T. Jennings and Malcolm Gladwell, "1,000 Rally for More Vigorous AIDS Effort," *Washington Post*, May 22, 1990, accessed January 5, 2024, https://www.washingtonpost.com/archive/local/1990/05/22/1000-rally-for-more-vigorous-aids-effort/6874f3c6-0732-46d8-9829-c2540f47a010/; "Storm the NIH," ACT UP Oral History Project, accessed January 5, 2024, https://actuporalhistory.org/actions/storm-the-nih/.

9. Jack Houston and John Kass, "129 Seized in Downtown AIDS Protest," *Chicago Tribune*, April 24, 1990, accessed January 19, 2024, https://www.chicagotribune.com/news/ct-xpm-1990-04-24-9002020963-story.html.

10. Rebecca Makkai, "They Were Warriors," *Chicago*, April 7, 2020, accessed January 5, 2024, https://www.chicagomag.com/chicago-magazine/may-2020/oral-history-act-up-chicago-aids/.

11. Later, the name was changed to Test Positive Aware Network (TPAN).

12. A small, sometimes laminated, card with an image of a saint or scene from scripture portrayed, and often with a prayer on the reverse side of it.

13. Father Kyprianos Bouboutsis died on December 6, 2019.

14. Father George Kaloudis died on November 13, 2024.

15. In Greek Orthodox tradition, a metropolitan is a church leader who is the head of a metropolis.

16. Metropolitan Christodoulos had a well-deserved reputation for being a loving leader. He was later elevated to lead the Greek Orthodox Church of Greece as archbishop. As archbishop, he actively and purposefully reached out to the youth of Greece. Once, when speaking to a group of young people, he said, "In the church, we accept everyone just as they are: women in pants or short-short

skirts, and men with earrings!" One of the youths in the audience said to another, "Christodoulos is awesome!" Overhearing this, the archbishop rejoined, "I think you're all awesome too!" The crowd responded with wild applause. His warmth drew many Greek youth back to the faith.

17. Elizabeth Glaser, "1992 Democratic National Convention Address," American Rhetoric, Top 100 Speeches, July 14, 1992, accessed January 9, 2024, https://www.americanrhetoric.com/speeches/elizabethglaser1992dnc.html/.

18. Mary Fisher, "1992 Republican National Convention Address," American Rhetoric, Top 100 Speeches, August 19, 1992, accessed January 10, 2024, https://www.americanrhetoric.com/speeches/maryfisher1992rnc.html/.

19. A catechumen is someone who is taking catechism classes in the expectation of converting (in this case, to Orthodox Christianity).

CHAPTER 9

1. Locke E. Bowman, "Desperate hours: Kokoraleis execution places us at a moral crossroads," *Chicago Tribune*, March 14, 1999, p. 43.

2. George H. Ryan Sr., with Maurice Possley, *Until I Could Be Sure* (Lanham, MD: Rowman & Littlefield, 2020), 41.

3. David Mendell, "Religious leaders call for halt to executions: Clergy ask governor to commute sentence," *Chicago Tribune*, March 15, 1999, p. 110.

4. Ryan, *Until I Could Be Sure*, 36–38.

5. Ryan, 19.

6. Ryan, 36–38.

7. Cornelia Grumman and Rick Pearson, "Ryan agonized, but confident he 'did the right thing,'" *Chicago Tribune*, March 18, 1999, p. 1.

8. Mendell, "Religious leaders call for halt to executions."

9. Michael Pearson, "Execution in limbo," *Southern Illinoisan*, March 16, 1999, p. 1.

10. "Court denies petition to stop executions," *Southern Illinoisan*, March 24, 1999, p. 5.

11. Ryan, *Until I Could Be Sure*, 40.

12. Jim Stahly and M. K. Guetersloh, "Kokoraleis pessimistic about delay," *The Pantagraph*, March 16, 1999, p. 1.

13. Christi Parsons and Cornelia Grumman, "Kokoraleis execution carried out," *Chicago Tribune*, March 17, 1999, p. 1.

14. Christi Parsons and Cornelia Grumman, "On the brink of execution," *Chicago Tribune*, March 16, 1999, p. 1.

15. Andrew's attorney, Alan Freedman, had previously filed two motions with the US Supreme Court—one for an emergency stay of execution and one petitioning the Court to review the state court's decision denying Andrew's appeal. Neither had been decided yet. Justice Harrison cited a statute that gave him the authority to unilaterally stay Andrew's execution until the US Supreme Court weighed in on the motions.

208   Notes

16. "Single justice issues stay; could delay execution," *The Taylorville Daily Breeze Courier*, March 16, 1999, p. 1.
17. Richard Goldstein, "Step by step: The last day in the life of a killer," *Southern Illinoisan*, March 17, 1999, p. 3.
18. Parsons and Grumman, "On the brink of execution."
19. "Appeals end; Kokoraleis executed early today," *The Pantagraph*, March 17, 1999, p. 1.
20. Goldstein, "Step by step."
21. Richard Goldstein, "Convicted killer gets lethal shot at Tamms," *Southern Illinoisan*, March 17, 1999, p. 1; Associated Press, "Clemency denied; convict executed," *Belleville News-Democrat*, March 17, 1999, p. 13.
22. Goldstein, "Convicted killer gets lethal shot at Tamms."
23. Ray Long, "Kokoraleis' Execution Carried Out," *Chicago Tribune*, March 17, 1999, updated August 11, 2021, accessed October 21, 2024, https://www.chicagotribune.com/1999/03/17/kokoraleis-execution-carried-out/.
24. Ryan, *Until I Could Be Sure*, 44.
25. Mark Hodapp, "Despite pleas Kokoraleis put to death," *The Messenger*, April 2, 1999, p. 2.
26. Ryan, *Until I Could Be Sure*, 47.
27. Goldstein, "Step by step."
28. Ryan, *Until I Could Be Sure*, 43.
29. Goldstein, "Convicted killer gets lethal shot at Tamms."

CHAPTER 10

1. The concept of AIDS buddies was started in 1982 by the Gay Men's Health Crisis in New York City. An AIDS buddy was a volunteer who would visit and assist someone living with HIV/AIDS. In Bob's case, his AIDS buddy was there only during the time Bob was in the hospital. He did not know her well, but she was a reassuring and helpful presence to Bob and his family.
2. "An Unprecedented Problem: The Clinton Administration and HIV/AIDS in the United States," Clinton Digital Library, accessed January 8, 2024, https://clinton.presidentiallibraries.us/an-unprecedented-problem-the-clinton-administration-and-hiv/aids-in-the-united-states#:~:text=On%20June%2025%2C%201993%2C%20President,AIDS%20policy%20guidance%20and%20coordinate/.
3. "History," National Institutes of Health, accessed January 8, 2024, https://www.oar.nih.gov/about/history#:~:text=As%20the%20expanding%20pandemic%20required,Public%20Law%20100%2D607/.
4. Later, he was ordained Reverend Stephen Martz, Episcopalian priest.
5. "Lewis-Thornton, Rae 1962–," Encyclopedia.com, accessed January 11, 2024, https://www.encyclopedia.com/education/news-wires-white-papers-and-books/lewis-thornton-rae-1962/.
6. Rae Lewis-Thornton shared her experience of living with HIV/AIDS in "Facing AIDS: I'm young, I'm educated, I'm drug-free, and I'm dying of AIDS," a

cover story for *Essence* magazine in December 1994. Her memoir, *Unprotected*, was published in 2022.

7. "Lewis-Thornton, Rae 1962–."
8. St. Demetrios Greek Orthodox Church in Weston, Massachusetts.
9. M. Cotter, "Marcha de las madres contra el SIDA" [Mother's march against AIDS]. *Sidahora*, 1995 Jun–Jul:16, Spanish, PMID: 11363208, accessed December 25, 2023, https://pubmed.ncbi.nlm.nih.gov/11363208/.
10. "Some protease (pronounced PRO-tee-ayz) inhibitors can be taken on their own (monotherapy), but many are used in combination with other antiviral medications. When they're used to help another medication be more effective, they're called a 'booster.'" From "Protease Inhibitors," Cleveland Clinic, accessed January 8, 2024, https://my.clevelandclinic.org/health/treatments/24937-protease-inhibitors/.
11. "To treat HIV, NNRTIs work by blocking an enzyme HIV needs to make copies of itself." From "How NNRTIs Work," International Association of Providers of AIDS Care, accessed June 17, 2024, https://www.iapac.org/?s=nnrtis/.
12. "A Timeline of the HIV and AIDS," HIV.gov, accessed December 13, 2023, https://www.hiv.gov/hiv-basics/overview/history/hiv-and-aids-timeline/#year-1994/.
13. This act later facilitated Operation Warp Speed, which resulted in the rapid development of vaccines for COVID-19 in the United States.

CHAPTER 11

1. The Very Rev. Demetri Kantzavelos, "Immoral execution," *Chicago Tribune* opinion page, March 27, 1999, p. 99.
2. "Costs," Death Penalty Information Center, accessed June 10, 2024, https://deathpenaltyinfo.org/policy-issues/costs/.
3. Raymond Bonner and Ford Fessenden, "ABSENCE OF EXECUTIONS: A special report.; States With No Death Penalty Share Lower Homicide Rates," *New York Times*, September 22, 2000, Section A, p. 1, https://www.nytimes.com/2000/09/22/us/absence-executions-special-report-states-with-no-death-penalty-share-lower.html/.
4. George H. Ryan Sr., with Maurice Possley, *Until I Could Be Sure: How I Stopped the Death Penalty in Illinois* (Lanham, MD: Rowman & Littlefield), 51.
5. Ryan, *Until I Could Be Sure*, 49–50.
6. Good Friday was April 2, 1999, on the Western calendar.
7. Steve Kloehn, "U.S. bishops renew plea to end death penalty," *Chicago Tribune*, April 3, 1999, p. 87.
8. Ryan, *Until I Could Be Sure*, 50–51.
9. Ryan, 50.
10. Ryan, 52.
11. Ken Armstrong and Steve Mills, "Death row justice derailed," *Chicago Tribune*, November 14, 1999, p. 45.
12. "America's US governor on Cuba mission," BBC News, October 24, 1999.

13. The Very Rev. Demetri Kantzavelos, "Illinois' needs," *Chicago Tribune* opinion page, November 15, 1999, p. 18.
14. Ryan, *Until I Could Be Sure*, 63–64.
15. Ryan, 64.
16. Ryan, 65–66.
17. Ryan, 67.
18. Steve Mills and Ken Armstrong, "Governor to halt executions," *Chicago Tribune*, January 30, 2000, p. 1.
19. Ryan, *Until I Could Be Sure*, 68.
20. David Schapter, "Former Illinois Gov. George Ryan Heading to Prison," NPR, November 6, 2007.
21. The Very Rev. Demetri Kantzavelos, "Ryan's politics," *Chicago Tribune*, opinion page, February 5, 2000, p. 22.
22. Julia Lieblich, "Clergy leaders stand with Ryan on death penalty," *Chicago Tribune*, January 31, 2003, pp. 1, 9.
23. Notes in preparation for May 12, 2000, meeting, private collection of Bishop Demetrios C. Kantzavelos; Ryan, *Until I Could Be Sure*, 85–86.
24. From 1986 to 2011, Chick Hoffman served as an assistant defender in the Supreme Court Unit of the Illinois State Appellate Defender, where he represented indigent defendants in capital cases, in both the trial court and on appeal. He served as the lead counsel in more than thirty death penalty appeals in the Illinois Supreme Court.
25. "How We Abolished the Death Penalty in Illinois," keynote speech delivered by Chick Hoffman at the "Life After Death Row: The Road to Death Penalty Abolition & Beyond in Illinois" event, Illinois Prison Project, January 2023.
26. "Former First Lady Calls for Moratorium on Executions," October 11, 2000, The Carter Center, https://www.cartercenter.org/news/documents/doc953.html/.
27. Ryan, *Until I Could Be Sure*, 107.
28. Ray Long, "Ryan to review Death Row cases," *Chicago Tribune*, March 3, 2002, p. 1, modified August 20, 2021, https://www.chicagotribune.com/2002/03/03/ryan-to-review-death-row-cases/.
29. Steve Mills and Christi Parsons, "Tears send a message: Hearings' emotional impact surprises death penalty foes," *Chicago Tribune*, October 27, 2002, p. 4-1.
30. Mills and Parsons, "Tears send a message."
31. Lieblich, "Clergy leaders stand with Ryan on death penalty."
32. "Prosecutors fire back at mass clemency bid," *Chicago Tribune*, October 1, 2002, modified August 20, 2021.
33. Ryan, *Until I Could Be Sure*, 171.
34. Mills and Parsons, "Tears send a message."
35. "Governor to Meet Murder Victim Families," *Los Angeles Times*, November 3, 2002.
36. David Mendell, "Ex-Death Row inmates stand against executions," *Chicago Tribune*, December 16, 2002, p. 1.
37. Ryan, *Until I Could Be Sure*, 196.

38. "'Exonerated' an enlightening evening for Ryan," *Chicago Tribune*, December 18, 2002, modified August 20, 2021; Ryan, *Until I Could Be Sure*, 197–98.

39. Eric Zorn, "Going-away gift for Ryan could be Nobel Prize," *Chicago Tribune*, February 19, 2002, modified August 20, 2021.

40. Ryan, *Until I Could Be Sure*, 231.

41. Cathleen Falsani, "Ryan draws applause, jeers—RESPONSE FROM RELIGIOUS LEADERS," *Chicago Sun-Times*, January 12, 2003, p. 7.

CHAPTER 12

1. Also known as the Malankaran Orthodox Syrian Church, or Orthodox Syrian Church of the East, the Church is a prominent member of the Orthodox Christian family, but it is not in communion with the Eastern Orthodox Churches.

2. "Mahapatra India overtakes South Africa as country with most HIV cases," *Seattle Post-Intelligencer*, September 2004, as cited in S. Solomon, S. S. Solomon, and A. K. Ganesh, "AIDS in India," *Postgraduate Medical Journal* 82, no. 971 (2006 September): 545–47, www.ncbi.nlm.nih.gov/pmc/articles/PMC2585722/.

3. "The Ecumenical Patriarch Bartholomew India Health Clinic Project: The Case for Support," prepared by the Greek Orthodox Metropolis of Chicago.

4. In the Greek Orthodox Church hierarchy, an auxiliary bishop is a bishop assigned to assist a ruling hierarch in meeting administrative and pastoral needs. He functions under the authority of the hierarch to whom he is assigned.

5. Maya A. Brachear, "Bishop Demetrios: From Altar Boy to Bishop," *Chicago Tribune*, December 8, 2006.

6. A brand of licorice.

7. The transition from a serious, fatal disease to a chronic, manageable disease has given the false impression that the pandemic has waned. People still get infected at high rates. Sadly, there is still a tremendous stigma attached to getting tested for HIV and for living with HIV.

In 2012, physicians began to prescribe a new medication to prevent HIV infection, called pre-exposure prophylaxis (PrEP). For the first time since the beginning of the pandemic, new HIV infections in the United States began to decline.

Several different categories of drugs and dozens of medications active against HIV are available. Resistance to drugs and side effects remain issues but much less so than previously.

A new class of antiretroviral therapy (ART) has recently been developed that offers new hope for multidrug resistant HIV. These long-acting HIV medications target the capsid of HIV-1, a conical structure that harbors its genome. One such drug, approved in 2023 by the FDA, is Lenacapavir. From Viviana Sofía Flores Rivera, "Lenacapavir: Drug Offers New Hope for Multi-drug Resistant HIV," Yale School of Medicine, published August 30, 2023, accessed October 21, 2024. https://medicine.yale.edu/news-article/lenacapavir-drug-offers-new-hope-for-multi-drug-resistant-hiv/.

CHAPTER 13

1. Rod Blagojevich, "Addressing the inequities of capital punishment," *Chicago Tribune*, April 23, 2002, p. 19.
2. George H. Ryan Sr., with Maurice Possley, *Until I Could Be Sure* (Lanham, MD: Rowman & Littlefield, 2020), 233.
3. Julia Lieblich, "Clergy leaders stand with Ryan on death penalty," *Chicago Tribune*, January 31, 2003, p. 1-9.
4. Michele Steinbacher, "Reverend seeks death-penalty abolition," *The Pantagraph*, October 2003, p. 11.
5. "Moratorium has been in place for more than a decade," *Chicago Tribune*, January 12, 2011, p. 1-9; Rob Warden, "How and Why Illinois Abolished the Death Penalty," *Minnesota Journal of Law & Inequality: A Journal of Theory and Practice* 30 (2012): 270–71.
6. In September 2005, the case went to trial, and in 2006, Ryan was convicted and sentenced to six and a half years in prison.
7. Warden, "How and Why Illinois Abolished the Death Penalty," 273.
8. Warden, 276.
9. Warden, 274.
10. Blagojevich was sentenced to fourteen years in federal prison on eighteen felony counts of corruption during his time as governor. Among these, he attempted to trade a US Senate seat for $1.5 million in campaign contributions, demanded $25,000 in campaign contributions from the chief executive of a pediatric hospital in exchange for increasing pediatric medical reimbursement rates, delayed the signing of legislation in an effort to obtain $100,000 in campaign contributions, and lied to the FBI.

President Donald Trump commuted Blagojevich's sentence after Blagojevich had served eight years.

11. John Keilman, "A dying message rewrites 2 lives," *Chicago Tribune*, April 7, 2010, pp. 1, 14.
12. Warden, "How and Why Illinois Abolished the Death Penalty," 279.
13. Kiera Manion-Fischer, "House officials pass repeal of death penalty," *Journal Gazette* (Mattoon, Illinois), January 7, 2011, p. 1; "Illinois House Passes Death Penalty Ban, Senate Next," Reuters, January 6, 2011, accessed June 25, 2024, https://deathpenaltyinfo.org/news/illinois-house-votes-to-repeal-death-penalty/.
14. Warden, "How and Why Illinois Abolished the Death Penalty," 281.
15. 725 ILCS 5/119-1.

CHAPTER 14

1. Immanuel Kant, *Prolegomena to Any Future Metaphysics*, trans. and ed. Gary Hatfield (New York: Cambridge University Press, 2004), 10.
2. On the Eastern calendar, St. Augustine's day is celebrated on June 15.

EPILOGUE

1. James Ramsey Ullman, *Kingdom of Adventure: Everest* (New York: William Sloane Associates, 1947), 385.

2. Diary entry by George Mallory, May 27, 1924, cited in Ullman, *Kingdom of Adventure*, 148.

3. Mallory and his climbing partner, Andrew "Sandy" Irvine, were last seen on June 8, 1924. Mallory's remains were found in 1999, some seventy-five years after his last attempt. On October 10, 2024, a portion of Irvine's remains were discovered on Mount Everest: a boot with a foot inside it and a sock with a red label with the name "A. C. IRVINE" stitched onto it. The question of whether the two men died in ascent or descent still remains a mystery. From Grayson Schaffer, "Exclusive: Remains of Andrew 'Sandy' Irvine believed to have been found Everest,' *National Geographic*, October 11, 2024, accessed October 23, 2024, https://www.nationalgeographic.com/adventure/article/sandy-irvine-body-found-everest/.

4. "But strive for the greater gifts. And I will show you a still more excellent way" (1 Corinthians 12:31, NRSV).

Index

Page references for figures are italicized.

abstinence, sexual, 95, 104, 109
ACT UP. *See* AIDS Coalition to Unleash Power
acquired immunodeficiency syndrome (AIDS): activism, 77, 97–99; anti-gay sentiment because of, 74; Bob's experience of, 67–70, 72; buddy, 130–31; death from complications due to, 71–72, 131, 139, 141, 142; first cases of in US, 70–72; health effects on women, children, people of color, 98; information about (in Greek/English), 72, 99, 101, 103, 142; lack of government urgency concerning, 76, 97; ministries, faith-based, 79–82, 133–34, 145; ministries, interfaith, 133–37; named by CDC, 73; pediatric quilt-a-thon, 138, *138*; questioning God over diagnosis of, 140–41; rapid spread of, 76, 142; risk factors for, 73; risk-reducing behaviors, 77–78, 95, 100, 104, 109; social stigma around, 72, 74, 109, 132; topic of mainstream politics, 106–7; treatment for, 97–98; virus that causes identified, 73. *See also* Congressional action regarding AIDS

AIDS. *See* acquired immunodeficiency syndrome
AIDS Coalition to Unleash Power (ACT UP), 77, 97–99
AIDS Pastoral Care Network (APCN) of Chicago, 96, 133–36, 142
"Amazing Grace," 140
American Bar Association (ABA), 52, 158
American Hospital of Paris, 75
Anders, Reverend David, 156
Angels in America, 132
Annas, Father Gerasimos, 21
Annunciation Greek Orthodox Cathedral, 47, 48, 115–18, 122, 125, 134, 187
Antonopoulos, Jeannie, 35–36
APCN. *See* AIDS Pastoral Care Network (APCN) of Chicago
Apostles, 172
Armstrong, Ken, 55, 152

Assembly of Canonical Orthodox Bishops of the United States of America, 188
assistants to Father Demetri, 116, 117, 177–78, 183, 185–86
Assumption Greek Orthodox Church, 15, 26, 37, 58, 171
Athens, 5, 35–36
Avero House, 188–89
Avramopoulos, Deacon Chris, 185–86
azidothymidine. *See* AZT
AZT, 97–98

Bahá'u'lláh, 134
Balourdos, John, 188
Bartholomew, Ecumenical Patriarch of Constantinople, 168–69
Basil, Saint, Bishop of Cappadocia, 180
Basil (volunteer driver for Bishop Demetrios), 192–93
Bastani, Ahmad, 134
Beckwith, Bishop Peter, 156–57
Bernardin, Joseph Cardinal, 62
Bettenhausen, Matthew R., 157
Bishop, Jeanne, 180–81
Bishop's Task Force on AIDS: alliances with other faith-based ministries, 96, 133–37; challenges encountered, 101, 104, 111; clergy retreat, 95–96, 107–10; completes its work, 175; composition of board, 96; conflict within, 138; discussion with Bishop Iakovos about starting, 80–82; expansion of ministry resources over time, 174–75; funding for, 111; Greek Orthodox Archdiocese of America, recognition by, 168; ministry beyond diocese, 140–41, 143–45, 168–69; ministry packets, 101–3, 111; outreach to Greeks and Greek Americans, 95–96, 99–100, 101–6, 107–11, 141–43, 144, 145; primary aims of, 99; speakers' bureau, 104–6, 111, 175; started because of Bob, 79, 129, 175, 191
Bissias, Father David, 186
Blagojevich, Governor Rod, 178–80

blood, donated, 74
blood, medical risk of exposure to HIV, 73–74
blood supply, US, test to screen for HIV exposure, 73
blood transfusion, 69, 73, 74–75, 106
Blue, Murray, 153
Bob (inspiration for Bishop's Task Force on AIDS): Angelike Mountanis's ministry to family of, 108–9, 110; death of, 129–31; family's reaction to, 68, 72, 78–79, 80, 108–9, 110; first meeting with Father Demetri, 69–70, 72–73, 78–79; his parish priest, 67–68, 69, 72, 81, 132; visit with Father Demetri at Pascha, 111–12
Borowski, Lorraine ("Lorry") Ann: abducted and murdered by Ripper Crew, 9, 31; A. Kokoraleis convicted of her murder, 3, 6, 27; A. Kokoraleis maintains innocence of her murder, 26, 29, 127; skeletal remains of, 10–11
Borowski, Raymond, 91
Borowski family, 90–91, 127
Bouboutsis, Father Kyprianos Elias, 101, 125
Bowman, Locke, 90, 115–16
Boyle, Francis, 163
Bright Week, 21
Burdusi, Manny, 36
Burge, Jon, 51
Burroughs Wellcome, 97–98
Burrows, Joe, 52–53
Bush, President George H. W., 78

Canaanite woman, 65
capital cases, additional review of in Illinois, 89, 90
Capital Litigation Trust Fund, 152
Capital Punishment Reform Study Committee (Illinois General Assembly), 179, 181
capital punishment: arguments against, 30–31, 150–51, 182–83;

arguments for, 30, 182–83; Church's opposition to, 4
capital punishment system in Illinois: commission to assess, announced, 156; commission to assess, proposed, 89, 115, 154; corruption of, 55, 149, 152
Carnahan, Governor Mel, 63
Carter, First Lady Rosalynn, 158
Carter Center, 158
cassock, 35–36, 37
Catholics Against Capital Punishment, 86
CDC. *See* Centers for Disease Control
Center on Wrongful Convictions and the Death Penalty, 151, 161–62, 181
Centers for Disease Control (CDC), 71, 73
Chacko, Reverend Koshy, 169
Chapekis, Fred, 185–86
Chapekis, Tina, 185–86
Chicago Council of Lawyers, 87
Chicago Tribune series on death penalty, 152
Chicago Tribune series on prosecutorial misconduct, 55
Christian unity, 137
Christodoulos, Metropolitan of Demetrias and Almyros (Greece), 103
Ciolino, Paul, 55
Clayburgh, Jill, 162
clemency, blanket, for those on death row: affirmed by Illinois Supreme Court, 178; Governor G. Ryan announces, 163–64; idea proposed, 158, 159; legal obstacle to, 159; obstacle overcome, 160; prosecutors's demand, 160; publicity campaign in support of, 161–62
clergy, closeted gay, 141
clergy, married, 39–40, 141
clergy, monastic (unmarried clergy), 40–42
Clergy/Laity Assemblies, 145, 168
Clinton, President Bill, 132–33

Cobb, Perry, 52
Combivir, 144
complicity of public in state executions, 31
condoms, 95, 100, 109, 136
confessions, coerced, 6, 26, 27, 51–52, 89
confidentiality, 32, 68, 112, 141, 167
Congressional action regarding AIDS: appropriates funds for research, 76; enacts FDA Modernization Act of 1997, 144; enacts National Institutes of Health (NIH) Revitalization Act, 133; enacts Ryan White Comprehensive AIDS Resources Emergency (CARE) Act, 78
Constantinople (Istanbul, Turkey), 168
Cook County Building, 99
Cook County Hospital, 99
Cook County Jail, 27
Corrigan, Reverend Jim, 133
Council of Religious Leaders of Metropolitan Chicago (CRLMC), 62–63, 160, 164
Coutretsis, Tom, 84–86, 116
Creticos, Catherine, 166
CRLMC. *See* Council of Religious Leaders of Metropolitan Chicago
Cruz, Rolando, 53
Culloton, Dennis, 154
cultures, duality of, 37

Daley, Mayor Richard M., 56
Davis, Rose Beck, 9–10, 27
Day, Doris, 75
Day of Prayer for People Living with HIV/AIDS, 134
Deadly Thrills, 88, 90
"Dead Men Walking" relay walk, 162
Death Penalty Focus, 158
Death Penalty Information Center, 52
Death Penalty Moratorium Campaign, 151
Death Penalty Moratorium Commission, 154, 156, 157, 158, 159; report by, 159–60, 179
death row, emptied, 164

death row cell, 27, 29, 87, 117
death warrant, 120, 156
Delaware, Sandra, 9, 27
Demetrios, Archbishop of America, 172, 186–88
Demetrios, Bishop of Mokissos, 177; at deathbed of Metropolitan Iakovos of Chicago, 185–86; ordination of, 171–73, *173*, *174*
Democratic National Convention, 106–7
Denove, Tom, *144*
differences, religious and cultural, 136–37
diseases, opportunistic, 70–71, 95, 98
DNA evidence, 6, 53, 54, 57, 152
Doppelt, Helen, 43, 49
Dreyfuss, Richard, 162
drugs, immunosuppressant, 70–71
Dugan, Brian, 53
Dulin, William, 52
DuPage County Jail, 27
Dwight Correctional Center, 121

East Georgia State College Baseball, 44
Ecumenical Institute (Switzerland), 169
eggs, red, 21, 111–12
Elpidophoros, Archbishop of America, 188, 190
Emmy Award, 135
Episcopal Diocese of Chicago's AIDS ministry, 96
Essence magazine, 135, *135*
execution, means of in Illinois, 83
execution chamber, 115, 126–27
The Exonerated, 162
exonerees in Illinois, 52–54, 55–56, 151–52, 158, 182
exonerees in US, 54, 162–63
exorasson (garment), 39

factor VIII (blood product), 74
Falconer, Michael, 52
Falsani, Cathleen, 164
families of death row inmates, 163

families of murder victims, 30, 150, 160–61, 180–81
A Family Like Ours, 143–44, *144*
Farrell, Mike, 158, 162
Feed the Hungry program, 47
Feingold, US Senator Russell, 158
Fisher, Mary, 106
Fletcher, Jaye Slade, 88, 90
Food and Drug Administration (FDA), 143, 144
Fred (attorney), 64, 92, 123, 183, 184; advocacy for A. Kokoraleis, 6; after A. Kokoraleis's execution, 147, 149; letter to Governor G. Ryan, 61, 63–64; Pontiac visit, 1–2, 7, 32–33, 58; at press conference, 118; at vigil, 125
Freedman, Alan: appeals to Illinois Supreme Court to grant new evidentiary hearing and delay of execution, 91; argues before Judge Ann Jorgensen for new evidentiary hearing, 88; files last appeals for A. Kokoraleis with US Supreme Court, 120; presents new evidence to Illinois Prisoner Review Board, 90
Freeman, Justice Charles, 151
Furman v. Georgia, 56
Furris, Nicholas J., *144*
Futorian, Aviva, 87

Gardner, Denise, 10, 11
Garmatis, Michael, 5
Garmatis family, 5
Gauger, Gary, 53, 162
Gay Men's Health Crisis (GMHC), 73
Gecht, Robin: adept at psychological manipulation, 60; A. Kokoraleis's anger at, 28; arrests, 11, *12*; breast fixation, 61; convictions, 27–28, 60; hires A. Kokoraleis, 3, 60–61; identified by victim, 61; sentence, 27–28
Gecht, Rosemary, 60–61
Glaser, Elizabeth, 106–7
Glover, Danny, 162
Glykeria, 169
GMHC. *See* Gay Men's Health Crisis

godparents, 43, 48
Greek America Foundation, 169
Greek Orthodox Archdiocese of America, 42, 168, 169, 172, 186, 187, 188, 189
Greek Orthodox Diocese of Chicago, 21, 168; advocacy for A. Kokoraleis, 29, 57–58, 62–65, 84–86, 90–91, 116–19; clergy retreat, 95–96, 99, 107–10; Father Demetri's place of employment, 38, 42, 187; geographical extent of, 38; improved interfaith dialogue, 137; Peter's visit to, 165–66. *See also* Bishop's Task Force on AIDS; Greek Orthodox Metropolis of Chicago
Greek Orthodox Diocese of San Francisco, 145
Greek Orthodox Metropolis of Chicago, 168, 169, 187–88. *See also* Greek Orthodox Diocese of Chicago
Greek Orthodox Youth of America (GOYA), 145
Gregg v. Georgia, 57
guided meditation, HIV/AIDS, 105, 107

HAART. *See* highly active antiretroviral therapy
Hampton, Lloyd, 83
Hanks, Tom, 132
Haralambos (Bob), 69, 72
Harrison, Justice Moses, II, 92, 123, 160
Heiple, Justice James D., 92
Hellenic College, 18, 20, 21, 35–36, 38; seminary-track program, 20, 35
Hellenic Foundation, 108, 142
hemophilia, 74
Hermes, 142
Hernandez, Alejandro, 53
highly active antiretroviral therapy (HAART), 143–44
Hillier, Polexeni (Polly) Maouris, 188–89, 193
His All Holiness (Bartholomew, Ecumenical Patriarch of Constantinople), 168–69
Hitler, Adolf, 5
HIV. *See* human immunodeficiency virus
HIV/AIDS, 107, 108, 109, 112, 129, 133
Hoffman, Chick, 158–60
Hoffman, Reverend Jane Fischer, 156
Holy Communion, 72–73, 103, 108, 112, 166, 194
Holy Cross Greek Orthodox School of Theology, 18, 20, 35, 39–40
Holy Spirit, 172
Holy Week, 39, 190, 192
Hudson, Rock, 75–76
human immunodeficiency virus (HIV), 67; abstinence to prevent transmission of, 95, 104–5; cause of AIDS, 73; educating students about, 136; HIV positive status, 69, 100, 108; human sexual behavior and, 77–78, 95, 104, 110; infection status unknown, medical challenges of, 73–74; panic concerning, 74; test for infection by (for military personnel), 73; test to screen US blood supply for, 73; transmission of, 75, 77–78, 95, 104; treatments for, 109, 143–44, 145, 166, 174; viral load, 136, 166

Iakovos, Bishop of Chicago, 5, 92, 129; advocacy for A. Kokoraleis, 29, 62, 84; Bishop's Task Force on AIDS, 81–82, 100, 103, 107; at clergy retreat, 107–8, 110; elected Metropolitan Iakovos, 168; Feed the Hungry program, 47; ordains Deacon Demetri to priesthood, 48; ordains Demetri to diaconate, 43, 44; recommends Demetri delay ordination, 42; relationship with Demetri, 20, 21, 38, 130; stands behind A. Kokoraleis, 64–65; as teacher, 46; as youth (Michael Garmatis), 5. *See also* Iakovos, Metropolitan of Chicago
Iakovos, Metropolitan of Chicago, 71, 168, 169, 170, *173*, 183–84;

220 Index

communications with Ecumenical Patriarch Bartholomew, 169; death of, 185–86; nephew of, 185–86; officiates funeral of Christ Kantzavelos, 171. *See also* Iakovos, Bishop of Chicago
ICADP. *See* Illinois Coalition Against the Death Penalty
icon, 72, 121
icon card, 101–2
icon screen, 14, 15, 117
Illinois, executions in, 6, 83–84, 126–27
Illinois Boys Reformatory School, 6–7
Illinois Campaign to End the Death Penalty, 151
Illinois Coalition Against the Death Penalty (ICADP), 87, 155, 181, 184; board discussions, 150; Father Demetri's outreach to, 58; new executive director, 179; and publicity campaign for blanket clemency, 161–62; representatives of, at press conference, 117–18; representatives of, at vigil, 125; urges abolition after moratorium on execution, 178–79
Illinois Coalition to Abolish the Death Penalty. *See* Illinois Coalition Against the Death Penalty (ICADP)
Illinois Conference of Churches, 156–57
Illinois General Assembly: enacts capital punishment system reform legislation, 179; enacts death penalty legislation, 57; enacts legislation to abolish capital punishment, 181–82; lacks authority to impose moratorium on executions, 89, 92
Illinois governor, authority concerning capital punishment, 92
Illinois House: approves reforms to reduce prosecutorial misconduct, 158; Judiciary Committee, 87; votes to abolish capital punishment, 181
Illinois Prisoner Review Board, 25, 159; A. Kokoraleis's hearing before,
90–91, 117; death row inmates's hearings before, 160–61
Illinois Senate votes to abolish capital punishment, 181–82
Illinois State Bar Association, 89, 179, 181
Illinois State Capitol, 177, 183
Illinois State's Attorneys Association, 152
Illinois Supreme Court, 120: allows forensic testing, 53, 152; *Chicago Tribune* op-ed urges postponement of A. Kokoraleis's execution by, 87; confirms legitimacy of Governor Ryan's moratorium on executions, 178; denies A. Kokoraleis's appeals for delay of execution and new evidentiary hearing, 92, 117; overturns Justice Harrison's solo stay of A. Kokoraleis's execution, 124; Representative Pugh's petition for stay of A. Kokoraleis's execution, 120, 124; reverses murder conviction of Steven Smith, 56; reverses two murder convictions, 158; seventeen-person committee and recommendations, 151, 152, 158
The Imaginary Invalid, 16
Imesch, Bishop Joseph, 156, 157
immigrants (Greek), 37, 57, 69, 108
immune system, compromised, 70–71
immune system, healthy, 70
Indian Orthodox Church, 169
"Interfaith Response to AIDS," 134
International Thespian Society, 17
Isaiah, Bishop of Aspendos, 43

Jackson, Reverend Jesse, 162, 163
Jenkins, Jennifer Bishop, 180
Jimerson, Verneal, 53
Job, Bishop of the Orthodox Church of America, Diocese of the Midwest, 62–63
John Chrysostom, Saint, 112
John Paul II, Pope, 63, 151

Joint Committee of Orthodox and Roman Catholic Bishops, 185
Jones, Emil, Illinois Senate Minority Leader, 151
Jones, Ronald, 151–52
Jones, Terrence, 53
Jorgensen, Judge Ann, 88, 91, 117
journalism students, 53, 55
judge, corrupt, 51–52
judging others, 105–6, 138–39, 145

Kallas, William, 185
Kaloudis, Father George, 101
Kant, Immanuel, 191
Kantzavelos, Bishop Demetrios. *See* Demetrios, Bishop of Mokissos
Kantzavelos, Christ, 13, *14*, 42–43, 48, 118, 173; allows Demetri to choose his own path, 38; death of, 170; view of capital punishment, 31, 54, 119; view of marriage, 41
Kantzavelos, Deacon Demetri, 44–48; ordination as priest, 48–49
Kantzavelos, Demetri: altar boy, 13, 191; changing understanding of ministry, 14–15, 33, 80, 190–91, 194 first visit with Bishop Iakovos of Chicago, 21; ordination as deacon, 43, *44*; priestly calling, family's views of, 19, 20, 38, 42; question of marriage, 39–41, 42; schooling, 15; seminarian, 38–42, 191; undergraduate, 35–38;
Kantzavelos, Father Demetri: after A. Kokoraleis's execution, 147–51; blanket clemency, 164; at Bob's deathbed, 131–32; character witness for Peter, 167; final visit with A. Kokoraleis, 87–88; first visit with A. Kokoraleis, 23–30; first visit with Bob, 67–70, 72–73, 78–79; letters critical of Governor G. Ryan to *Chicago Tribune*, 149, 152, 155; letter to A. Kokoraleis, 84; meets with Governor G. Ryan, 156–57; ordination as bishop, 171–73; religious leaders's press conference, 120; skepticism toward Governor G. Ryan, 122, 149, 155; speaks on A. Kokoraleis's behalf before Illinois Prisoner Review Board, 90; vigil for A. Kokoraleis, 125–27
Kantzavelos, George, 19, 48, 170, *174*
Kantzavelos, Kelly, 170, *174*
Kantzavelos, Maria-Magdalene, 19, 48, 170, *174*
Kantzavelos, Merope, 13, *14*, 42–43, 48, *174*; calls Father Demetri after press conference, 118; death of Christ Kantzavelos, 170–71; helps Father Demetri set up his home, 42; marriage discussion, 41; road trip to college, 35–36
Kantzavelos, Michael, 19, 48, *174*
Kantzavelos, Nick, 44
Kaposi's sarcoma, 71, 103, 139
Kartsimas, Dean, 177–78, 183
Killduck, John, 83
Kinsella, John, 88
Kokoraleis, Andrew, 155: arrest of, 11, 27; coerced confession of, 26, 27; controversy over, 57, 64; dependence on Gecht, 61; execution of, 126–27; execution of at center of moral crossroads, 115; expectations about legal appeals, 121; forgives brother, Gecht, and Spreitzer, 28; forgives Governor G. Ryan, 126; his hope concerning execution, 30, 148, 184; inspired anti-capital punishment activism, 33, 190–91; interviewed by press, 121; last hours of, 123–25; leaves home, 59; legal appeals for, 6, 25–26, 88–89, 90–91, 120; letters to Father Demetri from, 87, 147–49, *148*; manipulated by Gecht, 2, *12*, 54, 57, *60*; meets Gecht, 59; meets Spreitzer, 3, 59; mentioned in speeches by Governor G. Ryan, 159; new evidence supporting claim of innocence, 89–91; parents of, 3, 26, 28, 29, 59; police interrogation of, 27; siblings of, 26, 59, 123;

solitary confinement of, 27, 29; relationship with Theodora, 2, 3, 28–29, 124; relationship with Father Zacharapoulos, 2, 28, 121, 124; vigils for, 122, 125–26; visits by Father Demetri, 7, 23–30, 87–88
Kokoraleis, Costas, 3, 26, 28, 29, 59
Kokoraleis, Nick, 123
Kokoraleis, Thomas, 3, 11, *12*, 27, 60, 88
Kokoraleis, Wanda, 3, 26, 28, 29, 59
Kokoraleis family 58, 59
Koop, C. Everett, Surgeon General, 77–78
Kramer, Larry, 77, 97
Kushner, Tony, 132

Ladies Philoptochos Society, 47, 111, 138, *138*, 143
Langert, Nancy, 181
Langert, Richard, 181
Lawrence, Frankie, 63
Lawrence, Lloyd, 63
Lawrence, William, 63
Lawson, Carl, 53
laying on of hands, 43
Lewis-Thornton, Rae, 135–36, *135*
Libertin, Claudia R., 109–10
"Live from Death Row," 151
Living with AIDS, 135
Lukis, Jim and Diana, 139
Loyola University, 109
Lyon, Andrea, "angel of death row," 163

MacArthur Justice Center, 90, 115
Madigan, Lisa, 182
Madigan, Mike, 152
Mak, Shui, 9, 10, 27
Mallory, George, 195–96
Maloney, Judge Thomas, 51–52
Mandela, Nelson, 163
Manning, Steve, 153
Manuel, 83
marriage (after seminary), 39–41
Marshall, Lawrence C., 53–54, 151, 158–60, 162–63

Martz, Stephen, 133
Mavrakis, Carol, 91, 118, 123, 125, 184
McGarr, Frank, 156, 158, 159–60
McMillan & Wife, 75
Mease, Darrell J., 63
medical cases, baffling, 70–72
Midwest Center for Justice, 88
Miller, Father Tom, 126
Miller, Randall, 53
Mills, Steve, 152
Missouri Synod Lutheran: elementary/middle school, 15, 46; high school, 16, 37, 46
Montalvo Higuera, Archbishop Gabriel, Papal Nuncio, 63
Montgomery, Steven, 96
moratorium, de facto, 87, 154
moratorium on executions, 151, 155, 157; debate over, 25; Father Demetri's view of, 164, 178; Governor G. Ryan announces, 154; Governor R. Blagojevich's view of, 178, 179; Illinois first state with death penalty to declare, 154; new alliances in support of, 87; pressure on Governor G. Ryan to oppose, 119–20; pressure on Governor G. Ryan to impose, 115–16, 119, 149; requested by demonstrators, 86–87; requested by religious leaders, 117–18
Mothers March, 143
Mothers March Against AIDS, 142
Mountanis, Angelike, 108–10, 142
Mount Everest, 195–96
Murder Victims' Families for Reconciliation, 161–62
Murphysboro High School, 86, 154
Mussolini, Benito, 5

National Cancer Institute, 73
National Conference on Wrongful Convictions and the Death Penalty, 54
"National Gathering of Death Penalty Exonerated," 162
National Institutes of Health (NIH), 98

National Institutes of Health (NIH) Revitalization Act, 133
Newtson, Robert, 119–20
New Smyrna Colony, 189
New York Stock Exchange (NYSE), 98
Nicarico, Jeanine, 53
Nicene Creed, 19
Nicholas, Metropolitan of Detroit, 187
NNRTIs. *See* non-nucleoside reverse transcriptase inhibitors
Nobel Peace Prize, 163
non-nucleoside reverse transcriptase inhibitors (NNRTIs), 143
Northwest Ordinance of 1787, 83
Northwestern University, 53, 55
Northwestern University School of Law, 54, 151

Obama, State Senator Barack, 179
O'Connor, John Cardinal, 98
Onassis, Jacqueline Kennedy, 139
ordination of gay men and women, 136
organ transplants, 70–71
Orthodox Christian Mission Center (OCMC), 188
Orthodox Observer, 141
Ottoman Empire, 189

Papou (Grandfather), 22
Pappas, Carole, 10
Pappas, Father Eugene, 193
Pappas, Gregory, 169
Pappas, Milt, 10
pardons for death row inmates, 163
Pasteur Institute, 73
Patukas, Demetra, 141–43
Patukas, George, 141
Patukas, Kostantinos, 141
Patukas, Tom, 141
PCP. *See Pneumocystis carinii* pneumonia
Pediatric AIDS Foundation, 106
Peponis, Faye, 92
Persell, Bishop-Elect William, 92
Peter (soundscape therapist), 165–68, 173–74

Peter, Saint (the Apostle), 39
Peters, Pete, 119
pharmaceutical industry, 97
Philadelphia, 132
Philoptochos. *See* Ladies Philoptochos Society
plastic drop cloths, 68, 72, 80, 111, 112
Plato School, 15
Pneumocystis carinii pneumonia (PCP), 70–71
points of agreement, focusing on, 62, 137
Pontiac Correctional Center, 2, 6–7, 57, 87–88, 92, 121, 151, 163, 191
Porter, Anthony, 55–56, 58, 119, 159, 162
Possley, Maurice, 55
Potter, Gayle, 53
Poulos, Allen, 36
prayer of separation of soul from body, 126, 131, 171, 186
Prejean, Sister Helen, 158
press conference: as appeal to Governor G. Ryan, 116–18, 125; Bishop-Elect Persell's, 92–93; Governor G. Ryan, Death Penalty Moratorium Commission, 156; Governor G. Ryan, moratorium on executions, 154; Governor G. Ryan, report by Death Penalty Moratorium Commission, 159–60; Governor P. Quinn, abolition of capital punishment, 183–84; religious leaders's, 88, 91, 93, 116–18
Price, Leontyne, 139
prom, 69–70
protease inhibitors, 109, 143, 145, 166
Protess, David, 53, 55, 162
Pugh, State Representative Coy, 87, 120, 124, 151, 153
Pulitzer Prize for Drama, 132

Queens, the man from, 192–94
Quinn, Governor Pat, 177, 180, 182
Quinn, Lieutenant Governor Pat, 180

R & R Electric, 60
radio programs, 179–80, 190
Ramsey, Jane, 178
Rankin, Mary Alice, 57, 155, 184
Raoul, State Senator Kwame, 181
Rathje, Justice S. Louis, 92
Reagan, First Lady Nancy, 76
Reagan, President Ronald, 76
religious leaders advocating for clemency for A. Kokoraleis, 63, 88, 93, 116–18, 121
Republican National Convention, 106–7
resistance to drugs, 145
Ripper Crew, 3, 11, 24, 57, 61
Ripper Crew, victims of, 3, 6, 8, 9–11, 27–28, 29, 31
Roman Catholic bishops, 151
Rooney, Peter, 53
Rutgers, Reverend Paul, 160, 164
Rutherford, State Representative Dan, 121
Ryan, Bill, 151, 162–63
Ryan, First Lady Lura Lynn, 162–63
Ryan, George (candidate), 84
Ryan, Governor George, 25, 54; "agonizing" over A. Kokoraleis's execution, 147; applauded at *The Exonerated*, 162; blanket clemency, 159–61, 163–64; commutes sentences of death row inmates, 164; Cuba trip, 152; death warrant for A. Kokoraleis, 12; to determine A. Kokoraleis's fate, 116, 117; first governor to declare moratorium on executions, 155; guest speaker, 158, 159; indicted, 179; investigation of corruption, 155; letter sent to, by attorneys, 89–90, 115; letters sent to, by religious leaders, 63, 85, 93; meets Father Demetri, 156–57; in Murphysboro, 86–87; pardons four death row Inmates, 163; statement about A. Kokoraleis's execution, 125; stunned by Porter exoneration, 56; unmoved by press conference, 121; unveils report by Death Penalty Moratorium Commission, 159–60; urged to stay A. Kokoraleis's execution, 87, 89, 90, 120
Ryan, Jim, Illinois Attorney General, 151, 153; additional review of capital cases, 89, 91
Ryan White Comprehensive AIDS Resources Emergency (CARE) Act, 78

Saint John Chrysostom Monastery, 187
Saints Constantine and Helen Greek Orthodox Church, *138*, 140
Santini, Phyllis, 52
Scherrer, Father Carl, 126
Schneider, James, 53
Schroeder, Jeremy, 179
Schutte, Christian, 96–97
shackles, 2, 12, 23, 25, 29, 32
Simon, US Senator Paul, 156
Smith, Steven, 56
solo stay of execution, 123
Southern Illinois Death Penalty Moratorium Committee, 86–87, 126
Spectrum Films, 190
Spreitzer, Eddie, *12*, 28, 29; convictions, 27; flip-flops on Gecht's guilt, 88; introduces A. Kokoraleis to Gecht, 3, 60; manipulated by Gecht, 60; police interrogation of, 11
Spreitzer, Edward. *See* Spreitzer, Eddie
Spyridon, Archbishop of America, 63, 85
Staley, Peter, 98
Stamatakos, Bessie, 139–40
Stamatakos, Jimmy, 139–40
Stamatakos, Pamela, 139
Stamos, John, 143, *144*
St. Basil's Church, 13
Steidl, Randy, 182
Steinmetz High School, 59
Stevens, Justice John Paul, 124
St. John's Lutheran Church, 16
St. Patrick's Cathedral, 98
St. Patrick's Day, 92

St. Peter's in the Loop, 140
St. Photios Greek Orthodox National Shrine, 188–90, 193–94
Sullivan, Thomas, 156, 160
Sunday school teachers, 104, 145
Surgeon General's Report on Acquired Immune Deficiency Syndrome, 77
Sutton, Linda, 8, 9–10, 11, 27

Tamms Correctional Center, 92, 121–24, 126
Task Force. *See* Bishop's Task Force on AIDS
Task Force on Kaposi's Sarcoma and Opportunistic Infections, 71
Taylor, Elizabeth, 75
T-cell count, 136, 166
Terry, Don, 54
Test Positive Aware (TPA), 100, 142
Theodora (A. Kokoraleis's mentor), 59, 183, 184, 190–91; after A. Kokoraleis's execution, 147; as A. Kokoraleis's mentor, 2–3, 28, 29; before A. Kokoraleis's execution, 121, 124; Pontiac visit with Father Demetri, 8, 23–25, 32; seeks Father Demetri's help, 2–5, 6, 7
Thomas, Saint (the Apostle), 169
Thompson, J. Michael, 140
Tillis, Darby (Williams), 52
Tina (attorney), 63, 184–86
Tirado, Rafael, 10, 27
Tony Award for Best Play, 132
Torre, John, 90
Treantafeles, Father Demetrios N., 20, 21, 35
Turow, Scott, 156
Tutu, Archbishop Desmond, 163, 182

University of Illinois Law School, 163
US Supreme Court, 120; death penalty forbidden by Eighth Amendment, 56; declares death penalty unconstitutional, 56; denies A. Kokoraleis's last appeals, 124; *Furman v. Georgia*, 56; *Gregg v. Georgia*, 57; reinstatement of death penalty, 57; possible stay of A. Kokoraleis's execution by, 89, 92, 123

van (Gecht's), 10, 11, 61
Vasseur, Ernest, 96
Vatican, 163
Vazhuvady (India), 169
Venable, Captain Scott, 111–13
vestments, clergy, 14–15, 39, 43, 48
vigils, 122, 125, 126
Vranas, Bill J., 84, 86
Vsevolod, Bishop of Scopelos of the Ukrainian Orthodox Western Diocese, 62, 118

Walker, Charles, 83
Wallace, Bill ("Wallace"), 16–17
Warden, Rob, 151, 158–59, 161
Webster, William, 156
Welborn, George, 127
White, Ryan, 74; banned from middle school, 75, 76–77; death of, 78; welcomed to new high school, 77
White House, 142
White House Office of National AIDS Policy, 132–33
Williams, Dennis, 53

Yarbrough, State Representative Karen, 181, 182
Yiannias, Cynthia, 142
yiayia (grandmother), 22
Yiayia Lynn, 19, 36–37
Yiayia Maria, 137
York, Angel, 9
Young Adult League (YAL), 145

Zacharapoulos, Father Kallinikos, 28, 121, 124
Zorn, Eric, 58

About the Authors

Demetrios C. Kantzavelos, Bishop of Mokissos, has been an ordained clergyman for more than thirty years and a bishop for more than eighteen years. He retired from active ministry in early 2023 after a long career with the Greek Orthodox Metropolis of Chicago. Between 1992 and 2017, he was a dynamic leader in social activism, earning numerous awards for his groundbreaking AIDS ministry and his successful advocacy to abolish the death penalty in Illinois. His extensive interfaith, ecumenical, and Greek Orthodox networks, growing media presence, and broad social connections in Chicago have made him a recognized figure. He has been featured over a dozen times in outlets such as the *Wall Street Journal*, the *Chicago Tribune*, the *Philadelphia Inquirer*, radio, and YouTube. Bishop Demetrios resides in Chicago, Illinois, and in a rural village in the Peloponnese region of Greece.

Patra McSharry Sevastiades is the author of nine children's nonfiction books. In addition to being a writer, she was editorial director at the Rosen Publishing Group in New York, a freelance editor who had the pleasure of editing several fine books, and the executive director of the Duluth Library Foundation. She is the widow of Father Philemon Sevastiades, a Greek Orthodox priest. She was blessed to remarry, and she lives with her husband, Dean Casperson—a book collector and entrepreneur—in Duluth, Minnesota. They have seven children and nine grandchildren.